A History of
Italian Literature

A History of
Italian Literature

Volume 1

Eugenio Donadoni

With additional materials on Twentieth-Century Literature by Ettore Mazzali and Robert J. Clements

Translated by Richard Monges

1969
New York: New York University Press
London: University of London Press

© 1969 by New York University
Library of Congress Catalog Card Number: 68-13026
Manufactured in the United States of America

Foreword to the First Edition

In this volume I have outlined all that is essential to know about the history of Italian literature, with an eye to the works themselves, rather than on evaluations of them which have taken shape in the schools, more often dictated by laziness than by conviction. I have dwelt upon the major writers with emphasis, and passed rapidly over the minor ones, paying more heed to the significance of the work than to the facts of the lives. I have tried to give ideas rather than data, to say more and speak less than is customary in books of this kind, and to write a book, rather than compile a text. Twenty years of loving teaching of Italian in the secondary schools allow me to hope that I have not struck too wide of my mark.

Eugenio Donadoni

Foreword to the Fifth Edition

In the Foreword to the fourth edition (1960) we wrote:

In this new edition of the *Literary History* of Eugenio Donadoni — a work which every day demonstrates its robust vitality in Italian secondary schools — we have tried to accede to a wish which was made known to us by several of our friends: a desire, that is to say, that to so harmoniously proportioned a historical design there should be added timely pages on the more recent literature of Italy.

By its persistence, this same demand has persuaded us to prepare this new fifth edition which, from page 549 on, continues and concludes the *History*, treating more fully, as often happens when recent and contemporary matters are discussed, the late nineteenth century and the first sixty years of the twentieth. This completely new section was written by Ettore Mazzali (E. M.), who has also provided a brief account of Eugenio Donadoni. The generous chapters on Carducci, Verga, Fogazzaro, Oriani, Pascoli, and D'Annunzio, previously written by Francesco Flora (F. F.) for the third edition, have remained exactly as they were in the fourth edition, as there did not seem to be the slightest need for changing even a comma for this edition.

We are confident that this, the fifth edition, thus broadened and brought up to date — so that the twentieth-century account is the fullest and most complete that up to now has ever been written for a school text and covers works right down to the most recent 1963 publications — will encounter the old and unflagging approval and favor of the schools of Italy.

The Publisher
(Signorelli)

Contents

FOREWORD TO THE FIRST EDITION
FOREWORD TO THE FIFTH EDITION
PREFACE TO THE ENGLISH-LANGUAGE EDITION

1. Introduction 3
2. The Thirteenth Century (Il Duecento) 9
3. The Fourteenth Century (Il Trecento) 23
4. The Fifteenth Century (Il Quattrocento) . . . 127
5. The Sixteenth Century (Il Cinquecento) . . . 165
6. The Seventeenth Century 275
7. The Eighteenth Century 311
8. The Nineteenth Century 363
9. The Twentieth Century 549
   An Epilogue   663
   Index

Introduction to the English-Language Edition

It is a paradox that the English-speaking community, whose scholars have contributed so many important monographs on Italian authors, periods, and themes, has never produced a comprehensive and authoritative history of Italian literature that includes the twentieth century. The need for an adequate summary of Italian literature in English decided the Editors of the Gotham Library to bring out in translation the best brief history currently used in Italy. There were a number of most eligible literary histories to choose from, including those of Flora, Momigliano, Sapegno, and Cappuccio. After considerable reflection, it was decided to arrange for translation of the basic survey by the late Eugenio Donadoni, published by Signorelli. Indeed, this distinguished Italian house acceded to our request that they accelerate their revision of the twentieth-century materials, a task which they entrusted wisely to Professor Ettore Mazzali. Thus, the fifth Italian edition of this history represents the cooperative efforts of Eugenio Donadoni, Francesco Flora (whose chapters are initialed), and Ettore Mazzali.

Eugenio Donadoni of Bergamo, professor successively at Messina and Pisa, won critical esteem for studies on Foscolo, Fogazzaro, Tasso, Dante, and Manzoni. One notes immediately the temporal range of his interests. But it was his *Breve storia della letteratura italiana* that won him the affection of generations of Italian students at all levels. No one has ever met more convincingly the challenge of condensing the vast corpus of Italian literature into so few pages, doing full justice to the major figures and remaining just as solicitous about the minor and regional ones. Within the welter of facts, names, titles, and statistics inevitably presented, one observes throughout the serene and accurate judgments of the humanist and historian. Even more, one senses an exceptional personality, enabling us to understand at this distance Donadoni's popularity as a teacher. Donadoni believes in the traditional values of art. Literature must have form, substance, honesty, and purpose. It must be free, and he is the first to point out the encroachments of church, state, or maecenate system. Having lived in several regions of Italy, Donadoni nevertheless avoids the nationalistic bias that sometimes creeps into histories of French literature. A student of belles lettres in their fullest social and historical context, he brought (in Mazzali's words) "not just a rigorous philological and linguistic 'apparatus criticus,' but a total historical and moral culture, within which the history of the technical forms and of the language is hidden and almost disguised, refraining from any erudite arrogance whatsoever."

Donadoni does not shirk his task of constant synthesis and criticism by combining his history with an anthology. Studded with facts and interpretations without an idle word, this volume may be used successfully for quick reference. Yet even those who buy the book for its obvious merits as a reference manual should try at one point to read it from first to last page and enjoy the unfolding spectacle of the birth and growth of one of the world's richest and most varied literatures. Part of the great value of this volume for the English or American reader is that it offers him an Italian view of Italian literature and is itself an example of the Italian genius — intensely human, unfailingly religious, even in its most secular moods, and capable of a Roman seriousness. Those who believe that Italy was merely "a geographical term" until the nineteenth century, will find good cause to change their minds; they will find among Italian writers a sense of kinship that may be compared to that which the Hellenes felt and that which has preserved Jewish culture throughout its ordeals.

I cannot close without expressing my admiration for the manner in which Professor Richard Monges, a lifetime student of Italy, has captured the letter and the spirit of the original text. The American scholar Richard Fabrizio has discreetly modified the original text where modern researches required it. Thus, where Donadoni's generation taught that Boccaccio was born in Paris, scholars have now verified that it was Certaldo. Otherwise the translation stays as close as possible to the original text.

Robert J. Clements, 1969

A History of
Italian Literature

1.

Introduction

Persistence of the Latin Language Through the Middle Ages

Even through the long dark period of the Middle Ages, which lasted in Italy until some time in the fourteenth century, the cult of both the civilization and the name of Rome remained quite alive in the countries that had formed the Roman Empire, especially in Italy. A series of legends woven around the most important men of the Latin world and, indirectly, of the Greek world — Brutus, Julius Caesar, Trajan, Alexander the Great, Hector, Aeneas — took the place of forgotten and unfamiliar history. Schools of grammar kept alive the study of the Latin poets. Roman law was taught in the universities of Bologna and Padua; and the loftiest functions of collective life were expressed in Latin: sermons, teaching, laws, and public and private contracts. Therefore it is easy to understand how the language that Rome had implanted through all western Europe, with her conquests and her colonies, survived; not, of course, with all its elegance, but with its vocabulary, its grammar, and its syntax.

Nor did the Roman spirit ever die out completely in political life. The Catholic Church itself, in its hierarchy, in its capacity for ruling, in its moral and intellectual unity that it imparted to the world, may be considered as the heir of the Roman Empire: Roman values, of the industrious and practical life, offset the contemplative mysticism of the race; and even the monasteries had constitutions inspired by the requirements of social life. The election of Charlemagne, king of the Franks, as the new emperor of the West was a triumph of the Roman idea; and after the year one thousand, the glorious communes of northern and central Italy were not without memories of the ancient Roman *municipia*.

The Neo-Latin Vernaculars and The Volgare Illustre

Even before A.D. 1000, although it was still spoken and written to meet the requirements of upper-class life, Latin was less and less understood by the masses and began to find itself in approximately the same condition that it is in today: understood only by those who study it academically. Alongside Latin, the official written language, new vernaculars were developing in the various regions of the former empire. Spoken for quite some time before they were written, these vernaculars were the idioms of the populace, the *vulgus*, and so came to be called *vulgar* tongues. In time, refined by art and stabilized by writing, they became languages. The vernaculars that arose where Latin had previously been spoken were called neo-Latin, or Romance (from *lingua romana*); they were spoken in the areas we now call France, Spain, Portugal, Italy, and Rumania. From these tongues, originally very numerous since almost every city had its own, the modern languages derive. But obscurities concerning the origins of the vulgar tongues and their relationships with Latin are very numerous. The most widely accepted hypothesis is that the neo-Latin vernaculars do not derive directly from literary Latin but by corruption from a popular Latin or *sermo rusticus,* whose existence even during the most glorious days of Rome it is impossible to doubt. But it is not beyond the bounds of probability that in each region another vernacular was taking shape alongside the *sermo rusticus,* modeled partly on it and partly on the Latin of the schools. This so to speak typical vulgar speech was nobler and stood in the same relationship to the vernacular that language stands to its dialects. Dante called this higher vernacular the *volgare illustre.* In other words, besides the local dialects, Italy must have had a language that was common to the whole nation.

Characteristics of the Vernaculars

The vulgar tongues, then, took most of their words from Latin; but from Greek (the Church having developed first in the Greek world) they took many words dealing with the liturgy, and from the languages of the Germanic conquerors, many words referring to war and to the political and administrative system.

Even among the classical Romans the elision of some word endings in pronunciation caused an attrition of the cases and in their place prepositions, taking on new and fuller meaning, were substituted. The forms of the oblique cases, more frequently used than the nominative, often replaced it; simple morphological forms, such as that of the future tense, were broken up into periphrases; analogy was powerful in the inflection of verbs so that conjugations became confused with one another; ample adverbial periphrases replaced adverbs; and complicated connecting phrases replaced simple conjunctions. The Latin period, so complex and so solidly constructed, finally changed into a series of clauses with their elements arranged in logical order.

No less important was the transformation of ancient versification. The Latins had a sense of the quantity of syllables; the new tongues had only a sense of stress or accent, and their verse-lines were series of stressed and unstressed syllables, which produced a feeling of easy, singable rhythms. Also, the new versification gave great importance to that exact consonance of word endings (often originally substituted by assonance) much in use in the Latin poetry of the decadence. We allude to rhyme which was so important that in Dante's time *rima* meant simply a line of verse. From the varied coupling of rhymes, the first few simple strophes developed.

When the Vernaculars Arose

The formation and constitution of the vulgar tongues are lost to sight in the early Middle Ages. Even before the year one thousand, fragments appear that now are subjects for study by glossologists and philologists. But the important thing to note is that the vernaculars spread, grow stronger, and pass from oral to written form when the social classes using them acquire political importance and become material for history. During the invasion and establishment of the barbarians one ecclesiastical class enjoyed a spiritual superiority as representatives of the surviving culture. After the year one thousand two other classes opposed to the clerics emerged: the powerful, dominating conquerors, almost all of Germanic origin, who found their ideal expression in chivalry and their concrete expression in the feudal regime; and the ancient, conquered populace of predominantly Latin origin. At first this latter class lived a life of slavery and obscurity and then, in reaction to feudalism, acquired consciousness of its rights and of its power, gradually becoming the wealthy and industrious middle class of the towns, the bourgeoisie. The vernaculars followed the rise of these two classes which until then had remained without a voice, because they lacked consciousness of self. And first (approximately from 1000 to 1200) the speech of the warrior classes asserted itself in praise of the legendary undertakings of a Charlemagne and the still more legendary exploits of a King Arthur and his knights of the round table, while songs of love and of deeds of arms, and sometimes anticlerical satires, resounded in the castle halls of Provence. Thus the early French and Provençal literatures took form: the French, being called *langue d'oïl* (*hoc illud:* modern *oui*) from its affirmative particle the Provençal, *langue d'oc* (pronounced *o,* Latin *hoc:* this).

From 1200 on, then, the vernaculars developed and became increasingly important, whether to express pure meanings of love and joy and the raptures, hopes, and terrors of religion or, for purely practical purposes, to satisfy the needs of that culture, encyclopedic, if elementary, which was growing ever more necessary to the men of the communes. So it is that the Italian vernaculars, or at least Italian popular literature, arose when primitive French and Provençal had already worn themselves out. And if the Italian vulgar tongues and popular literature were the last to assert themselves, if during their first century they appeared both in form and in spirit to be borrowed from those of France and Provence, they nevertheless bore within themselves fecund germs of thought and art that were later to be developed amply.

2.

The Thirteenth Century (*Il Duecento*)

The Poetry of Love

Thirteenth-century poetry is largely the expression of the most elementary and primitive of feelings: love. Dante stated it simply when he wrote that the first man to write poetry in the vernacular did so in order to declare his love to a woman who did not understand Latin. This love poetry is basically courtly: the poetry which flourished at the courts of Provence, and this origin explains the artificiality and conventionality of so much of it, composed in order to pay homage to a lady of the court rather than to make love to a woman. Provençal troubadours brought it to Italy after Provence, accused of favoring heretics and having become a victim of the greed of the French crown, had disappeared as a nation and as a literature.

These troubadours found hospitality in the courts and the republics of northern Italy, where there were many Italians who wrote poetry themselves in Provençal, in forms that by now had become stylized and rigid. One of these was Sordello of Mantua, a man of loves, of courts, and of arms who died about 1267, and who plays an important role in one of the loftiest cantos of Dante's *Purgatory*. Among the few surviving fragments of his poems, there is a *complainte* or lament on the death of the noble knight Blacatz. Foreshadowing the vigor of Dante, it resolves into harsh criticisms of the abased princes of Europe who, contrasted with this deceased nobleman, personified the disappearing chivalrous virtues of courage and loyalty.

The troubadours were also welcomed in the South, at the Sicilian court of the last and greatest of the Suabian emperors, Frederick II, the high-minded sovereign who was long remembered as the highest ideal of royal munificence, and who died in 1250. Indeed, to his court flocked not only poets, but men of all manner of attainments: philosophers, doctors, naturalists, historians, and jurists; that proud adversary of ecclesiastical authority felt the importance of that culture, which was the strongest weapon of the Church.

The Sicilian School of Poetry: (Scuola Siciliana)

The rhymers who graced Frederick's court were very numerous and constituted what we call the Sicilian [School of Poetry], although we have Dante's assertion that poets of other regions were also called *Siciliani*. Many of the verses of those primitive poets are still preserved. In most of them the Provençal manner is noticeable in the artificial images and lack of personality, in the rhetorical reworking of conventional themes, in overlong meters, and in the complicated strophe of the *canzone* or song. But at the same time and possibly earlier, there flourished in southern and central Italy a poetry not very different from that which even now sounds spontaneously in many parts of the Italian lands. The sonnet itself, an original creation of Sicilian poetry derived not from the strophe of the *canzone,* but from popular rhythmic harmonies such as *nona rima* and *ottava rima,* is evidence of an indigenous poetry. And what are the names of the Sicilian poets? Of the many, a few suffice: that of Frederick himself and his son Enzo (who died a prisoner of the Bolognese); Frederick's secretary Pier della Vigna (who was far more deserving of praise as a secretary than as a rhymer, one of the greatest statesmen of his time and the fearless defender of the laicality of the State as is apparent from his letters) ; Guido delle Colonne of Messina, a judge, and author or translator of a Latin *History of Troy*; and Giacomo da Lentini, also a man of the law and a notary, the Emperor's chancellor. All these men represent the Provençal manner. Other poets derive from the popular manner: Rinaldo d'Aquino with his lament of a lover departing on a Crusade; Ruggero da Palermo as a lover lamenting the departure of his lady for Syria; Odo delle Colonne; Giacomino Pugliese; and Cielo d'Alcamo, whose long *contrasto* or dialogue of the lover and his beloved, richly spontaneous and dramatically alive, is written in deft strophes of three double *septenarii* and two hendecasyllables, which have no precedent in Provençal poetry.

The Tuscan Lyric of the Thirteenth Century

In Tuscany, contemporary with, or a little later than the Sicilian poetry, a related type of artificial poetry of Provençal inspiration flourished. We remember Buonagiunta Urbiciani of Lucca, whom Dante was to teach (in canto XXIV of the *Purgatory*) that without inspiration there is no poetry; Chiaro Davanzati of Florence, who wrote not only love verse but composed a *sirventese,* a topical narrative poem, dealing with the rout inflicted in 1260 on the Guelfs at Montaperti; A *canzone* had been written on this subject by one who once was considered the greatest of these old Tuscan rhymers: Guido or Guittone del Viva, of Arezzo (d. 1294), one of the Knights of Santa Maria or "jolly friars" (*frati gaudenti*). In his youth he wrote love poetry; at a riper age he disdained profane subjects and composed moral or religious rhymes and political admonitions addressed to various cities of Tuscany. He also left us his *Letters,* which have pretentions to elegance and reproduce the rhythm of classical Latin. By the content of his writings, no less than by that artificiality which in unsophisticated cultures is taken for art, he earned a reputation as a superior man. Dante neglects no occasion to disparage him. (He is not to be confused with the Guido d'Arezzo, 990–1050, who was a famous musician.) Also worthy of mention are the Florentine, Ciacco dall'Anguillaia, whose famous *villanella* derives from the *contrasto* of the Sicilian School, and the Florentine poetess, La Compiuta Donzella, to whom we owe a lovely sonnet, "In the Season when the World Leafs out and Blooms."

Religious Poetry

Francis of Assisi

Thirteenth-century religious poetry enjoyed great favor, especially because of the great Franciscan movement which, in the field of religion, has a certain analogy with that of the Communes in secular politics. Saint Francis, born at Assisi (1182–1226), was the initiator of the movement. For him, God loses the dread with which He had been regarded in the feudal age, and is close to all who seek Him with purity and fervor. Loving God becomes equivalent to loving mankind. The "convent" (in the sense of a religious community) replaces the monastery; the prior and abbot, titles of superiority, give way to *padre* [father] and *fra* or *frate* [friar, brother], names of equality and affection. Asceticism, so important in the older orders, loses importance in the Franciscan. The soul is what God asks for. For although Saint Francis preached utter poverty, it was only as a means to more ardent charity. This is revealed in his "canticle of the creatures," a kind of psalm in which he blesses all created things: the sun and the moon, air and water, earth and fire, exalting himself to praise God the Father for all of them, calling them all brother or sister — even Death, which even then was fluttering about the Saint. It is a very simple, ardent canticle written in a meter or rather, an irregular sing-song, which calls to mind the performance of liturgical chants. For Saint Francis, therefore, God becomes more inward, more intimate; the voice of religion has a more humane sound. The more familiar and more moving characters, scenes, and themes are preferred; later there would be the marvelous series of paintings by Giotto, the supreme artist of the Franciscan spiritual movement, which happened to coincide with the old beliefs about the end of the world and the approaching Kingdom of God. So, a few decades after the death of the Saint, in order to be prepared for the great day, the preaching of repentance was entrusted to companies of fanatical flagellants who increased in numbers from 1258 on, especially in the region that would always be the most mystical in Italy: Umbria. To these companies of penitents is due the diffusion among the multitudes of a religious poetry, of which the primitive form was the *laude* [laud]. In town squares and streets the lauds replaced the hymns and sequences sung in churches; they were sung by the people, related the important events in the life of the Christ and of Mary, and told of Christian belief. The favorite, most popular meter for these songs was the *ottonario,* an eight-syllable line with rhythmic accent on third and seventh.

Jacopone da Todi

Few writers of lauds are known by name, but some details are available for one very prolific such writer: Jacopone da Todi or rather, Jacopo Benedetti, born about

1230. Grieved by the sudden death of his beloved wife, he withdrew from worldly life and gave himself up wholly to God, choosing whatever forms of penitence would make him appear most ridiculous and contemptible. After some twelve years of this discipline, he entered the Franciscan order, joining the strictest, sternest party, the one most opposed by the Church. He took part in a rebellion of the Colonna party against Boniface VIII. In prison he did not soften his fierce animosity against that pope, whom Dante also saw as a corrupter of the Christian spirit. Jacopone died in 1306.

Innumerable compositions are attributed to him. He left many satires scornful of the world and of everything that the world extols most; in these pieces there is in truth little or nothing of the Franciscan spirit that blesses life. He also wrote many lauds in which the pure religious feeling bursts forth, although in a humanizing of the religious story or tradition. One of these lauds, although of uncertain attribution* is a tender hymn to Mary contemplating the infant Jesus; another tells of Mary witnessing the crucifixion. In still others Jacopone feels all the terror of the day of universal judgment. Although Jacopone is sporadically a poet, he is never an artist; he lacks the sense of fitness, of propriety, of restraint. He passes from the delicate to the coarse with no intimate fusion of the two elements. At times his mystical language is an ardent stammering which expresses nothing. He repeats the same themes endlessly and becomes lost in interminable sermons. From this "madman of Jesus Christ," as he was called, a work of art is not to be expected. Art is the product of the most exquisite spiritual balance.

---

* This laud has also been attributed to the Dominican Giovanni Dominici or to the priest Leonardo Pisano; its composition dates from the end of the fourteenth or the beginning of the fifteenth century.

The Little Flowers of Saint Francis (I Fioretti)

All the spirit of the Franciscan movement is revealed in a book in prose, written in the vernacular in the fourteenth century; but it is included here because the originals from which it derives belong certainly to the thirteenth century, and because few books are so substantially poetic as this prose. It is called *The Little Flowers of Saint Francis*. The book is not a life of the saint, but a collection of facts, sayings, and miracles presented in a barely discernable chronological order. The virtues of the Saint most stressed are his humility and his cult of poverty, together with the inner joy that comes from renunciation of all worldly joys. Some of the fifty-three little chapters or *capitoletti* are childishly ingenuous, such as the sermon to the Sultan of Babylon; the sermons of Francis to the fishes and to the birds; and the conversion of the ferocious wolf of Gubbio, which the Saint induced to change from a devastator of the countryside into a well-behaved wolf living on the spontaneous gifts and offerings of the citizens. Several of the "Little Flowers" are dedicated to the earliest followers of Saint Francis, men no less saintly than simple: Brother Bernard, Brother Egidio, Brother Leo, Brother Giovanni della Penna, Brother Pacifico, Brother Umile; two of them belong to history: the ardent preacher, Saint Anthony of Padua, and Saint Clare who, on the example of Saint Francis and to encourage him, founded the feminine counterpart of the Franciscan order, the Clarisses. The life and teachings of Brother Egidio and the life of Brother Ginepro complete the book. Brother Ginepro is the very figure of simplicity of the spirit, and commits several acts which, although hierarchically and socially reprehensible, are directed toward charity. Thus, on one occasion he cut off the foot of a hog in order to help an invalid, and one Christmas Eve he plucked some silver bells of great value from the altar and gave them to a poor woman in dire need. The "Little Flowers" are of interest also for a certain simple and inimitable grace, a childlike spontaneity that is part of the soul of the pious compiler. Free of any artistic pretentions, they are more moving than a formal work of art, and arouse an unconscious suggestion of some primitive painter.

The Poetry of Religious Morality

But a less enthusiastic and more moralizing literature also flowered among the commoners of the thirteenth century, of whose authors it will suffice to recall two names. Giacomino da Verona, a Franciscan monk who lived in the second half of the century, wrote two little poems: one on Paradise and the other concerned with Hell, entitled *De Ierusalem celesti* and *De Babilonia civitate infernale*. These two vernacular poems deal with a subject very popular in Latin-Christian literature, which later was to be treated by Dante: the next life. Giacomino presents in a very realistic way, the most ferocious tortures in Hell and the grossest pleasures in Paradise, especially those of gluttony, since the common idea of Paradise was summed up in the dominant desire of the wretched, impoverished lives of the people. Bonvesin de la Riva, a Milanese and a friar of the Umiliati order, wrote much, both in Latin and in the vernacular, and died after 1313. He was chiefly an author of moral works and made frequent use of the form known as *contrasto,* which resembled the disputations of the schools and churches. Among his many compositions of this sort, he wrote a contrasto of the soul and the body, another of the rose and violet, one on the fly and the mosquito, still another on the twelve months of the year and their arguments with one another, and a contrasto of the Virgin Mary and the Devil. His little poem *De quinqua-*

ginta curialitatibus ad mensam [*The Fifty Rules of Good Manners To Be Observed At Table*] is interesting in the history of customs because of the gross usages of the lower and middle classes that it implies.

Allegorical Poetry: Brunetto Latini

Deeply rooted for centuries in the traditions of the schools, and which was to endure for many more centuries, was the conception of a poetry that would make learning agreeable by its use of images, imagination, and ornamentation. Such a concept is entirely repugnant to the idea we now have of poetry as inspired and spontaneous. The most widely used form for this purpose was the *allegory*, which gives sensible form to abstract concepts or, more concretely, personifies them. This does not mean, as it does in more realistic poetry, the creation of plausible human characters and themes; it means to wander about outside of any reality, to delineate beings who are all outward form, inanimate beings of literary convention. The Middle Ages had produced several famous allegorical poems in Latin, which later served as models for the rhymers using the vernacular. About the middle of the thirteenth century in France, an immense poem, *Le Roman de la Rose*, appeared, the first part of which, amid a choreography of personifications of the moments of love, teaches chivalric or courtly virtues. In the second part, it gives way to orgies of learned digressions and to violent satires aimed principally at women.

One of the followers of this poetic manner was the Florentine Brunetto Latini, a notary. Politically a Guelf, he passed a long period of exile in France after the victory of the Ghibellines at Montaperti and returned to Florence only after the defeat of the Ghibellines at Benevento in 1266; there he died in 1294 or 1295. In a very broad sense he was Dante's teacher, and in *The Inferno*, the poet addresses him with a reverence (mingled perhaps with irony) and places him in a circle that does him no honor. Brunetto was a scholar above and before anything else. While in France he composed the books of the *Trésor* [*Treasure*], an encyclopedia in eight books, which treats of astronomy, geography, the Church, Roman and medieval history, natural sciences, rhetoric, and morality. An appendix includes a subject that was particularly important to the life of the commune: the appointment of the *podestà* or chief magistrate. The contents of the work expressed the doctrines and summarized the famous books of the schools, for the edification of a literate middle class. It is at once an exposition of the knowledge and a document of the ingenuous ignorance of the times, particularly in the field of the natural sciences. The work is written in French prose, because the Italian vernaculars were not yet well enough developed for handling speculative and scientific subjects as was French, already more than two hundred years old. But the learned notary felt the need of increasing his reputation in another work also, this one in the vernacular, which, on account of being much shorter than the *Trésor* was called *Il Tesoretto* [*The Little Treasure*], but had no connection with the longer opus. The *Tesoretto* is an allegorical poem of which the hero is the author himself, who travels through the kingdoms of Nature, of chivalric virtue, of love (where the great classical poet, Ovid, whose love poetry was popular during the Middle Ages, becomes his teacher), until the pilgrim arrives on Mount Olympus, where the geographer, Ptolemy, gives him a lesson in physics. Here the poem breaks off.

It is easy to perceive in the *Tesoretto* an allegorical voyage like that of Dante in the *Commedia;* the passing of the author from the sensual to the contemplative life (symbolized by Mount Olympus) is also a fundamental concept of Dante's poem. These analogies have conferred on the writing of Brunetto an importance that it does not really deserve. Dante, the sovereign artist, who classes Brunetto with the plebeian writers, could feel no sympathy for that miserable poem whose heaviness is aggravated by a meter, septenarii rhymed in couplets, of intolerable monotony. Although the *Tesoretto* may have the *Roman de la Rose* as a distant model, the famous French book also had more direct reworkings in Italy: in an anonymous *Detto d'amore* [*Story of Love*] also in *septenarii,* and in *Il fiore,* a series of over two hundred sonnets attributed to a Ser Durante, whom some scholars, with little justification, have thought might be Dante Alighieri.

Historical Poetry and Chronicles

Nor does the thirteenth century lack examples—(which must have been far more numerous than the few which have reached us) of a popular poetry that found its material in the more sensational events of the troubled life of the communes. In such compositions, it would seem, the *sirventese* was the most frequent form. But by the thirteenth century, contemporary events found more natural expression in the prose chronicles of the various cities. The chroniclers were sometimes maintained at the expense of the Commune, or were commissioned to write for it. In the thirteenth century, from a sense of dignity, the chroniclers continued to write in Latin, as did Fra Salimbene of Parma, the most eloquent and lively of them all. But even then anonymous chroniclers were writing in the vernacular at Pistoia, at Lucca, at Siena. One Ricordano Malespini had already written, or was thought to have written, a chronicle of Florence, which reaches to 1282, but in all probability this is a much later compilation of data taken from Villani. Municipal pride is discernible in the old chroniclers and was to continue for centuries. For each of them, his own city had a most ancient origin, connected with the noble history of Rome or the even more ancient history of Troy, and romantic legends of feats of arms and tales of love are grafted upon the lives of his heroes. There are many anachronisms in the chronicles: Greek and Roman personages are given such titles as baron and knight; in Malespini's chronicle, Catilina, encamped near Florence, goes to hear mass in the rectory of Fiesole. But when they deal with contemporary events, those storytellers take pains to adhere to the truth, as far as partisan passion allow.

The Novella

The legends of antiquity and of chivalry also enjoyed a fairly widespread popularity, although most of them were translations from the French, such as those centering on the Round Table, and the *Romance of Tristan,* the *Noble Deeds of Alexander the Great,* or those of Caesar and the *Tales of the Ancient Knights*. But these legends, together with those of Charlemagne and his paladins, gathered into various poems which, even in Italy, were written in French or the Franco-Venetian dialect, were barely kept alive until in the fifteenth and sixteenth centuries they found their own Italian poets. The men of the Communes had greater fondness for the short stories known as *novelle* or *novità*, which were as useful in satisfying public curiosity about famous persons and events as they were in supplying entertainment. The most noteworthy collection of tales in the thirteenth century was the *Libro di Novelle e di bel parlar gentile* [*Book Of Novellas And Of Elegant Noble Speech*] also known as the *Novellino* or *Cento novelle antiche* [*The Hundred Old Tales*], to distinguish it from the more recent *Cento Novelle* or *Decameron* of Boccaccio. There are various editions of the *Novellino* differing considerably one from another. The subjects are taken from a wide range of material: from the ancient world, Priam, Antigonus, Hippocrates, Aristotle, Seneca, Cato, Trajan; from the world of chivalry, Tristan, Isolde, Meliadus; and from the lives of the troubadours. Great men of the past appear: the Emperor Conrad, Frederick II, Charles of Anjou, Saladin, King John of England. There are memorable deeds and clever sayings, with no pretentions to art but for that very reason, greatly aided by the precise Tuscan tongue, not lacking in vigor and beauty.

Il libro dei sette savi [*Book Of The Seven Sages*] is an ancient collection of novellas of Indian origin, translated in the Middle Ages into Latin, Arabic, Hebrew, French, and toward the end of the thirteenth century, into Italian. A son of the king resists the evil desires of his stepmother who, offended, accuses him to her husband. The seven wise men charged with the education of the young prince know, through astrology, that to ward off a great danger he must not speak for seven days. They speak for him, and each day one of them narrates to the king a tale about the iniquity of women, while each evening the stepmother relates a tale illustrating the iniquity of sons. Finally on the eighth day the young prince can speak, and by means of a novella he exposes the perfidy of his stepmother, who is burned at the stake. The idea of gathering many stories around a central point, enclosed as in a picture frame pleased the greatest Italian writers of novellas of the following century and their countless imitators. Although it is a work of a different nature, mention should be made here of the anonymous *Libro dei cinquanta miracoli della Vergine* [*Book Of The Fifty Miracles Of The Virgin*], which probably was written at the end of the thirteenth century.

Educational Literature

Not much interested in poetry perhaps, but imbued with a sense of the practical, the Italian middle class aimed at the conquest of that learning which had made the clerical class so powerful. They wished to assimilate, to epitomize, and to render in the vernacular that learning. Therefore, near the end of the thirteenth century, shortly after the *Trésor* of Latini, we find other encyclopedias, for example the *Composizione del Mondo* of Fra Ristoro of Arezzo. Morality and rhetoric were considered singularly interesting in this period. Fra Guidotto of Bologna composed the *Fiore di retorica* [*Flower Of Rhetoric*], and a *Fiore di virtù* was contributed by Tommaso Gozzadini of Bologna. There were more than a few translators of famous books, sacred and profane. An anonymous writer of Siena translated Aesop's fables with admirable vigor. Translations from Cicero and Sallust were formerly attributed to Brunetto Latini. The most copious translator was Bono Giamboni of Florence who, among other things, made vernacular versions of Latini's *Trésor*, the *Art Of War* by Vegetius, and the *Garden Of Consolation* [*Viridarium consolationis*] by Jacobus di Voragine, bishop of Genova, who is best known as a hagiographer for his *Legenda aurea* [*Golden Legend*], a collection of saints' lives.

3.

The Fourteenth Century

Transformation of the Love Lyric

The poetical literature that has been discussed so far has rarely ever reached the level of art. Even the rhymers of the Sicilian school, whether they were imitating the Provençal poets or learning from the simple popular poetry, were closer to artfulness than they were to art; by later standards their work was rough and unpolished, for art is measure, proportion and selection. From crude expressions of love early artistic poetry developed amid an atmosphere of culture in places like Bologna and Tuscany. Without the stimulus of active thought and refinement poetry is a specter, a flower without roots.

In Bologna, philosophy and theology were in flower, as was the juridical culture. Thus, it was natural that the poetry of love, passing in that city from the courtly society to the cultured middle classes, became tinged, in a manner of speaking, with philosophical elements. Love was regarded as a power of the soul and confused with will itself. Woman was no longer the lady of Provençal or Sicilian poetry but an intermediary of God; perfect beauty that reveals itself to man either as grace that touches the heart, or as truth that illuminates the intellect.

But if the new poetic school seemed to translate love into philosophy, in reality it made love more inward and more intimate: homage was converted into adoration; gallantry became passion, sometimes serene, more often sorrowful. Love was carried from the courts into the shrine of the soul. Inspiration was therefore the fundamental canon of the new poetry which, with a phrase from Dante's *Purgatorio,* canto XXIV, was called *Dolce stil nuovo.*

Guido Guinizelli

Dante and his contemporary Tuscan rhymers are the true poets of this *Dolce stil nuovo.* Dante himself, however, in the *Purgatorio,* recognizes a native of Bologna: Guido Guinizelli (c. 1240–1276), a doctor in jurisprudence as his "father," or as we would say, precursor in the new love poetry. Canzoni, ballads, and sonnets — almost exclusively concerning love — have come down to us from Guinizelli's pen. He began as an imitator of Guittone of Arezzo, and several of his canzoni are the typical pretty things, compliments and despairing laments, in the Provençal or Sicilian manner. But in one canzone, *Al cor gentil ripara sempre Amore* [*Love Always Takes Shelter in the Noble Heart*], he gave a strong statement of the principle of the equivalence of love and nobility of heart. Going a step further, he affirmed the oneness of the feminine and the divine, so that when God reproves the poet for having loved a woman more than Him, the poet defends himself by saying that the woman seemed an angel from Heaven. Actually, the sonnets extolling the pure grace-giving beauty of woman are perhaps more beautiful than this abstruse canzone; traces of them are visible in Dante's rhymes. Sprightliness, delicacy, and concision are the virtues of

Guinizelli's rhymes, but harshness is frequent, and the travail of thought is felt more often than the impulse of passion.

Il Dolce Stil Nuovo

The new lyric found the proper climate for its continuation in Florence rather than in learned Bologna, for Tuscany had already developed that sense of form and measure that for centuries would characterize the art of the region. Because of the democratic make-up of the city, popular poetry — sometimes gentle, sometimes proud, now amorous, now satirical — could mingle with learned poetry and give it greater vigor of imagery and loftier expression. Here at last love poetry found its most apt instrument in a vernacular which, if it were not the "illustrious" one envisioned and sought after by Dante, stood out above the others for its precision, its fullness, and its harmony.

Thus it came about that in the last decades of the thirteenth century and the first of the fourteenth century, the poets of the *Dolce stil nuovo* flourished in Florence. Let us recall a few names: Gianni Alfani, who sometimes lets us hear the sad notes of exile; Dino Frescobaldi, who comes nearest to the joyous ecstasies and the melancholy of the verses of Dante; Lapo Gianni, a notary, who recalls the freshness of the popular *rispetti* (a sort of *ottava rima*, of which the first four lines have alternate rhyme and the next four are in couplets); Guido Orlandi, Lapo degli Uberti, Sennuccio del Bene, and outside of Tuscany, Guido Novello, Lord of Polenta, who was Dante's last patron. In its popular form, the *rispetti* did not necessarily end in two couplets, but sometimes in *abcc*.

The love expressed by these poets has a mystical character. The woman they love is nameless, or else has a name symbolizing her virtues or her power. There is no mention of her feminine, bodily reality nor of her historical identity. She is an angel who is on earth for a fleeting moment, for the joy and comfort of mankind, but she is awaited in Heaven. The theme of love ends or merges with that of death. Because of their unreal character it was thought that the women spoken of by the *Dolce stil nuovo* poets were allegorical. Some took them to be figures of philosophy, or of revelation, and there were those who held them to symbolize perfect beauty. But perhaps in all pure and chaste love, like that expressed by these early poets, there is an inherent and ineffable and unreal quality.

Three poets of the *Dolce stil nuovo* stand out: one is Dante; another is Guido Cavalcanti, the greatest friend of his youth, and one who died before him; the third is Cino da Pistoia, who outlived the great poet.

Guido Cavalcanti

Guido was of a noble family: son-in-law of Farinata degli Uberti, the Ghibelline captain who inflicted the defeat of Montaperti on the Guelfs. When Florence was divided among the White Guelfs and the Black Guelfs, he was included with the Whites, who were sympathetic to the Ghibelline cause. In 1300, while Dante was serving as one of the priors of the city, it was decided that the leaders of the Blacks and the Whites should be sent into exile so that the citizens might have some peace. Guido was held at Sarzana, in the Lunigiana district, where he fell ill of malaria. He died soon after his return to Florence in August of 1300. Several women appear in his poetry, or *canzoniere*, a certain Giovanna, called Primavera [Spring], and a Pinella from Bologna. During a pilgrimage that he made to Santiago de Compostela in Galicia, he fell in love, at Toulouse, with a Mandetta. From his pen we have *canzoni*, sonnets, ballads. Perhaps he was also the author of more than sixty anonymous sonnets, which speak of *il ben servire* [loyal service]; that is, how to woo a lady. He concerned himself deeply with those same questions of love dealt within Provençal poetry, and on the origin and nature of love he wrote one of the least felicitous and most famous of *canzoni, Donna mi prega, perch'io voglia dire* [*A Lady Entreats Me That I Fain Would Say*]. Several moral *canzoni* were also attributed to him, but we find the real poet in a handful of poems about love and gallantry: in sonnets that describe the beloved; in a ballad in the Provençal manner in honor of Mandetta of Toulouse; in the poems in which he analyzes and paints his sadness in love; and in a celebrated ballad *Perch'io no spero* [*Since I Have No Hope*] sent during his exile to his lady, to whom this ballad is to carry the poet's last greeting. Guido interests us with his immediacy, his directness, and his ability to express with gracefulness, lightness, and individuality, the concepts and the images of the poetry of his time.

Cino Da Pistoia

Cino was a great jurist, and wrote a commentary on the first nine books of the Codex of Justinian, entitled *Lectura in Codicem*. He taught law at Siena, at Perugia, at Naples, and again at Perugia. He died in his city of Pistoia *circa* 1337. He carried on a correspondence with Dante through an exchange of sonnets. He composed a *canzone* on the death of Beatrice and another on the death of Dante himself. He also wrote one for the death of the emperor, Henry VII (*Arrigo*) in whom he, Dante, and all those who deplored the discord in Italy had placed such hopes. Another *canzone* written at Naples and full of yearning for his home is *Deh, quando rivedrô il dolce paese* [*Ah, When Shall I See Again the Beloved Country*] is "a true satire," as the poet himself says, on the customs of that city. But more than anything else Cino da Pistoia was a poet of love. The lady he loved was named Selvaggia [Wild], which probably corresponds to the nature of a woman averse to the desires and entreaties of the poet, as is made clear in many of the verses. Those verses sing of her as she was in life, and in sometimes heartrending accents, of her in death.

The poetry of Cino is an abundant and deep analysis of the passion of unrequited love; no longer beatitude as in the other poets of the *Dolce stil nuovo,* but travail and sadness, and despair find new and stronger expression. Here we are already in the poetical world of Petrarch, who greatly admired Cino and from him derived more than one inspiration.

Dante Alighieri

His Life, to the Time of the Priorate

In the superb XVth canto of the *Paradiso,* Dante encounters in the heaven of those who fought for the faith his great-great-grandfather, Cacciaguida, a Florentine who was knighted by Emperor Conrad and died in the Holy Land. Cacciaguida's wife was from the *Val di Pado* [the Valley of the Po], an expression too indefinite to permit a guess at what city or region of Upper Italy Dante had in mind; with her came the surname of Aldighieri or Alaghieri, later Alighieri. Dante's father, Alighiero, was a Guelf, apparently a man of no great importance and one about whom little is known. After the defeat, which in 1260 the Ghibellines, led by Farinata, inflicted on the Guelfs at Montaperti, he was probably banished. He was able to return home before 1266, the year in which the battle of Benevento, which weakened the Ghibelline party throughout Italy, reestablished the Guelfs in all cities.

Dante was born in Florence a year before that battle, in May, 1265. His mother, Bella, died when her son was ten years old, and a stepmother took her place in the home. It seems likely that the boy was brought up by the Franciscan friars in the convent of Santa Croce. The mysticism that was to inspire the young man's loves may have been strengthened not only by the sadness of those early years but by an austerely religious education.

The mystical youth was a citizen of old, noble Florence, and the events of Florence were his own. In the *Commedia* are deeply felt memories of public happenings of his early years and even mention of some that took place before his birth. He participated in some of the many small wars that Florence waged against cities that were her enemies and rivals. In 1289 he was in the battle of Campaldino in the Casentino region, where the Florentines defeated the men of Arezzo, and later that year, he was present at the surrender of the castle of Caprona. The youth had the soul of a knight and was a poet with a rich inner life. It was probably Guido Cavalcanti, ten years his elder and the man he called his best friend, who caused him to fall in love with the beauty of the Tuscan tongue. Tradition holds that he was also a friend of Giotto, prince of painters. He paid court to several women; he timidly and fervently adored one — Beatrice.

Giovanni Boccaccio, the first of Dante's biographers, and Pietro di Dante, in his commentary on his father's poem, maintain that Beatrice was the daughter of Folco Portinari a rich and liberal citizen. It is known that a Beatrice Portinari did in fact exist, and that in 1283 she was the wife of Simone dei Bardi; also, that she died, as did the Beatrice of whom Dante speaks, in 1290. Surely the adoration of the poet is for a real women. His throbbing poetry could not be for an abstraction, although in the mystical light of love, her bodily reality becomes hazy and indistinct. She becomes an angel who cannot bear the sadness, the wretchedness, or the vulgarities of life, and so quickly returns to heaven, from which she has descended to give a moment of peace and comfort to mortals. His adoration of Beatrice was a capital fact in the inner life of the poet. Beatrice disappeared from the earth, but in

Dante's heart she did not die. She remained as a vision of heaven, a vision to which the man turned again and again in the darker moments of his life. She was the distant generatrix of the *Commedia.* Never was a poet's love for a woman purer, more exalting, or more fecund.

After the disappearance of Beatrice, Dante fell into a deep depression. For consolation, he gave himself up to the study of philosophy, in particular, moral philosophy. His learning was not yet great. He possessed the art of composing poetry, he knew the French and Provençal languages, some Latin, and perhaps the elements of drawing and music. He had the culture of a youth more familiar with the profession of arms than with letters. Now he began to frequent the schools or, as we might say, the circles of the philosophers. It is probable that at this time he cultivated relations with old Brunetto Latini, the previously mentioned author of the *Trésor,* and began the study of the ancient poets, especially Ovid and Vergil. He and his contemporaries took notice to such a degree of the moral sense of these poets that they became the embodiment of philosophy. Dante's amorous interest in the woman who in his *Rime* [minor poems] is called Pietra falls probably within this period. It is not too astonishing that this love was quite different from that which he felt for Beatrice. The loftiest spirits are often those who most feel the weight of the flesh. Dante married Gemma Donati,* a relative of the Corso Donati who was to become the head of the party that drove him into exile. By Gemma he had children: Jacopo, Pietro, Antonia, and perhaps others.

---

* Dante scholars attribute the poems concerning Pietra to 1296, or to 1306–1307, or even to 1310. The date of Dante's marriage to Gemma Donati is unknown, but it was certainly later than 1287. His daughter Antonia may have become a nun with the name of Beatrice.

Political Conditions in Florence: Dante in Political Life

Dante the citizen participated in what must have seemed to his virile conscience a duty, and to his desire for glory, a suitable field: public life. But here it is necessary to say a few words in order to give a general idea of the constitution of Florence and the political conditions in the city. That constitution was very changeable, and continued to be thus for a century. The poet had occasion to remark, satirically, that laws decreed in mid-October did not remain in vigor until mid-November. The fact is that in Florence, at that time the most civilized city in all Italy, the factions were in unceasing conflict, and struggle was a necessary condition of life. Control over Florence, a rich city established for over a hundred years as a free commune, was the aim of the Ghibelline lords, who had been severely checked but not destroyed in the battle of Benevento. Then the city became the objective of the Angevins, and of the Papacy jealous of the Angevins, although the latter had been called into Italy by the popes. As early as 1280, Nicholas II sent Cardinal Latini to Florence, where he made peace between the Guelfs and the Ghibellines, or rather, disarmed the latter. A new power, however, had very effectively imposed itself upon the situation: the class of the capitalists and producers — the wealthy middle class, which in the picturesque expression of the times was called *popolo grasso* [lit. "fat people," as opposed to *popolo minuto,* the laboring classes or "small people"]. The capitalists were opposed to Guelfs and Ghibellines alike, whom they considered to stand for idleness, parasitism, and pride.

This rich bourgeoisie formed itself into *arti maggiori* [guilds or economic corporations], of which there were seven: judges or notaries; merchants of Calimala (or foreign cloths. Calimala was the name of the street in Florence where the cloth-merchants were located) ; money changers or bankers; wool dealers; merchants; doctors or apothecaries; and furriers. Each guild had its own statutes and its own consul. The lesser merchants, workers, such as carders or combers, were also emerging from servile obscurity. The time of their self-assertion in the history of Florence was still far off, but already they had organized into *arti minori* [minor guilds]. However, they were still at that time a humble multitude, now exploited by the grandees, the "greats," against the rich middle class, but more often by the rich bourgeoisie against the nobles. The *priors*, something like the present-day Italian municipal councilors, were six in number and held office for only two months; for, to accommodate widespread political ambition high offices had to fall vacant frequently. In theory, the *priors* were representatives of the city: in fact, they represented the corporations, nominated as they were by the Council of the Sages and by the *capitudini* [the consuls of the guilds]. With the *priors* were two executive magistrates who as a safeguard were to be of another city: one was the *podestà* [equivalent to a mayor] with judicial powers, and the other the *capitano del popolo* [captain of the people], who was head of the armed forces. Everything was governed by councils, or parliaments. The upper-council was called the *Consiglio dei Cento* [Council of the Hundred], and it passed first judgment on governmental measures. Thus organized, the rich bourgeoisie aimed at humbling the nobles as much as possible, imposing upon them the burdens of the State, and keeping them out of government posts and the magistracies. Since the Guelf nobles were a great factor in the defeat of the Aretines at Campaldino and threatened to regain control of the government again, the *gonfaloniere di giustizia* [gonfalonier of justice] was set up, with one hundred soldiers, as a sort of national guard to keep the nobles tied down, and also in 1293, the Code of Justice of Giano della Bella was agreed upon for the same purpose. Giano, although a noble by birth, was elected in that year a *prior* and used his power to expel the nobles from the priorate, from the other magistracies, and from the councils. He obliged them to be bonafide members of one of the guilds if they wished to have the honor of governing Florence. This caused the ostracism of the nobles, who quickly retaliated with calumnies. Giano was accused of favoring the Ghibellines; he was sent into exile and his house looted.

No measure was successful in bringing harmony to the citizens. Ruling Florence aroused too many ambitions and satisfied too many interests. Two powerful men had divided the citizenry between them. Vieri dei Cerchi, who, like Giano della Bella, had forsaken the nobles for the people, came from a family not indigenous to the city, and was looked down upon by the real Florentines, although he was wealthy. The other man was Corso Donati, of an ancient patrician family, a shrewd, violent man, representative of the class and the spirit of the nobles and hostile toward the bourgeoisie. Dante did not hesitate to consider him the principal cause of the city's disorders. The partisans of Cerchi were called Whites, those of Donati, Blacks — the terminology was derived from the struggles of the White Cancellieri in Pistoia against the Black Cancellieri; the heads of these two factions had moved to Florence.

The Whites, substantially democratic and attached to the Commune, could agree with the ideas of the Ghibellines and consider themselves as old noble families because of their antipathy to the Blacks who, for the sake of winning, did not hesitate to ally themselves with the politics of the Church. And the Church, or rather the Papacy, wanted to exercise its supremacy over Florence and Tuscany.

In 1294 a pope ascended the throne of Peter who, even considering his excessive ambitions for sovereignty, was a man of uncommon greatness: Boniface VIII, who in the Jubilee of 1300 saw at his feet the power of the whole Catholic world. Like Gregory VII and Innocent III, he cherished the dream of a universal domination over the kings of the earth. In the first years of his pontificate, he planned to subjugate Tuscany. In keeping with the policies of his predecessors, who had created the Angevins, a monarchy in the South devoted to them, he determined to win central Italy to the Papacy. Therefore, in April 1300, he eagerly approved a conspiracy in Florence that would put the city in the hands of the pontiff. The conspirators were discovered and sentenced to a fine of two hundred liras and to having their tongues cut out. The Pope intervened, and tried to impose revocation of the sentence by threating excommunication but it was in vain, the people would not yield. Then the Pope sought shrewder and more peaceful methods. He sent the Cardinal Friar Matteotto d'Acquasparta to Florence, supposedly to calm the factions. The Cardinal remained to protect his Blacks. The people decided to assemble the army of the League of the Tuscan Communes for protection against external enemies. Dante was sent to San Gimignano in Val d'Elsa to ask that commune to send delegates to the parliament of the league.

What role, up to that time, had the poet played in public life? Not a great one, it would seem. A member of the guild of doctors and apothecaries, which also included painters and artists, he participated occasionally in the councils. In 1300, however, a high honor was accorded him which, in some later moments of depression, he regarded as the beginning of all his woes: from June 15 to August 15 he was one of the six *priors*.

A high sense of justice and a strong desire for harmony seem to have inspired the performance of Prior Alighieri. Noble but not rich, and not therefore committed to any great family, he was accustomed to consider things more in theory than in reality. He determined to carry out his duties with that absolute independence that arouses everyone's wrath if it is not completely successful. The *priors* reconfirmed the sentence against the conspirators. Because the factions of the Cerchi and the Donati became more unruly than ever, they decided to banish the leaders of the two parties. Of the Whites, Dante's beloved friend Guido Cavalcanti went to Sarzana, where he fell victim to the fevers that resulted in his death shortly after returning to Florence. The Blacks, protected by Cardinal d'Acquasparta, first refused to leave, but after the Cardinal's flight to Rome where he saw his machinations had been discovered, they accepted exile in Castel della Pieve, from whence Corso went to Rome to intrigue with the Pope.

Dante's political activity did not cease with the priorate. In April of 1301, he was appointed to oversee the repairs of the San Procolo road. In June of that year, he was a member of the Council of One Hundred. To a request from the Capitano del Popolo for one hundred knights for the service of the Pope, to subdue under the command of the Angevins the Sicilian rebels of the Vespers, he repeatedly answered "No": *"Quod de servitio faciendo domine papae nihil fiat."* The name of Dante occurs also in other, lesser council meetings of that year, but that repeated and imprudent No! is more than sufficient to explain the hatred of the Pope's partisans for him, and the vengeance they were to take.

The dissensions in Florence grew worse. In a moment of popular indignation the partisans of the Donati were driven from the city. The Cerchi had the upper hand, but their triumph was brief. Charles de Valois, the brother of the king of France, had entered Italy with the title of Captain General of the Church supposedly to put down the insurrection against the Angevins in Sicily, and later, to lead a crusade to the Holy Land. Charles de Valois was jestingly called "the king without a land." He had vainly courted fortune fighting against the Aragonese in Spain, just as he was to do in Sicily. His route took him to Milan and to Bologna, where he received emissaries from the Whites and the Blacks. The Pope then sent him to Florence as a peacemaker. This was a serious moment. Ambassadors from Florence were sent to the Pope to calm him. According to Dino Compagni, Dante was one of these. The Pope sent back two of the ambassadors with soft words; he did not allow Dante to return, perhaps because he well knew that soft words did not quiet Dante. Meanwhile Charles de Valois encamped before Florence. The *priors* were powerless to resist. On All Saints' Day in 1301, he entered Florence by treachery, "with the lance," the poet would say later, "with which Judas jousted." There followed days of pillage and massacre for the Whites, until new *priors*, all Blacks, were named, and a *podestà* elected — Conte dei Gabrielli of Gubbio — these measures gave legal form to the iniquitous proceedings. Later, filled with hatred, the previously beaten Cardinal d'Acquasparta returned, the better to spread charity and peace. The trials of the Whites were begun.

One of the first of these trials was the one that condemned Dante and four other men. The sentences have been preserved. They speak of his and their crime of fraud, or barratry: not offering any proof but common knowledge. They speak also — and this is the real crime — of the opposition of Dante and of the other four to the coming of Charles and their aversion to the pontiff. They did not appear, and on January 27, 1302 they were condemned and sentenced to restore what they had extorted, to pay 5,000 small florins each, to banishment for two years, and to loss of all civil rights in perpetuity. On March 10, these five and ten others, were condemned a second time and sentenced by default to die on the stake should they ever fall into the hands of the Commune. Dante was either still in Rome, or on his way home. One thing is certain: he never again set foot in Florence.

Dante in Exile

The six-hundred Whites banished from Florence — Dante among them — thought about what is the main concern of every exile: return. Their attempts were many and unsuccessful. Dante, perhaps an unheeded counselor, parted company with his companions in misfortune. He felt alone and wanted to be alone. In a world divided into Cerchi and Donati, into Blacks and Whites, and into Guelfs and Ghibellines, he made in his own words *"parte per se stesso"* [a party by himself]. Men like Dante can only be solitary; solitary he had always been even in his public activities. He considered the eternal value of ideas, with their intransigent imperatives more important than men in their concrete wretchedness; Dante was not a politician, if politics means knowledge of men and the art of exploiting them.

In exile and in solitude, he thought again of the celestial Beatrice and the sadness of human life. The past merged with the present, the moral loftiness of man with the hatreds of the exile, and so the *Commedia* was born.

The sufferings of the exile were great. Banishment, in those times, was civil death. Dante suffered difficulties of every sort. He went about, "begging," as he says in the *Convivio,* over most of Italy. He suffered a heavier sorrow than that of being separated from "the most beloved" things, of eating "the bread of charity," and of "descending" in disappointment and "mounting" in vain hope "the steps of another's house," as is foretold him in *Paradiso* by his glorious Cacciaguida. He tasted the gift that humiliates, when it is granted after so much asking. He wandered confused amid so many anonymous men. His self-esteem must have suffered even more than his heart and his body. And he was not alone in his suffering; his children suffered with him while his wife remained in Florence.

Dante's pride did not allow him to tarry long in any

of the courts which granted him hospitality. Foretelling Dante's exile in the *Paradiso,* Cacciaguida names as Dante's first refuge the Scaligers of Verona. He went to that city for the first time around 1303 and was there in 1304 as the guest of Bartolomeo della Scala. He returned in 1312, when the lord of Verona was Can Grande, spoken of by the poet as the restorer of Italy and of society.

Of another host Dante leaves a less formal but perhaps more tender souvenir in canto VIII of the *Purgatorio:* this is the Marchese Malaspina of Valdimagra [Valley of the Magra] where Dante went in 1306. It is not known which of the three Malaspina brothers — Moroello, Franceschino, and Corradino — was Dante's host. In the preceding year Moroello in command of the Blacks of Florence and Lucca had defeated at Campo Piceno the forces of Pistoia backed by the Whites; a defeat most harmful to the Whites. But now and henceforth Dante felt himself outside and above any party. From the Lunigiana region, through Liguria, he went, perhaps, to France. In a letter of 1307 to Uguccione della Faggiuola, a certain Friar Ilario of the monastery of Santa Croce del Corvo relates how one evening he saw in his convent a stranger who, to his question What are you seeking? answered one word, "Peace." That stranger was on his way to lands across the Alps. The letter, previously considered apocryphal because it mentions the *Inferno* as already finished and ready to be sent to Uguccione della Faggiuola, has been looked on more favorably by later Dante scholars, who attribute the composition of the poem to the first years of exile. The supposition that Dante attended the University of Paris for a short time cannot therefore be entirely ruled out; perhaps such a belief is due to the fact that Dante shows himself uncommonly well versed in theology, of which the most celebrated masters were to be found in that city. In reality, all traces of Dante's whereabouts are lost until the time when the Emperor Henry VII came into Italy.

Public Events

Boniface VIII passed the last years of his life in an all-out war against Philippe le Bel, king of France. It was a struggle which, even in its intemperances, does honor to that Pope. In 1301 he published several bills, in the most famous of which he declared himself constituted above kings and kingdoms, and he convoked the French bishops to Rome to resist the king. Most of them remained faithful to the king; Philippe le Bel seized the property of the few who came to Rome. In April of 1303, the Pope excommunicated the king, but the States General of France, as they had often done before, proposed to appeal the excommunication to the council. Guillaume de Nogaret, minister of Philippe le Bel, came to announce this decision to the Pope, who at the time was sitting in Anagni. In union with the Colonna family, personal enemies of the Pope who belonged to the Caetani family, the Frenchman took possession of Rome. It is said that on that occasion the old pontiff was slapped. He died of grief a few days later, in October of 1303. Dante, the fierce judge of Boniface, curses the sacrilege committed against the Vicar of Christ by the house he hated above all reigning houses, and not only because Charles de Valois was of that lineage.

An austere and pious pope succeeded Boniface: Benedict XI, the only one of the popes of his time that Dante does not condemn, although he does not deign to mention him. His was a short pontificate, of less than two years. It continued the fierce opposition to the policies of France, until in 1305 the French cardinals succeeded in having a French pope elected, Clement V, who was subservient to the wishes of Philippe le Bel. It was he who authorized the trial for heresy against the military and religious order of the Templars, so that the crown might be fattened with their possessions. He also transferred the pontifical seat from Rome to Avignon, where it was to remain for seventy years. Dante, who had limitless hate for Boniface, covers Clement V, "the Gascon," with horrible scorn, and once he couples him with his sorry successor, John XXII, "the Cahorsin." When Clement died in 1314, Dante wrote a letter to the cardinals gathered at Carpentras for the election of the new pontiff, exhorting them to put an end to the grave scandal of the Church of Avignon.

In Florence, Corso Donati was the turbulent manipulator of the city. With the help of the *popolo minuto* [lower classes], he stirred up the *Grandi* [Nobles] against the rich bourgeoisie. Benedict XI, toward the end of 1303, had sent Cardinal Niccolò of Prato to Florence in a vain attempt to arrange a truce with the political exiles. The city remained in the clutches of Corso Donati, who in 1308 tried to make himself its sovereign. The attempt failed. Corso tried to escape but, falling from his mount, he was dragged along the road by the animal and killed, as Dante has Corso's brother Forese prophesy. The good men of Florence could no longer bear the violent state of affairs. Dino Compagni hoped for an act of God's justice and believed his hope was realized with the arrival of the Emperor in Italy.

Elected king of the Romans at Frankfurt and crowned at Aachen in January 1309, Henry VII came into Italy in 1310, activated by the idea of restoring the Ghibelline party and pacifying the factions. Pope Clement V in an encyclical proclaimed him the maker of peace. He reached Turin by way of the Mont-Cenis pass and went on to Milan. Many cities sent representatives to pay him homage, but not Florence; instead, Florence asked for the help of Robert d'Anjou and Philippe le Bel against him. In northern Italy some cities that had previously resisted Frederick Barbarossa were unwilling to accept the domination of his descendant. Cremona was stormed and pillaged; Brescia surrendered, on honorable terms, after the emperor had lost a large part of his army around it. Then, through the Ghibelline cities of Genoa and Pisa, he proceeded to the city where pontifical consecration awaited him. But the Pope had already abandoned his cause. He was crowned unostentatiously in Saint John in Lateran by two cardinals. The Pope sent him word to leave the Papal States. Furious, the emperor turned around and laid siege to the city that opposed him most strongly, Florence. The siege lasted through September and October of 1312. The Florentines did not yield, and their resistance saved Italy from the imperial yoke.

The emperor returned to Pisa. The king of Sicily, Frederick II of Aragon, invited him to participate in an expedition against the Angevins. Pisa and Genoa allied themselves for the undertaking. Henry once more started to march southward, but in August of 1313 he died at Buonconvento, near Siena. There was no longer a place for emperors in Italy. Henry had come to find out that the Holy Roman Empire was, as before long Petrarch was to call it, a vain name without substance.

Dante wholeheartedly welcomed the undertaking of Henry VII. In the emperor he saw God's messenger, who would bring justice and peace to Italy and return him to his native city. It is probable that he went to Milan to pay homage to the Emperor in 1311. During the early times of the expedition he wrote three letters in Latin, varying in tone but all three filled with passion. One, undated, but surely written in 1310, when Henry had just crossed the Alps, is addressed to all the kings of Italy, to the senators of Rome, to the peoples, and to the nations. It is a hymn of jubilation for the coming of Caesar: a message of hope for the Italians, and a warning and exhortation to all oppressors to receive worthily the lord of the world. But the exile's hope soon had to vanish. The stubborn opposition of Florence to the Emperor filled Dante with anger. He wrote another letter, this time to the *scelestissimis florentinis intrinsecis*, [the horribly wicked Florentines], who had remained within the walls. The letter was dated March 31, and was written near the source of the Arno, in the first year *faustissimi cursus Henrici Caesaris ad Italiam* [of the propitious voyage of the Emperor Henry to Italy], that is, in 1311, because for Dante a new epoch in history began with the coming of Henry. The letter dwells on the premise that all men owe obedience to the Imperial authority, willed by God, and that liberty is lacking for all where observance of the laws is lacking. He goes on to threaten imminent ruin to the Florentines who resist Caesar. The city will experience the punishment that Milan and Spoleto previously suffered for having resisted the first Frederick. The bitterness of a great disappointment may justify Dante's imprecations against his native city, but he went further. On April 16, 1311 in his name and the names of all Tuscans who desired peace, he wrote to the Emperor not to waste time besieging Cremona, but to strike without delay the city that was fomenting the insurrections against the Empire: Florence, the fetid fox, the viper that throws itself against its mother, the infected sheep that spreads infection among the healthy ones! We do not accuse, we do not defend; Dante was a man of his age, stubborn in his loves and implacable in his hatreds. Henceforth the battle between the exile and his city was not to be hidden.

The death of Henry must have greatly saddened the poet and perhaps he gathered and concentrated all his powers in himself and in his poem; bitterness has the power to sublimate heroic souls. It is probable that he return to Verona, where Cangrande was collecting the disappointed Ghibellines. He probably also approached another powerful Ghibelline, Uguccione della Faggiuola, who held power in Pisa, extended his sway over Lucca, and defeated the Guelfs at Montecatini. Perhaps in that year Dante was also in Lucca, where a woman, Gentucca, as he says in the *Purgatorio,* made him like that city, which had seemed to him a haven of demagogues and swindlers.

Meanwhile the Angevin vicar in Florence, Raineri di Zaccaria of Orvieto, issued a decree of amnesty for those who, like Dante, had not directly taken part in the emperor's undertaking against Florence. He changed the punishment of exiles condemned to death to that of temporary internment, provided they put up a cash guarantee and agreed to be "offered" as penitents by the bishop to Saint John, on that saint's day. Several of Dante's companions in exile were pardoned in this way. A friend pressured Dante to make the necessary request and accept the pardon. The exile responded with an undated letter *"to the Florentine friend":* Not thus, with so much humiliation, must Dante Alighieri return home after fifteen years of unjust exile. If there is a more worthy way to return, he will accept it gladly; if not, no, he will never return again to Florence. He can look at the sky everywhere, nor will he lack bread.

The Commune responded to this letter, one of the loftiest and strongest statements of human dignity. In November of 1315, the above-mentioned Angevin vicar reconfirmed the sentence against those banished in 1302, granting leave to anyone, in accordance with the dreadful customs of the times, to injure them in possessions or in body; and it was ordered that they should be decapitated if they ever fell into the power of the Commune. Among these exiles were Dante and his children. Perhaps it was then that the poet cried out his ineffable paternal grief in the canto of Ugolino.

But in April of 1316, Uguccione was driven from Pisa and Lucca and took refuge with Cangrande. It is not impossible that Dante followed in his wake. It is certain that he was again in Verona in 1320, where he read a dissertation in physics, *On Water and Earth,* which now is attributed to his pen. But since 1317 he had accepted residence at Ravenna, where he had been invited by Guido Novello of Polenta as a man of letters and doctrine, rather than as a courtier.

Filled with souvenirs of Justinian and the last emperors and where, in the ancient Byzantine churches, the saints are triumphant in the golden mosaics, Ravenna was the proper refuge for the singer of the Empire and of Paradise. Here he had his children with him. One daughter took holy orders and entered the convent of Santo Stefano dell' Ulivo, perhaps taking the name of Beatrice. At Ravenna Dante, already famous, had pupils and admirers. A certain Giovanni del Virgilio, reader in rhetoric at Bologna, invited him to come to Bologna, assuring him of coronation as a poet. Dante did not accept; he wanted to receive the laurels in his own Florence. Two of his eclogues in reply to the persistent invitations of that grammarian are extant.

In 1321 he went as Guido Novello's ambassador to the Venetian Senate, which was threatening Ravenna with a war of reprisal for the capture of some ships of the Republic. Dante did not have great success in his mission; the senators pretended to understand neither his Latin nor his Italian. A few months after his return on September 14, 1321, he died at the age of fifty-six. He was buried with great honor in the church of Saint Francis. In 1482, when Ravenna was ruled by Venice, the magistrate, Bernard Bembo, had the tomb built or restored by Pietro Lombardi. The tomb bears an inscription in distichs, which certainly dates back to the original burial, and was perhaps composed by Dante himself. It ends with a melancholy reference to Florence, *madre di poco amore* [unloving mother].

We have a few ancient portraits of Dante that all agree with the written one by Boccaccio: "the face long, the nose aquiline, the eyes more large than small, the jaws big, the upper lip extending beyond the lower"; physical signs of the man's character such as his iron will and proud scorn. The oldest of those portraits was discovered in 1840 in the hall of the Bargello in Florence; it was formerly attributed to Giotto but is probably the work of one of his followers. But the figure of Dante finds its most spiritual expression in the bronze bust in the Museum of Naples, formerly attributed to Donatello, but probably a work of the late fifteenth century.

The Minor Works of Dante

The *Vita Nuova*

Toward the last years of the fourteenth century, when his Beatrice was dead, Dante gathered together the poems he had written during her life and after her death, according to whether love or sorrow were his inspiration; before each of the poetic compositions, he set one in prose, in which he told of the occasion that had given rise to the poem. Then, following the scholastic custom of the day, he added another, didactic, prose composition, which explained the parts into which the poem was divided and cleared up some of its difficulties. It is not unlikely that, since the book was written after death had already transformed the girl into an angel, the poet may have made additions, to better describe the appearance of the heavenly woman. It is certain in any case, that he did not include all the lyrics written for Beatrice in the *Vita Nuova*.

Actually, in the *Vita Nuova* the young poet only recounts a few things, unimportant in themselves. He relates how when he was nine years old he saw for the first time the little girl, almost a year younger than he, whom men called Beatrice [she who gives beatitude] "because they were unable to give her any other name". The name became hers, although it might not have been her baptismal name. The mere sight of her was enough to make the boy feel pure and to enable him to pass through the years of early adolescence without any disturbance of the senses. Nine years later Dante saw her again and received her first salutation; nor did he ever receive from her anything more than a salutation. It filled him with bliss. He dreamed of her; of her and of love: a dream prophetic of death, for the presentiment of death accompanies the joy of love in the young man. Dante feels filled with gentleness and charity for all; he looks for the lovely girl, and follows her into church, where she is listening to words of the Virgin Mary. His eyes are fixed on her but his gaze falls, or appears to fall, upon another noble lady, and there are some persons who believe he is in love with this other woman. Dante, who wishes to keep his passion hidden from everyone, pretends to pay court to this other lady, *dello schermo* [of the screen] as he calls her; and he writes poetry for her. And, after that woman, he serves another "lady of the screen" so actively and indiscreetly that Beatrice withholds her salutation.

Then, dejected, he meditates in his room and weeps, while Love appears to him and admonishes him with obscure words to be more constant in his love. With the counsel, then, of some young women, Dante decides to sing directly to Beatrice, and to sing *of* her. He tarries for some time "with desire to speak and with fear of beginning," so difficult does the subject seem to him; but one day, while walking alongside of a beautiful stream, his tongue speaks of its own accord "as though moved by itself", and it says: *Donne, ch'avete intelletto d'amore* [Ladies, you who have understanding of love], the first line of the first *canzone* of the *Vita Nuova*. Then comes the most delicate part of this most delicate book: Beatrice appears not as a mortal woman but as an angel that Paradise wishes to take back. But God, pitying man and wanting to comfort him, allows her to remain on earth a little longer, a miracle has come to earth from Heaven. At her greeting, men have a feeling of well-being and of shame for their wretchedness.

Dante's love is ecstatic and contemplative, a story of inner beatitude without external episodes, unless that term may be used for the death of Beatrice's father, on which occasion Dante speaks, or imagines that he speaks, to the women who had seen the daughter weeping. Shortly afterwards, he too falls ill, and the idea of the beautiful girl's death, born in him when first he saw her, takes on a concrete form in his physical and moral dejection. In feverish trevail he dreams of an earthquake and a cataclysm. A friend leads him to the bed on which Beatrice is lying peacefully in death, and the angels return to Heaven, preceded by a small cloud. He awakens with her name on his lips, but fortunately this is not heard by those around him. On June 19, 1290 Beatrice dies in fact, and Dante stops in the middle of a *canzone* which he was writing in her honor and gives way to despairing laments. He also writes a Latin letter, *To the Princess of the Earth,* which means, probably, to its leading citizens, although even with this interpretation such a manifestation of affliction seems very strange. This letter, mentioned by the poet, has not come down to us. Without her presence, the city to him seems a desert, as did Jerusalem to the prophet Jeremiah, and all during that year he writes poems full of yearning for death.

But in the presence of an attractively real, live young woman, the dead girl's image begins to fade from the mind of the young man of twenty-five. One day as he is weeping, he becomes aware that a girl, young and very beautiful, is gazing at him piteously. Her pity awakens Dante's emotions and he experiences a feeling for that young woman which is very much like the love he would like to repress. He writes some poems to that *donna gentile* [kind lady, even noble] in which the contrast between his love for the dead girl and his love for the living is expressed with delicate vigor. He seeks her out and, to his sorrow, discovers that he no longer has the strength to remain faithful to a memory. Remorsefully he battles with his thoughts and curses his eyes, but from the depth of his conscience Beatrice rises again. She reappears to Dante in a vision just as he first saw her, an image of immaculate purity. With all his soul he returns to her. She reappears to the poet in a final heavenly vision the details of which the poet finds himself powerless to tell. Perhaps the triumph of Beatrice in Heaven was shown to him, and with it the first idea of the *Commedia*. Certainly Dante determines to speak no more of Beatrice until he is able to say of her what never before was said of any woman. The tale of love comes to an end with a thanksgiving to God *qui est per omnia saecula benedictus* [who is blessed for all time].

In truth, the book is so pure that it might be read by a saint or an ascetic. It is the love of the cloister rather than that of the world. It is a fervent and humble adoration, as a tremor of one in the presence of the supernatural. On one occasion Dante is presented to Beatrice amid a group of women and is forced to lean against the wall so as not to faint with emotion. No physical description is given of Beatrice; even her paleness "color of pearl" is barely mentioned, but that is not all. In all the pages of the tale the notes of reality are suppressed. Not one name of a person or place occurs. Dante, who in the *Commedia* was to be the sovereign poet of the real, of the characteristic, of the concrete, here shuns any definite presentation; the divine ecstasy of love would be too troubled and distracted by any note of miserable daily reality. The single reference to reality is the date of the Beatrice's death but Dante the mystic, discoursing on the number nine that appears in that date, finds a means of proclaiming the divinity of

Beatrice, since nine is the number of the miracle, as a multiple of three, the symbol of triune God.

This vagueness and mystery in Dante's story, such as the recurrence of the number three, and the frequent visions, has caused many readers to think that Beatrice never existed in reality, and that she was an allegory, perhaps that of Divine Grace, which speaks to the heart of the elect in the earliest years of life. Dante himself attests, in the *Convivio* [*The Banquet*] that the kind lady with whom he fell in love after the death of Beatrice was Philosophy, and the fact that in *Paradiso* Beatrice reappears, certainly, as both symbol and allegory, supports that hypothesis. That does not, however rule out the possibility that Beatrice and the *donna gentile* appeared to the poet in the first place as real people. The allegory may well have been superimposed at a later time. Certainly whoever reads it without preconceptions feels strongly in the *Vita Nuova* the notes of a true love in the poet's bashfulness and in his trembling in the presence of the divine. This love of Dante's was very pure but it was also real; and it was a love that remained as the center of his whole inner life.

The artistic value of the *Vita Nuova* is such that for the first time in Romance literatures we find an ingenuous and delicate probing of the life of sentiment done in a prose that has all the strength of sincerity and of simplicity. At first the rhymes are stiff and harsh, but then they become refined, and softer. The first *canzone* in praise of Beatrice, although slightly complex, the other in which Dante envisions Beatrice dead, the sonnets on the grace that her appearance diffuses and her salutation, the others in which he tells of his falling in love with the "kind lady," and the tear-filled sonnet to the pilgrims passing by Florence: these — and more — are among the purest and most exquisite things which the Italian lyric of any age possesses.

The Canzoniere

Dante wrote many other lyrics, most of them before his exile or during its first years. A few are related to the *Vita Nuova;* they were probably not included in its because they did not correspond to the mystical spirit in whose light Dante later saw his youthful passion. A considerable number of others are love poems for other women, perhaps for the women "of the screen," and certainly for the "kind lady" of the *Vita Nuova:* are remarkable. The two *canzoni* for her: *Voi che intendendo il terzo cielo movete* [*You Who Move to the Sound of the Third Heaven*], in which the poet expresses his struggle between his love for the dead Beatrice and the new love which is rising; and *Amor che nella mente mi ragiona* [Love which in my mind speaks to me], which sings of the serene victory of the new love. For other women there are other poems; some, as has been said above, name the beloved Pietra [Stone] probably as an indication of her hardness of heart in response to the entreaties of her lover. Of these, the sestina *Al poco giorno ed al gran cerchio d'ombra* [I have reached, alas! the season of dwindling day, and the great circle of shade] is powerful in its portrayal of the desolation of winter. The one that begins *Così nel mio parlar voglio esser aspro* [In my speech fain would I be as harsh] is warm with desire. Among the love lyrics there are also those, delicate and airy, which bring back typical attitudes of the *Dolce stil nuovo*. Some of them are ballads such as *Io mi son pargoletta bella e nuova* [*I Am Small and Pretty and Young*], and *Deh, Violetta, che in ombra d'amore* [*For Pity, Violet, that in Shadow of Love*]; and some sonnets, like *Chi guarderà giammai senza paura* [*Who Will Ever Look without Fear*], and *Guido, i'vorrei che tu e Lapo e io* [*Fain Would I that Thou and Lapo and I*], which is a desire of the poet to lose himself on the sea, far from men, in a perfect joy of love. The allegorical *canzoni* are much less beautiful and spontaneous: the allegories are more cerebration than feeling, more imagination than fancy. In any case they are few. The most famous is the one that begins: *Tre donne intorno al cor mi son venute* [Three women surrounded my heart], which dates from the beginning of Dante's exile, and in which Justice and, it would seem, Generosity and Temperance join in lamentations with the banished one and seek refuge in his magnanimous heart. Some of the doctrinal and moral canzoni are hard, dry, and prosaic, for all that fanatical admirers of Dante have extolled them. They are conducted in the manner of scholastic discussions: one on Nobility, another on Lightness, and one on Avarice. All this is matter that will become imagery and poesy in the *Commedia*.

The *Convivio*

The name *Convivio* is metaphorical, and refers to the banquet of science and wisdom that Dante is offering to his readers. A commentary on fourteen of his *canzoni* was to have been devoted to such a purpose. These *canzoni* were already known to the public and were "concerning love as well as virtue." The commentary was intended to be like that customary in the schools which, starting with the words of the text taken by in and of themselves would wander through all the fields of the knowable, out of which would come a sort of chaotic encyclopedia, an unorganized exposition of doctrines. In reality, Dante succeeded in giving a commentary on only three *canzoni:* the two on love mentioned above for the "kind lady" of the *Vita Nuova;* and a moral one on Nobility. Three *canzoni* constitute the body of the *Convivio,* to which an introductory *canzone* is added, resulting in a work of four treatises instead of the fifteen that were the author's original intention.

From allusions to political conditions and facts belonging to Dante's youthful years, it must be assumed that the treatise composed first was the fourth, written perhaps when the author was still at home. On the other hand, the introductory treatise states that the author, a wanderer and beggar, has visited almost all Italy. The author manifests a weary desire to return to Florence, so that it is quite possible that it was written after the death of Henry VII. The other two treatises were composed in the interval between the fourth and the first.

Perhaps because he devoted himself so wholly to the *Commedia,* the author abandoned this other work which would have added little to his stature. The treatises of the *Convivio* are an expression, not of Dante, but of scholastic culture. The first one is the finest. In it the author feels the need of rehabilitating himself in the eyes of all those, far too numerous, who have seen him in the wretchedness of exile or have believed him to be a fickle lover. He proposes to demonstrate that many of his love poems are to be understood allegorically, as cloaks for a doctrine into which he will now initiate, not so much the multitudes, as the knights and the noble ladies, in short, that social class which could not be instructed in Latin and toward which went the sympathies of the "fleeing Ghibelline." The author knew that for the first time the vernacular was adapted into a properly scientific or scholastic prose — a daring which until then had only been permitted to the French language. Dante has angry words for those who slander their own language and extol the virtues of other nations' tongues. He proceeds to demonstrate, all too pedantically, that a text in the vernacular can be accompanied only by a commentary also in the vernacular. All of this is presented with full awareness of the worth of his native tongue, which seemed to him to be the glorious language of the future.

In the second treatise, he states that all writings are to be understood in four senses: the literal, which is what the word means by itself; the allegorical, which is the conceptual truth represented by the literal meaning, i.e., Orpheus moving stones signifies the sage who moves cruel hearts; the moral, which is a lesson for one's life that can be extracted from some narration, as happens for different gospel selections; the anagogical (from a Greek word meaning *to lead up*) which consists of relating the facets of earthly life to a supernatural meaning, as the passing of Israel from Egypt into the promised land is the passing of the soul from the earth into heaven. Dante then sets aside the moral and anagogical meanings as not pertinent to his poems and expounds, first literally and then allegorically, the *canzone Voi che intendendo il terzo ciel movete*. The literal exposition gives him occasion to dwell on the fields of learning, as was customary in those times. The first line alone allows the author to speak of the heavens according to the Ptolemaic system, and of the relationship between the seven heavens and the sciences of the trivium (grammar, logic and rhetoric) and the quadrivium (arithmetic, music, geometry and astronomy); i.e., the seven liberal arts. In the allegorical sense the *donna gentile* is, or more probably, for the Dante of the *Convivio,* has become, Philosophy, and any mention of the lady is to be considered as a reference to philosophy; her eyes are the demonstrations, the lover's tribulations are the doubts, and so on. The praises of philosophy are as generic as they are abundant. It goes without saying that for Dante philosophy did not mean new interpretation of life and freedom of investigation, as it has come to mean today, but rather a fervent love of knowledge and a guide to theology.

In the third treatise, which comments first literally, then allegorically, on one *canzone Amor che nella mente mi ragiona,* the generic praises of philosophy and wisdom continue. Perhaps only his theory of love is important. We find it stated here not very differently from in the *Commedia:* love is the soul's will, conscious or unconscious, to join itself to its original source, which is God.

Considerably fuller, the fourth treatise has no bond with those which precede it. It comments on the moral *canzone* about Nobility, *Le dolci rime d'amor, ch'i solìa* [*The Sweet Poems of Love, Which I Used*] and since the *canzone* is not allegorical, there is only the literal commentary to be made. The same Dante who, when he reached the highest of the heavens, boasted of the nobility of his blood, here, when he defines nobility or, as he says, *gentilezza* [gentle, in the sense of *gentle*man, gentle birth; gentility], attaches no importance to the antiquity of the family line, nor to its wealth, but brings it all down to a practice of virtue. He thereby disputes a definition of Emperor Frederick II, and mention of the emperor presents him with an occasion to speak of the divine origin of the empire and of its nature. He does not, however, mention its independence of the Church, as he did later in *De Monarchia*. The theory of the origin of sin, deriving from the soul's error of seeking happiness in earthly things, and relying upon them to hold it (a theory later expounded in a canto of *Purgatorio*), forms one of the most remarkable pages of this treatise.

The *De Vulgari Eloquentia*
[*On Eloquence in the Vernacular*]

This work might be considered in connection with that first treatise of the *Convivio*, in which the praises of the vernacular are sung and in which, indeed, the present work is pointed to, as to a book meditated by Dante. Its composition is attributed to the early years of his exile. It is written in Latin because it was intended to reach all scholars, even those who did not understand the vernacular, or would not have read a book written in it because of their scorn for the common tongue. The work was to have consisted of four books, but we have only the nineteen chapters of the first book and fourteen chapters of the second. The principal part of the writing aims at determining the characteristics of the common or vulgar speech and more precisely of the *volgare illustre* [illustrious vulgar], the language in which prose and poetry of the loftiest style were to be written. It is probable that the word *eloquence* simply signifies *language*. Following the manner of the scholastics, the author digresses into premises which for us no longer have the slightest value. Out of the confusion of the tongues around the tower of Babel three groups of languages arose: that of the inhabitants of southern Europe (French, Spanish, Italian); that of the inhabitants of the North (corresponding to the languages of Germanic origin); that of the Orientals, which, according to Dante, was represented by Greek. Since, however, languages are always being corrupted for various reasons, there is need for a language guided by immutable norms and principles, a language of art, which the author calls *grammar*. For southern Europe, Latin was that language. Latin, therefore, in Dante's view, did not precede those languages which we today call neo-Latin languages because they are derived from Latin. For Dante Latin came into existence after the vernacular languages and was always a literary language learned in the schools and not from the mother. Confining himself to the vernaculars of southern Europe, he distinguishes the language of *oïl* or French, of *oc* or Provençal and Spanish, and of *sì* or Italian. He pauses to discuss the language of *sì*, especially the form of it that he calls *volgare illustre,* which should be written rather than spoken by Italians, at least in the higher forms of composition.

Dante does not say what the origin of this illustrious vernacular might be; he speaks of it as already existing. It is probable that he recognizes a state of affairs concerning speech not very different from that of today; that is, the coexistence of the different dialects and of a universal language for the educated classes. He calls the dialects *volgari municipali* [local vernaculars] and has various appellations for the higher vernacular: *illustre* or *cardinale,* because it should serve as a model — as the grammatical language that it is — for all the local vernaculars, and *aulico* or *curiale* (both mean "courtly") because it should be spoken at court, if Italy had a court. Dante finds that it is in use in the two principal areas of Italian culture: that of chivalry and of the schools: by the poets of the Sicilian school and by the poets of Bologna or at least by the "greatest" poet of Bologna, Guido. The illustrious vernacular is present in every Italian city, but it resides in none of them. Dante judges all the dialects unfavorably. That of the Romans is the vilest of all dialects; those of the inhabitants of Ancona and Spoleto, of Milan and Bergamo, are scarcely better. The Sardinians do not even have a vulgar tongue; they are apes who imitate Latin. What can be said of the Genoese, whose dialect would be nonexistent if the letter "z" were taken away. What of that of Romagna, soft and effeminate? He rips to pieces the dialects of Tuscany, as he does those of the Florentines, the Pisans, the Lucchese, the Sienese, the Aretines. The dialects of Tuscany are not vernaculars, they are a *turpiloquio* [base and vile speech], and their rhymers, with Guittone (Guido of Arezzo) at the head, are detestable, although there have also been among them some, such as Cino da Pistoia, who could use the illustrious language.

The second book starts off with the statement of a serious esthetic principle: not all those who write in the common tongue should cling to its illustrious form, because there must be proportion and suitability between subject matter and linguistic form. Those concerns most important for man — love, arms, and rectitude — have to be sung in the illustrious language. In this connection the poet remarks that in Italy love was sung in *volgare illustre* (as was done by Cino) ; rectitude also, (as by Cino's friend, Dante himself, in the allegorical and moral canzoni) ; but no one has yet arisen to sing of arms. The author then goes on to distinguish, as used to be customary, the various kinds of styles: the tragic, or higher; the comic, or lower; the elegiac, or style of the unhappy ones. It is fitting to use the "illustrious" for the tragic style; for the comic it may be proper to employ the medium, or the humble vernacular; this latter is the one to adopt for the elegiac style. The author proposes to speak about all styles, and of the compositions suitable for each. For *canzone,* the highest style, inspiration is not enough, but great learning and art are essential. This is a thrust at the presumptuous ones who, lacking both requirements, and trusting to nature alone, undertake to sing of the loftiest matters in high style, as geese trying to emulate the eagle. The remainder of the book is a study of the metrical constitution of the stanza of the *canzone.* The author also discusses at length the nature and beauty of the words: shaggy or combed, rustic or urban, masculine or feminine; stressing how much hidden art there was in the Provençal *canzone,* from which, chiefly, he derives his rules.

The *De Monarchia*

The *De Monarchia* is the expression of Dante's ideas concerning the perfect government for human society: a work intended for philosophers and jurists and, like the preceding work, written in Latin. Perhaps it was written in the years of Henry VII's entry into Italy, although allusions to men and events of the time are lacking. The work has value by itself and in itself, and for this reason some critics have thought that it was not a work of polemics but of meditation, written in Dante's mature years.

The monarchy is the empire, and the purpose of the work is to show the need for it and its independence of ecclesiastical authority. By "empire" Dante does not at all mean a tyrannical authority that suppresses liberty and destroys the physiognomy of the individual nations; even under a sole empire the nations may maintain their own internal governments according to their own laws and customs. The empire is necessary to maintain universal peace. The importance of the treatise, then, is that the author gives an entirely rational basis to politics, separates the state from theocracy, and with a clear conscience opposes the civil domination of the Church; Dante would permit it to possess wealth not in the role of proprietor, but rather as administrator or dispenser of it to the poor. Even if the fundamental ideas of the treatise are before their time, the reasonings are truly of the times and have little or no value in themselves.

The treatise is divided into three books. In the first, the necessity for a single emperor is upheld both as an example of the unity in world order, to which Dante aspires in all possible ways, and because of need for peace in the world, since only with peace can man develop the higher life of the spirit, contemplation. The second book demonstrates that God has conferred the right of empire upon the Roman people, who the author believes are a chosen people as were the people of Israel. The history of the Roman people is a history of miracles, because in Dante's view such are the heroic deeds of that people. God was always with them nor did they abuse the divine favor, since they did not aim at conquest but at the dispersion of justice throughout the world. Nor is that all. Jesus Christ himself, by his birth under Octavian, and by his having been judged by Pontius Pilate, the representative of Tiberius, recognized and sanctioned the Imperial authority. In the abstract, then, the Roman people are the electors of the emperor, regardless of the fact that he was then a German. For Dante, the fact never detracts from the right. The right of the Roman people had passed to the great electors of Germany. Certainly, however, Dante thought — as stated in the *Commedia* — that the emperor should reside in Rome; he would like Italy to rule the world. The third book is the most daring, and it attacks most directly the authority of the Church, or rather, the decretalists or interpreters of canon law, who maintained that the emperor was subordinate to the pope. Dante victoriously fights the sophisms of the decretalists, who largely depended on allegorical interpretations of the sacred books, interpretations which make us wonder how they could ever be considered proofs. Thus, for example, the sun and the moon signified — in a famous document by Gregory VII, the most autocratic of the pontiffs — the Papacy and the empire. As the moon receives its light from the sun, so the empire should find, in the Papacy, its reason for existence. Peter, in a passage of the Gospel, is said to have two swords; so the pope as Peter's successor must also have two swords, which represented spiritual and the civil power. The historical arguments were stronger: Constantine (as it was then believed) had personally ceded Rome to the pontiff. Dante remarks that Constantine simply did what he could not do, because by its very nature the empire was one and indivisible. If the pope had crowned Charlemagne, the first of the new emperors of the West, he had merely recognized an already existing authority. Against all the sophisms Dante repeats the passages in the Old Testament which forbade the priesthood to possess earthly goods, the passages in the Gospels which condemn riches, and the unequivocal response of Jesus to Pilate: "My Kingdom is not of this world." Towards the end of the treatise Dante eloquently states his own political principles. Man is a citizen and a Christian; he lives in this life and he will live in the next one. The empire, historically more ancient than the Church and in the divine idea, eternal as the Church is eternal, is the civil man's guide in this life, just as the Church is the spiritual man's guide in the other life. Just as the Church rests upon theological teachings, the empire rests upon philosophical teachings, which also emanate from God. Empire and Church are not subordinate one to the other, but are both coordinated under God.

Seven years after the death of Dante the *De Monarchia* was ordered burned because of its daring ideas, by Cardinal Bertrando del Poggetto, the Pope's legate in the region of Lombardy. It remained for many years on the Index of Prohibited Books.

Other Latin Writings By Dante

We have already mentioned the *Quaestio de aqua et terra* [*Problem of Water and Land*], a dissertation which Dante read in public, as a note at the end says, in January, 1320, at Verona. Likewise we have touched on two Latin eclogues to Giovanni del Virgilio of Bologna, which were also works of his last years, and we have mentioned several letters written by Dante. Among the remaining letters, a long one in Latin merits attention: this is the one in which the exile, in his implacable hatred of his native city, calls himself *florentinus natione, non moribus* [Florentine by birth, not by customs], and dedicates the third *cantica* of the *Commedia*, the *Paradiso*, to Can Grande della Scala. It is of interest, chiefly, for understanding the allegorical sense of the *cantica*.

Works Attributed to Dante

Some scholars attribute to Dante a series of over two hundred sonnets that translate the liveliest and most scabrous passages of the principal French allegorical poem, the *Roman de la Rose*. Its adapter was named Durante and was a Florentine at the end of the thirteenth century. Even if the form of those sonnets were worthy of the poet of the *Vita Nuova* and the *Commedia*, and overlooking the fact that so lengthy a collection remained unknown to the oldest biographers of Dante, who do not mention it, it remains difficult to admit that Dante, whose work is characterized throughout with events, moments, and inspirations of his own life, would have been able to devote himself to such a long work, remote from his conscience as a man and a citizen, and which sometimes indulges in the grossest sensuality. Undoubtedly false, also, is the attributing to Dante a clumsy paraphrase of the *Credo,* the *Paternoster,* and the *Salma Penitenziali* [*Psalms of Repentance*] known by the name of *Credo di Dante.* The claim was probably invented to prove to doubters the perfect attachment of the poet to the Catholic creed, or to correct misunderstanding of some parts of the *Commedia.*

La Divina Commedia

Inward Genesis and Chronology

It is conceivable that the last marvelous vision of the *Vita Nuova,* about which Dante gives no information, was Beatrice triumphant amid the souls of the blessed. In Dante's mind was the theme of a divine story, a still undefined synthesis for whose development the poet would require years of meditation and study. In 1300, the Year of the Jubilee which was dedicated to repentance, redemption, and extensive divine pardon, the poet, having been distracted by other loves, and saddened by his first contact with the iniquity and coarseness of mankind, may have experienced the nostalgia of innocence, the need to become pure again, to live according to reason and not according to instinct. Beatrice, still living in his heart, came to him then as the guardian angel of his moral life, like the voice of God within him, if not yet the enlightener. Although later dates are suggested, it is not impossible that the poet began his work in 1300 or the year following, since Boccaccio, asserts that Dante wrote the first seven cantos of the *Inferno* before his exile. There are, however, concepts carried in one's heart throughout a lifetime, which continue to develop, take shape, and grow ever brighter, increasing with all the new impressions of life: such as Goethe's *Faust*. The *Commedia*, germinating as an indefinite yearning in the times of the *Vita Nuova*, was begun perhaps ten years after the death of the Beloved. The idea changed with the broadening of experience, with the growth of learning, and with the transformation of Dante's thought and nature. He worked on the poem during all the years of exile, putting his whole self into it, with his sorrows, his bitterness, his enthusiasms, his knowledge. All went into the poem, which was to be his glorification and his victory. The *Inferno* was probably ended, if not finished, about 1308 and the *Purgatorio*, about 1313. In 1318, in his Latin commentary on the *Documenti d'amore*, Francesco da Barberino mentions the *Inferno* and the *Purgatorio* as known. The *Paradiso* was the work of Dante's last years and was not published until after his death; according to Boccaccio, the last cantos were lost and found again later by Dante's son Iacopo, in ways that seem miraculous.

Such, approximately, was the inner genesis of the poem and the chronology of its composition, according to the latest opinion of scholars engaged on this very difficult problem. However, the more common opinion until a few years ago, one which is still held by many famous and learned Dantists, is that the *Commedia* is the work of the last years of his exile and that Dante worked on it zealously after the death of Henry VII when he had lost hope of return and had retreated into his inner world.* The principal argument in favor of this hypothesis derives from the allusions in the *Commedia* to events after the death of Henry VII, even in the *Inferno*. Foscolo had already advanced the hypothesis that Dante did not write the cantos of the *Commedia* one after the other, from the first of the

---

* A conciliating opinion is much favored: that the first two parts were composed before the death of Henry VII or shortly afterward, and the *Paradiso* in the poet's last years.

Inferno right down to the last of *Paradiso,* and this belief is shared by more than one scholar. Having the plan of his work firmly in mind, he could, as events influenced him, go back over cantos already written and complete them or change them. On the other hand, it would be hard to reconcile Dante's character, or that of any other great poet, with the possibility that many years after the events he would come back to them "in cold blood," so to speak, and write pages about them burning with lyricism and satire. It would be almost absurd, for example, to suppose that the stormy invective against Italy in canto VI of the *Purgatorio,* where God's justice is invoked against Albert of Austria for abandoning the nation to its dissensions, was written after the death of Henry VII, the second successor of Albert.

The Title of *Commedia*

This name probably refers to the style or quality of the poem's language rather than to the dramatic content or to the fact that it has a "happy" ending. In *De Vulgari Eloquentia* we learn that for Dante the tragic style is the loftiest style (or phraseology) and suitable for the greatest compositions, such as the canzone. *Commedia* therefore is a name that implies modesty on the part of the author, either for the style or the content; and *commedia* is what Dante called his poem, whereas he calls the *Aeneid tragedia.* The adjective *divina* does not refer to the religious material, but to the artistic excellence. It appeared in the printing of the poem that was edited at Venice in 1555, and remained a part of the title from then on. This is the place to add that although there is not the slightest gap in the *Commedia,* and it is in its entirety as Dante composed it, we are nevertheless unsure of the exact reading of many passages. The same may be said of his other works. Whatever the reasons may be, the original copy of the poem and the copies made from it have been lost, so it is probable that the transcribers have often altered the text according to their own judgment. It may be admitted that they generally tried to make the more difficult and personal passages easier, or more in accord with their own understanding and taste. Therefore, in a passage of which we have several readings the least common variant is closest to the original. In the sixth centenary of the poet's death (1921), the *Società Dantesca* [Dante Society] published together in a single volume (Florence, Bemporad) the *Commedia* and the other works of Dante. It was a critical edition, which may be considered fundamental and perhaps definitive. In 1965 the organizers of the seven-hundredth Anniversary Congress published *Dante Nel mondo,* a bibliography of world-wide scholarship on Dante.

The Animating Spirits of The Poem

The opening motif of the poem is the sinner's conversion to God. Dante was not the first to deal with this subject, one well known to mystic writers, among them it suffices to mention here Saint Pier Damiano, Saint Bonaventure, and Saint Bernard. The conversion is the salient moment, the typical and decisive crisis in the story of the Christian soul, for the saint is always a convert or at least one who has, thanks to God, overcome the world. It is necessary to add that Dante's conversion is not only that of an individual who takes refuge from the world in God. Asceticism, in Dante, never effaces social man. He tries not only to raise himself to the kingdom of God, but to lift up all men. He has faith in a transformation of the corrupt church, in a divine appearance on earth sooner or later, bringing back not only the Christian virtues but also the human and civil virtues, justice above all. One of the conceptions concerning the end of the world that existed in Dante's time, and particularly in certain fervent currents of Franciscan spirituality, was the expectation of a mysterious Reformer. There are frequent and very obscure prophetic references in the poem to this personage and to the change in conditions that would accompany him.

The story of the soul's conversion to God is allegorically narrated as Dante's voyage to the kingdoms of the hereafter: the kingdom of sin, which is Hell; that of repentance or expiation, which is Purgatory; and that of the soul's grace, which lies in God; final destination of the understanding and the will, which is Paradise. Thus the work of Dante coincided with the literature of the hereafter, those descriptions of voyages to the other world which, beginning with a vision attributed to Saint Paul, extend down to Dante's time. It is debatable, however, whether the austere and cultured spirit of Dante was even acquainted with the awkward and clumsy monastic literature of those unknowns, who were wrongly called his precursors, for in the structure and in many details, of the *Inferno,* and here and there in the *Purgatorio* as well, Dante had in view a very different model: the voyage of Aeneas to the lower regions in Book VI of the *Aeneid.* For some characters and passages of the *Paradiso,* he was mindful of Cicero's *Dream of Scipio.* Aristotle was in his thoughts when he was evaluating faults and virtues. It has been said wisely, however, that the *Divine Comedy* has no sources. The intention of the pretended medieval travelers to the other world was to find out information which was of interest to the living and to confirm the belief of the faithful in a life of repentance and sacrifice (sometimes there were more egotistical churchly aims as well). Dante, like those mystic travelers, thinks of himself as a humble man whom God has accepted into his grace, but at the same time, one chosen by God to reveal to the world His infallible judgments and the eternal principles on which the spiritual and temporal salvation of man rests. He feels in some way like the prophets of Israel who God ordained his messengers and announcers to the peoples and the kings and the priesthood itself. For this reason the opinion of certain Dante scholars should not be disregarded; they believe that Dante himself is the Reformer whose coming is foretold in the poem.

Dante brings into the poem about the other world the whole reality and experience of the earth with all its learning, insofar as this was knowledge of life, all its passions, its loves, its hates, its memories, and its hopes. The man, in Dante, is much stronger and richer than the mystic. In the *Commedia*, mysticism stands as the antecedent, the presupposition of the poem; it is like the medulla, the pith, of the great green plant which grows into a humanity perhaps fuller and more varied than has been seen in any work of poetry.

Schema of the Poem

The *Commedia* is divided into one-hundred cantos, of which the first may be considered an introduction; the remaining ninety-nine cantos are divided equally into three cantiche, or parts: *Inferno, Purgatorio,* and *Paradiso.* Each canto is written in *terza rima* (terceto rhyming *aba, bcb,* and so on). The mystic number 3, it is clear, is dominant in the constitution of the poem, which begins with a completely allegorical stanza. In 1300, midway through his life, Dante hears a call to return to God; that is, he wants to find his way out of a wilderness (the life of disorder). Three wild beasts block his escape — a panther, a lion, and a she-wolf. They are symbols of the lusts which incline the soul towards sin — lust, pride, and avarice. As Dante in despair seeks a way out, Vergil, the symbol of reason, comes to his aid. He speaks of a time when the greyhound — the reformer — will drive away the she-wolf, but for the present there is no safety from her. Vergil offers to act as Dante's guide through Hell and Purgatory, for only by seeing the consequences of sin and by following the paths of castigation and expiation can he free himself from evil.

Dante gratefully accepts, but he is also fearful of having accepted. How will he, poor man, be able to bear the sight of things of the other world? Nor, while still alive, is he worthy of viewing the kingdoms of the dead. He is not Aeneas who, in the Elysian fields, heard the prophecy of the greatness of his descendants and was strengthened in his mission to conquer Latium; He is not Saint Paul who in heaven found comfort and solace in the Christian faith. He learns, though, that Vergil has been sent to his aid by Beatrice herself, who represents that divine grace without which not only conversion is impossible but also the will and desire to achieve it. When he hears that the proposed journey is willed by her, his courage is renewed, (though it will fail him again), and he entrusts himself to his guide.

Hell is an immense abyss that narrows as it extends down to the center of the earth, closed over by a ceiling formed by the earth's surface, on whose highest part stands Jerusalem. Christ the Redeemer came to vanquish Hell, and Hell stays thus, materially, beneath Jerusalem. The abyss has a vestibule or antechamber to which the greater part of mankind descends: those beings who while living did neither good nor evil, and never realized that life is a battle for an idea. This ante-inferno extends to the river Acheron, beyond which lies Limbo, the place for those who died unbaptized through no fault of their own, and thus did not sin. The poets and great men of the ancient world are also there, and Dante is elated to see them (Circle I).

Then the real Hell begins. For Dante, sin is most serious when it has violated that part of man which is most divine, that which the schools called "the rational soul," or the intellect and will. Less serious are the sins of passion and sensuality which are therefore the first that the pilgrim sees punished. The first of these and the least serious in Dante's view, are the sins of love (Circle II). Next come the gluttons (III), the misers and prodigals (IV), and the quick tempered, the proud, the slothful and the envious (V). Within the iron walls of Dis is the deepest part of Hell where the heretics suffer (VI), and then (VII) subdivided in three concentric rings are those guilty of violence against others, such as tyrants; or against themselves, such as suicides; or against God, such as blasphemers. Dante puts with the suicides those who squandered their possessions; there is little difference between taking one's own life and wasting one's means for living. He places with the blasphemers those who, with debased, degrading affections, violated the holy law of nature; and the usurers who outraged art, the daughter of nature, by practicing that industry which should never exceed the limits that nature sets on the thirst for gain. In the eighth circle, the deceivers are divided among ten compartments, which the poet, not without satirical intention, calls *bolge* [valises, bags]. The lowest circle, the ninth, is for the artists of sin; the wretches that Christian conscience, no less than the standards of chivalry, considered as unworthy of any pity, the traitors. They also are divided among various compartments, according to whether they betrayed relatives, friends, or benefactors. At the bottom of the abyss, imprisoned beneath the whole terrestrial mass and a little below the center of the earth, rises erect into the hemisphere of Jerusalem the gigantic bust of the archangel who was hurled down from heaven, the father of pride and rebellion, Satan or Lucifer. He is imprisoned in ice from the chest down, his legs stretched out into the opposite hemisphere. In his three mouths the fallen angel crunches Judas, the betrayer of Christ, the founder of the Church, and Brutus and Cassius, betrayers and slayers of Caesar, the founder of that other institution that Dante held equally divine, the Roman Empire.

Each circle is watched over by one of the pagan

divinities that Christianity thought of as demons. As in the *Aeneid,* Charon is the harsh and ancient ferryman of souls. Minos the judge, made monstrous by a long tail, is at the entrance to the circle of the lustful, i.e., the ante-inferno. Cerberus, the three-headed dog, guards the gluttons. Pluto the god of riches, changed into a wolf, keeps the misers in order; the Furies appear on the walls of Dite. More beast than man, the Minotaur stands at the entrance to the circle of the violent; The harpies are in the wood of the suicides, and the centaurs around the brook running blood, in which the bloodthirsty are boiling. The flying serpent-man, Geryon, swims about in the murky air of the deceivers; while the Giants, who threatened Jupiter, are dazed and in chains around the circle of the traitors. The devils of Christian belief are crowded behind the walls of Dis to keep the pilgrims from passing; others appear as torturers in the *bolgia* of the pimps and go-betweens and in that of the cheats and swindlers. Undesirable companions, they accompany the two poets. Dante has depicted them in their fearsome traditional appearance but has made them beings of a lower yet very lively moral life.

The punishments, which differ for each particular sin, follow the law of correspondence with the nature of the fault that Dante himself calls *contrappasso* [retaliation]. In general, the punishments are analogous to the sin and are almost perceptible representations of its effects; thus, the lustful are agitated by an unceasing gale, which may signify the tumult of the passions by which they were troubled in their lifetime; the simoniacs, attached to money and mistaken in their evaluation of things, are planted upsidedown in the ground; the spreaders of scandals and schisms that divided the family, the city, the Church, or whatever constitutes a single unit, carry around their own bodies, rent and divided. However, it is not always easy to discern in the punishment the law of retaliation and the figuration of the sin. We can only say that the punishments are always dictated by a burst of scorn and a strong, fierce imagination.

In each circle Dante speaks with one or more of the damned, who belong to his own generation or are alive in his memory or conscience. Only in the abode of the misers does he speak with no one; their vice has made them unrecognizable. He often discusses current events; those occurring after 1300, the supposed year of the vision, are mentioned in a prophetic manner, since Dante recognizes the ability to foresee the future not only in the souls of Paradise or Purgatory, but even in those of Hell. This device permits him to include in his poem the whole history of his age. The pilgrim descends painfully from circle to circle, skillfully guided by Vergil. In dangerous moments such as crossing the Acheron or entering the city of Dis against the opposition of the devils, a miraculous help intervenes. He crosses the river of blood astride a centaur. He goes down among the deceivers on the back of the monster Geryon. To come up out of Hell he clings to Satan who is imbedded in the center of the earth, and he emerges through a narrow opening in the Antipodes of Jerusalem in the Atlantic Ocean. The journey through Hell had lasted three days.

A tremendous cataclysm had accompanied the fall of Lucifer. The land lying in the southern hemisphere, terrified at the sight of the monster, hid beneath the waters and fled, emerging in our own hemisphere, which was contaminated by the mere sight of the monster. That part of the terrestrial mass displaced by the fall of Lucifer left the opening by which the pilgrims, moving in the opposite direction, arose out of the empty waters, forming a great mountain. This mountain, after Christ's sacrifice, became Purgatory. No living man had ever reached it, except Ulysses, the explorer of the uninhabited world, who perished within sight of it when he was sunk by a tempest. An angel guides the souls of those destined for redemption from the mouth of the Tiber, which symbolizes the authority of the Church, as far as the mountain which rises high above the sea. At a point where atmospheric disturbances are no longer troublesome, Purgatory proper begins, encircled by a wall. At the base and on the first part of the mountain are scattered the souls of those who died in the grace of God, but without having made repentance, because they were under the ban of excommunication, because they were surprised by a violent death or simply because they were lazy. In a flowery valley off to one side live the princes of the world who did not heed the duties of their office.

Purgatory is divided into seven ledges or terraces, on each of which is expiated one of the seven deadly sins — pride, envy, anger, sloth, avarice, gluttony, lust. The penalties are not so much punitive as corrective: they are to redeem the soul from its inclination towards evil that it has brought with it from the world and to restore to it the freedom of will that it had abused by leaving the hands of God. The punishments are, therefore, hard disciplines, which are in contrast with the nature of the sin being punished. The proud and the haughty who went about on earth with heads held high, drag themselves along the first ledge of the mountain bent under enormous weights. The envious, who on earth aimed their desires on the felicities of others, there on the mountain have their lids sewed tightly together with iron wire. Leaning against the mountain wall, they who in life felt only hatred of their neighbor charitably lend support to one another. The slothful who were inert on earth are forced to run continuously up and down and so on. Often, too, the souls chant liturgical prayers, for according to the teachings of the Church, prayer brings about and accompanies contrition of the heart. In order that the corrective purpose of the penalty be most effective, however, it is always accompanied by ample exemplification of the virtue contrary to the vice being expiated or of the punishment which that vice served earlier in history, or in legend, which for Dante is also history. That exemplification is offered in a multiplicity of ways: there are carvings on the walls and on the pavement, as on the ledge of the proud; or mysterious voices passing by, as in the circle of the envious; or ecstatic visions, as in that of the wrathful. The examples of vice punished and virtue extrolled are taken from ancient or from Church history, since for Dante the Graeco-Roman world had reached human perfection. The souls may pass through different circles according to the manner in which they were blemished here on earth. When purged, naturally, they leave the mountain and amid thundering chants of jubilation mount toward Heaven. The peak of the mountain is the site of earthly paradise, the home of the first man. It is not difficult to understand why the poet places the earthly paradise on that peak; it is the symbol of the innocence and the happiness of the Christian soul whose baser instincts are all subdued by repentance.

At dawn the two pilgrims have reached the foot of the mountain. Venerable Cato greets them. He, who died in Utica to keep himself free of obedience to Caesar, in the bold Dantean allegory signifies that freedom from sin, or freedom of will, which the Christian could win by penitence. He, the guardian of the sacred island, obliges Dante to bind a reed about his forehead as an image of humility, or of man's losing himself in God, without which penitence is impossible. The pilgrims spend a whole day on the first section of the mountain, and Dante falls asleep in the little valley of the princes after having seen the serpent-tempter put to flight by two angels sent by Mary. In his slumber, Lucy, Divine Grace, bears him upward to the gate of Purgatory, for without help from above it is impossible for man to repent. On the morning of the second day, an angel confessor introduces the pilgrims into the first circle; previously, he has, with the tip of his sword, marked seven P's for *Peccato* [sin] on Dante's forehead, for absolution has removed the actual sin but not the tendency toward sin, indicated by those seven letters. Then, as Dante proceeds upwards from circle to circle, another angel cancels one of the P's with a brush of his wing. Dante feels progressively lighter and the climb grows easier. These are Angels of Forgiveness, and each of them chants one of the beatitudes pronounced by Jesus in the Sermon on the Mount. As soon as he enters each of the circles, Dante perceives the examples of the virtue being exalted. Then he speaks with one or more of the penitents and perceives the examples of the vice being punished. Dante spends two days in Purgatory. The Latin poet Statius accompanies the two pilgrims beginning with the circle of the misers. Dante imagines that Statius died a Christian, in great measure due to Vergil; that is, by having interpreted the fourth eclogue of Vergil as a prophecy of Christianity. When they have reached the last circle, Dante is constrained to pass through the fire which cleanses the lustful and the thought that he will soon see Beatrice encourages him in the terrible trial. Beyond, on the peak of the mountain in the divine forest of the earthly paradise, Dante encounters a creature of celestial serenity and beauty, Matelda; it is not known who she is, perhaps a symbol of primitive innocence. Then he witnesses a complicated procession in which the dominant feature is a carriage, signifying the Church. The representation of the Church is appropriate in the earthly paradise, where man is innocent, as the intermediary of divine grace by which man is purged of original sin and, through repentance, given back the innocence of Adam.

On that carriage, in triumph, Beatrice the divine enlightener descends from Heaven and greets Dante with words in which the most ardent love is mingled with the most feminine jealousy. Vergil, gentle father, has disappeared. Penitent and weeping, Dante is immersed in the river Lethe, which washes away all memory of sins committed. Then the mystic carriage is tied to a great tree, the Tree of Life, which is spoken of in Genesis but here appears to signify the imperial authority, that is, according to Dante, the source of earthly felicity of man to which he is destined by nature and which he could have preserved had his lusts not led him astray. Then the carriage undergoes a series of monstrous transformations that show the exterior history of the Church, the corruption and deterioration by which it has been abased, and by which it has reached its lowest point — its enslavement by the house of France. The transfer of the pontifical seat to Avignon is portrayed by the domination of a giant over his paramour. Beatrice, like Vergil before the journey to the underworld, announces a Reformer, symbolized by the number five hundred and ten and five (D X V), which appears to be the monogram of Henry, the emperor in whom Dante had placed so many vain hopes. Then the pilgrim is immersed in the river Eunoé, which awakens in him the joyful memory of the good works performed in his life. Now he is pure and ready to mount to Heaven. Purgatory is completed.

Beatrice looks toward Heaven (theological speculation, of which here she is the symbol, can receive its effectiveness only from God) and Dante looks into the eyes of Beatrice; like a flash of lightning he is lifted after her on high, now that none of the lusts bind him to earth. In each of the seven heavens exult those souls who in life felt its particular influence and turned that influence to good works. The Heaven of the Moon is, so to say, a pre-Paradise; there rejoice the souls of those who failed in their monastic vows, not of their own volition but by not having offered a heroic resistance to the wills of others. Even these souls, however, are perfectly blessed since, as one of them explains to the poet, grace consists in the consonance of one's own will with that of God, in this is the supreme "virtue of charity." The souls of the moon circle, who did not triumph over all terrestrial weaknesses, have a shadowy human appearance, but those of the other heavens have the appearance of flames, which become brighter as their devotion to charity increases. In the Heaven of Mercury are the souls of the spirits who worked for good, but more for their own glory in the eyes of men than for God. In the Heaven of Venus are the spirits that here on earth were conquered by love. The theologians rejoice in the Heaven of the Sun; the spirits of just kings and princes in the Heaven of Jupiter; the fighters for the faith of Christ in the Heaven of Mars; the contemplatives and mystics in the Heaven of Saturn. Beyond, in the Heaven of the Fixed Stars, the pilgrim witnesses the triumph of the flames of Christ and of Mary; when he has passed beyond, he undergoes, before Peter, James, and John (and ultimately Adam too) an examination on the theological virtues of faith, hope, and charity. After which, from Peter, he hears the fiercest invective to be found in the whole poem, one against the corruption of the Papacy, and then a prediction of restoration. Higher up, in the Crystalline Heaven or Primum Mobile, Dante gazes upon the seven angelic choirs, arranged in concentric circles, of which the most rapidly moving might be expected to be the slowest, because it is closest to the center, God. He then ascends into the tenth heaven, the Empyrean, a metaphysical heaven outside of time and space, which is the proper seat of divinity, the supreme desire of all. Here the Primum Mobile turns so rapidly as almost to merge with it and impresses its whirling movement upon the heavens lying below, more and more weakly until at last its motion ceases on the unmoving earth. Angelical intelligences preside over the movements of the various heavens and their influence on mankind, which is not of a nature ever to destroy his freedom of will. In the Empyrean there is that which is properly called paradise, the paradise of the contemplative. Beatrice explains that the souls of the blessed appear to be distributed through the different heavens to give something of an image of the scale of human activities from the practical to the contemplative. But the souls, which therefore are gifted with ubiquity, have each their allotted place in the Empyrean where they are no longer flames but human countenances of divine beauty and delight in the vision of God. They are arranged as in an amphitheater; on one side sit the souls of the just of the ancient law; on the other, those of the just of the Christian age. On this same side there are also a few seats vacant (one is for Henry VII), a sign that the end of things is not far off. Amid a fluttering of angels, Dante notices the Virgin Mary; he perceives the principal saints and beautiful Eve. Beatrice too has taken her place, and the most ardent of the mystics, Saint Bernard, now offers himself as guide to Dante, for not by the light of reason but only by rapture will it be possible for him to complete his journey; that is, to see God and to lose himself in Him. Saint Bernard first prays to the Virgin that she may grant so much to this man; and then Dante — he can find no words to say how — sees. In the light divine he sees the mystery of the Trinity, and that of the Incarnation; and as he struggles to penetrate the meaning of those mysteries, like the geometer who seeks vainly to square the circle, suddenly a light illumines him.

And here ends the poem of a soul's journey to God.

The Poetry of Dante

The over-all lines of the material and the allegorical construction of the *Commedia*; are such that it is possible to discern from them the majesty, the unity, and the admirable order of the whole tremendous organism. That unity, however, permits maximum variety; there is room for the representation of all the phenomena of being and of all levels of life, from the demon to the angel, to God; from the criminal, to the hero, and to the saint. Truly, as Dante says, "Heaven and earth have lent a hand" to the "sacred poem." But the Dantean poetry resides principally in the *truth* of the representation of the external world, and still more of the psychological world, which interests Dante even more than the concrete. Dante is a psychological poet, like Shakespeare; while in the countless characters of the *Commedia* he portrays the most diverse aspects of the most uncommon souls, it is in the portrait of himself, a traveler in the kingdoms of the beyond, subject to fear, pity, scorn, curiosity, and amazement, that he depicts the most representative and universal humanity. He can speak about himself for a hundred cantos without ever wearying us, because in him there is no attitude or pose, but only that humanity which, in the long run, is the most interesting. No less true, but loftier and more exquisite, is the humanity of his mentor, Vergil, who is not a teacher in the common and scholastic sense, but alternately is paternally tender and nobly admonishing. In the *Purgatorio,* especially, he is ineffably melancholic in his awareness that salvation is not for him, and beneath his stoical demeanor surge the passions of a man. While the principle of inspiration that generates the lyrics of the *Vita Nuova* is valid for the *Commedia,* here the poet formulates another esthetic canon for which he hopes to find even harsher words to tell of the horror in the depths of Hell. It is the canon of perfect agreement of content with form, which for us means the perfect identity of the two. This simple law allows of no unnecessary rhetoric, no tried conventionalism; there is no shred of either in Dante's poetry. On the other hand, it sometimes sins in its formal obscurity and reveals the struggle of the poet, who has not always succeeded in putting that law into effect and finding an adequate expression for his world. Dante often mentions the difficulty of the poetic art, especially in *Paradiso,* where he must express the inexpressible and, therefore, sometimes prefers silence to words.

With Dante, for the first time in the modern age, there arises esthetic consciousness, the artistic sense, awareness of art's difficulties and of its joys. Art is principally a "brake," that is, proportion and eurythmy of the parts with respect to the whole, the ability to compress much into little, and to reduce the fantastic into the most expressive lines. Concision, brevity, strength, and directness, are indeed — even when the poet is most tender and delicate — the outstanding characteristics of the Dantean style.

If one wishes to know something more definite concerning the poetry of the *Commedia,* the *Inferno* is the cantica of the most tangible beauties. It is the most human of the *cantiche,* for what is more human than sin? Here the subject matter is more plentiful than in the other two divisions, and the limits are the same, so the presentation gains in efficacy what it loses in extent. In the *Purgatorio* there is less vigor. The penitent is like a man cut in two. But those penitents, still gripped by the world, and moved by the longing for God, become figures of an exquisite spirituality. An elegiac sense runs through the entire cantica, and in it are perhaps the most delicate beauties of Dante's poetry. In its fundamental inspiration the *Paradiso* is a lofty lyric, a song of victory and exultation. Human passion, however, is incorporated in it. It rings with the voices of the earth far more than with angelic chants, and the vehemence sometimes assumes the language of the liveliest satire. In the Empyrean, the paradise of the contemplatives, the poet has performed miracles. Here the human word has reached its maximum power. Fantasy has become ecstasy.

To be sure, not every part of the *Commedia* is equally felicitous. But a long and loving reading of the poem, with meditation, convinces the reader more and more of its beauties, which often are deeper when less evident. It may be said that public agreement has made a selection from among the hundred cantos. Of the most-read passages of the *Inferno,* there is the third canto with its heroic conception of life, battle and duty; the fifth, or the canto of

Francesca, about a love that reaches its sublimity, and its punishment, in being stronger than death and Hell; the tenth, that of Farinata, the superb portrayal of the Ghibelline who loves his city even more than his party; the thirteenth, of Pier della Vigna, the suicide of "scornful preference"; the nineteenth, of the simoniac popes; the twenty-fifth, of the robbers; the twenty-sixth, of Ulysses, the hero of voyage and knowledge; the thirtieth, about Ugolino, the tragedy of paternal love. Casella, Manfred, and Pia of Siena are among the gentlest figures of the *Purgatorio* (cantos II, III and V); Sordello (VI and VII) is one of the most magnanimous. Among the wrathful, Marco Lombardo (canto XVI) expresses harshly the moral and political credo of Dante. The appearance of Beatrice to Dante and her chiding (canto XXX) is full of magnificence and passion. Among the most-read cantos of the *Paradiso* is that of sweet Piccarda (III); the one in which the emperor Justinian celebrates the history of Rome (canto VI); and the panegyric of Saint Francis (canto XI); admirable are those in which Cacciaguida speaks of old Florence, prophesies Dante's exile, and encourages him to truth (cantos XV–XVIII); the thundering invective of Saint Peter against the degenerate popes (canto XXVII); and the fervent prayer to the Virgin in the last canto.

Science and Philosophy in the *Commedia*

It was not always understood that Dante was essentially a poet, and that in the last analysis his whole world took on the character of poetry. In former ages what counted most was that which Dante had in common with his own time, doctrine and allegory. Endless discussions were carried on about obscure and enigmatic lines in which Dante is not Dante, or at least not entirely Dante. Certainly, doctrine, restrained in the *Inferno*, assumes considerable importance in the *Purgatorio*, where questions of moral and natural philosophy are touched on, and it abounds in the

Paradiso, where quantities of theology are grafted onto moral philosophy. There are allusions to the astronomy of the age and to physics. Needless to say, the poet takes pleasure in showing his learning in the field of mythology. But human interest predominates in the poem, and culture is never an end in itself. The history of Rome and the empire, for example, which is narrated in the *Paradiso,* aims at showing how unimportant the Ghibellines and the Guelfs really are. Even the theological discussions are never useless. Also, the problem of the nature of vows resolves into hostile remarks about the monastic orders, who profited by allowing the substitution of alms for the fulfilling of difficult vows. It is noteworthy that the saints whom Dante meets in the heavens are recent saints or, at any rate, still very alive in the consciousness of his age; the Scholastics, not the Fathers; Saint Thomas, not Saint Augustine. For Dante, theology is not so much speculative as practical; fundamental to the faith, which he knows by its very essence cannot be discussed. Often, in the form of theology, it is the ethical problem which is urgent, the most highly human problem, such as the one to which he often returns, the freedom of will.

The erudition of Dante, then, in itself, in its individual elements, is completely medieval, with the possible exception of his political ideas. Intellectual presuppositions, however, are one thing, the sentimental attitude is something else. In this respect Dante is already ahead of his times: detached from ideas characteristic of the Middle Ages; advanced in universal ideas, and a precursor of the Renaissance. In his work the cult of the Greek and Latin worlds finds significant expression. Thus, he assigns a special and glorious place in Limbo to the great figures of antiquity: making use of allegorical interpretation, he saves Cato; he makes Ulysses pronounce the words most expressive of human greatness; in the moral lessons of Purgatory he does not hesitate to alternate examples from the history of Greece and Rome with those from sacred history; and he celebrates the history and the epic of Rome amidst the lightning flashes of Paradise. For Dante the human and civic virtues exist close to faith. God does not destroy man but uplifts him in all his activities. Truly Dante is the greatest advocate and the most eloquent poet of human values; his is perhaps the highest conscience that the Western world had even seen.

Therefore, the *Commedia* is a book that can remake a generation, morally, and the Italian writers who contributed most to the *Risorgimento* [revival] of Italy: Alfieri, Foscolo, Mazzini, looked to Dante as a spiritual father of the nation, which first recognized and asserted itself in him. So the cult of Dante has been clouded over in the lowest moments of Italian history and in the loftiest again shone brightly. For those Italians who do not live by bread alone, the study of Dante should be a moral duty, far more than a requirement of culture.

The Contemporaries of Dante

Didactic and Doctrinal Poets

While accepting the literary and cultural currents of his age, Dante, by the extraordinary strength of his individuality and the vigor of his presentiments, surpasses them all. Minor spirits, his contemporaries, or those of the following generation, continued those currents. Mediocre versifiers persisted with moralizing poetry in allegorical form. Francesco da Barberino a notary who died in Florence in 1348, the year of the Great Plague of Val d'Elsa, left the *Documenti d'amore* [*The Treasurer of Love*], dictated by Love himself and written down by Love's retainers. The *Documenti* are precepts for the moral life, in twelve chapters of *septenarii* (seven-syllable lines) rhyming in couplets, one of the most boring metrical forms. Of no value artistically or in thought, the work nevertheless had the honor of a Latin translation and a Latin commentary by its author. Nor was another work by Barberino any better: *Del reggimente e costume di donna* [*On the Conduct and Manners of a Lady*]. It is in twenty parts with lines of varying length and, for the first time, in rhymeless or free verse. Some novellas are scattered here and there through it. In the work Honesty dictates precepts to Eloquence to be written down by the author which refer to the norms of life for woman in her various ages; the book has some value for the history of dress. The lady who ushers the poet into the presence of Honesty is thought by some scholars to represent "universal intelligence," one of the chief components of scholastic philosophy known also as "active intelligence," or that which awakens the intellect ("potential intellect") of man to knowledge.

Almost certainly universal or active intelligence is allegorized in an anonymous fourteenth-century Tuscan poem (perhaps by Dino Compagni of whom we shall hear more later) called *Intelligenza*. It is in *nona rima,* an ancient meter of a popular nature. The main character is a beautiful woman dressed and adorned with an oriental wealth of detail, dwelling in a palace whose walls are painted with the most glorious events of world history. The poet himself unveils the allegory, explaining that the lady is intelligence and that her palace is the human body. Very pleasant verses, great abundance of descriptions — what is lacking is that soul, that inspiration, without which there is no poetry.

More important than the two preceding poets was Cecco or Francesco Stabili of Ascoli, professor of astrology (then ranked as a science) at the University of Bologna. After an adventurous, wandering life, he was accused of heresy by the Inquisition and burned alive at Florence in 1327. In the very last years of his stay in Florence, he composed the poem *Acerba* [*Sour*], perhaps to indicate that, like green, unripe fruits, it would be difficult for the ignorant to chew and digest it. The unfortunate poet, in fact, assumes the tone of a wise man and pedant in this encyclopedia of his which, like Latini's *Tesoro*, talks about everything, from astrology to morality, the qualities of animals, the virtues of stones, but also like Latini, all he does is copy and compile. He writes in extremely modest verse, in a sort of six-line strophe that tries to be more varied than the tercets of Dante against whom the pedantic author makes several hostile allusions. He promises the reader that in *his* work there will be no Francesca, Paolo, King Manfred nor Count Ugolino, nor "vain things"; in short, there will be no imagination, no poetry, and he keeps his promise.

One of Dante's sons, Jacopo, who perhaps died as a result of the plague of 1348, also attempted a didactic poem, the *Dottrinale* [*Doctrinal*] in sixty little *capitoletti,* each of sixty septenarii. Within those narrow confines he squeezes all the knowledge of the schools. Not a spark of the flaming paternal soul passed down to Jacopo, and yet he wrote a commentary on the *Inferno,* as his brother Pietro did for the entire poem, and wrote in tercets a summary of the *Commedia.*

Realistic and Comic Poems

The lyrical production of the age of Dante is far more poetical. We have already spoken of the last and greatest lyric poet of the *Dolce stil nuova,* Cino da Pistoria. Here, instead, let us mention that the same poets of that *stil nuovo,* the singers of the angel-woman — Dante, Guido Guinizelli, Cavalcanti — tried now and again to achieve in certain of their sonnets a realistic and satirical note. The Italian spirit, beside or in comparison with the poetic dream, never forgot the necessities of prosaic reality, and from this was born that comic poetry, which derides and mocks any higher spirituality and is unenviably abundant in Italian literature.

Thus, opposition to the angel-woman of the *Dolce stil nuovo* appears in several rhymes of a strange contemporary of Dante, Cecco [Francesco] Angiolieri of Siena, a quarrelsome busybody, of whose fines and sentences documents are extant. His amorous troubles with Becchina and his spite for his stingy father, whose death he hoped for, his rancor against the world, which he would have liked to see burnt to a cinder, are the salient notes of his 150 vivid sonnets, which gave him a reputation as a comic poet, the oldest of the Italian humoristic poets. Humor that seems to be mirthful but is really a spasm of a noble and wounded conscience is wholly a modern product, and for Angiolieri we can speak only of burlesque poetry, or at most, satire. Some of his sonnets against Dante try to be satirical. Satirical, as well as obscure and abusive, are the sonnets that the Florentine Forese Donati wrote against Dante, which the poet answered with rhymes. [Forese and Dante each wrote a series of three so-called satirical sonnets against each other; yet, after Guido Cavalcanti, Forese was Dante's most beloved friend: cf. *Purgatorio,* cantos XXIII–XXIV, passim]. Among the mirthful poets are to be remembered Rustico di Filippo and Folgore da San Gemignano.

Religious Literature in Prose

With the decline of the Franciscan movement, religiosity continued at a less fervent and more restful pace. Domenico Cavalca, a Dominican (d. 1342) from Vico Pisano, stands out above several obscure writers. There are many ascetic treatises which he wrote or which are attributed to him, but his major work is a translation of a part of the *Vitae Patrum* [*Lives of the Fathers*]. These Fathers were the religious men who, around the third and fourth centuries A.D., abandoned Alexandria, Egypt to go and live in the solitudes of the Thebaid, like Saint Paul the hermit, Saint Anthony, Saint Hilarion, Saint Malco, and others, to fulfill the perfect life of repentence and contemplation. Saint Jerome wrote, or translated, the legends about them to which the name of *Vitae Patrum* was later given. The book remained extremely popular during the following centuries and was amplified from time to time with other "Lives." Cavalca's translation is free, passionate, vigorous, and spontaneous.

Jacopo Passavanti, another Dominican, was prior of the monastery of Santa Maria Novella in Florence, where he died in 1357. The sermons he preached there are collected in Latin for clerics, and in Italian for laymen. They make up the *Specchio della vera penitenza* [*The Mirror of True Repentance*] in which definitions and teachings on penitence are alternated with examples or with ascetic tales, designed in particular to strike the sinner with terror. Because of the vigor of the narration, these constitute the most interesting part of the book. Such examples are also important because they are linked to themes of religious legends, which flourished widely in the Middle Ages, for the most part outside of Italy — apparitions of the dead, infernal hunts, miracles of the Virgin. It is apposite to mention here another fervent ascetic, Friar Giordano da Rivalto (d. 1311), a Dominican. His impetuous and biting Sermons, preached in Florence, have been preserved; they are important for knowledge of the moral environment of the city and the age of Dante.

Works for the Dissemination of Culture

No less abundant than religious writings were the works aimed at spreading culture. There are numerous translations and adaptations from the best known ancient writers: Sallust, Ovid, Valerius Maximus, Boethius; and from sacred writings, beginning with the Bible. Bartolomeo of San Concordio, a Dominican (d. 1346), compiled in forty chapters, the *Teachings of the Ancients*. These were short moral sayings, chosen from the classics, the Bible and the Church fathers, a sort of *vademecum*, which would be useful to the teacher as well as the preacher.

Various moral or historical compendiums were widely utilized under the name of *Fiorite* or *Fiori* [Blooms, Flowers], akin to our anthologies or Florilegia. In the first decades of the Trecento, the judge Armannino of Bologna gathered in a *Fiorita*, tales ranging from the Creation to Julius Caesar; and, as an afterthought, he added the deeds of the Round Table. More popular was Guido, a Carmelite friar of Pisa, who in seven books, under the title of *Fiore d'Italia* is supposed to have narrated the history of Italy from the age of fable down to his own times. Of this work only the first two books are extant, the second of which is known under the name of *Fatti di Enea* [*Deeds of Aeneas*]. These *Deeds* are partly a translation of the *Aeneid*, and in part a résumé of the book, and the compiler reverently quotes Dante whenever he gets a chance.

Chroniclers and Historians

Another writer of the age of Dante is important for entirely different reasons: the Venetian Marco Polo, who in the last quarter of the thirteenth century took a journey to the lands of the Tartars, to Mongolia, China, and other regions of eastern Asia. After his return home and his capture by the Genoese in the battle of Curzola [1298], he dictated the story of his travels in French to his companion Rusticiano of Pisa, when he was in prison in Genoa. It was called, for no known reason, the *Milione* [*The Million*], probably because of the vast distances and sums with which he embellished his oral accounts. It is said that his house was known as "the house of the millions," and he was known as "Marco of the millions." To this day there is in Venice a quarter "of the Million."

Translated into Italian at the beginning of the fourteenth century, the book is interesting for its geography and history, the substantial veracity of which modern criticism has recognized.

Of the chroniclers, the most eloquent is Dino Compagni, a Florentine and partisan of the popular reforms of the Commune which raised Giano della Bella to leadership. Gonfalonier of justice and *prior* in 1301 he was like Dante, a fierce adversary of Boniface VIII. He left us a *Cronica* [*Chronicle of the Things Occurring in His Own Times*] in three books. It is a history of the events of Florence from 1280 to the siege of the city by Henry VII, written with the passion and the eloquence of one who has seen what he describes and who has defended himself. He reveals himself to be a small man living amid great times. He does not understand the parties and deplores the discords of the city, as well as the demands and vexations of Corso Donati, Boniface, and Charles de Valois. His moral conscience, though, is wounded and therein lies his strength. His is the first personal voice to animate the as yet anonymous material of the chronicles.

After the age of Dante, the chronicle seems to resume its objective impartiality. The outstanding chronicler is Giovanni Villani. He was a merchant and, as we would say today, a stockholder in the bank of the Bonaccorsi family; in that capacity he traveled to France, Flanders, and Naples. A leading citizen, he was twice a *prior* and filled other important offices in his city, about which he speaks in his *Cronica*. He died in the year of the plague, 1348. While still young, he went to Rome in 1300 for the Jubilee proclaimed by Boniface VIII. The appearance of the city and the reading, or rather an indirect and very superficial acquaintance with the ancient historians and poets of Rome, inspired him to narrate the history of his own Florence, the daughter of Rome. This the author himself tells us in Book VIII where, coming to the year 1300, he touches on the Jubilee. He set to work forthwith, on a work which lasted for the rest of his life, since it breaks off with the description of the pestilence that carried him away. It is divided into twelve books; his brother Matteo continued it down to 1363, and the latter's son, Filippo, to 1364. The *Cronica* narrates not only events of Florence, but those of Italy, France, England, and the Orient, year by year. In the first two books he accepts the fables and the legends concerning the founding of Florence, but as the work goes on, in time, it acquires great historical importance in spite of the credulity of the chronicler, his ingenuousness, and inability to separate the big facts from the minor ones. It becomes indeed one of the principal sources for the history of the late Middle Ages. The information about the financial conditions of Florence is of special interest, for the republic was tending more and more to become a plutocracy, and Villani was proud of the wealth of his city. Although a partisan of the Blacks and the rich middle class, which held the power, he displays equable and serene judgment and great respect for the truth. He provides the oldest information available on Dante. Villani's style is colorless and cold; he lacks that passion which makes the pages of Dino Compagni so endearing and alive. Even when he writes about contemporary events, Villani is not involved in them and remains aloof.

Francesco Petrarca [Petrarch]: His Life

The poet's father, Petraccolo di ser Parenzo (a name his son later changed to the more euphonius Petrarca) was a Florentine notary belonging to the White party. Sentenced to have a hand lopped off, and pay a fine of one thousand liras in the same year that Dante was condemned, he succeeded in fleeing to Arezzo where, on July 20, 1304, his son Francesco was born. The child was taken to the family villa at Ancisa in the Arno valley and lived there for several years; there too his second son, Gherardo, was born. With the death of Henry VII, all hope of returning to Florence vanished, and the notary determined to go to Avignon, where the papal seat was situated and where he might have good hope of earning a livelihood. He in fact was appointed *scriba* at the pontifical court, and established himself in the village of Carpentras. Thus, from birth Petrarch was a "man without a country," and such he remained for the whole of his lifetime; this had great influence on his poetry and literary production, which is without any municipal or regional content or spirit. His father wished to make a jurist of him and sent him while still a boy to the University of Montpellier. But the lad was passionately fond of Cicero and the ancient poets; perhaps too in that city he became acquainted with Provençal love poetry, then still a living tradition. Literature was the morrow, and jurisprudence, was the past. From Montpellier the youth went to "learned Bologna." Here he was more attentive to diversions than to study, perhaps because he was unaware that among those professors of law was the men who would become one of his future teachers of poetry, Cino da Pistoia. In Bologna he began some of the friendships that he cultivated in great numbers throughout his life, such as that with the Roman prince Giacomo Colonna. The death of his father called him and his brother Gherardo, who was with him, back to Avignon. Gherardo entered the Carthusian order. Young, vain, elegant, handsome, and well-off, Francesco gave himself up to a life of pleasures. On Holy Friday in the year 1327 in the church of Saint Clare in Avignon, he saw the woman who was to be his inspiration, in life and in death: Laura, since 1315 the wife of Hugues de Sade. She was to die in 1348, the mother of at least eleven children. However, the poet has so completely suppressed every note of prosaic reality concerning his lady and has so completely transformed her in the heaven of beauty, that the certain identification of Laura, is probably insoluble. Meanwhile, the limited wealth left him by his father was dwindling, and Petrarch had to conquer his disposition to contemplative idleness and study in order to live, and try to engage in some settled occupation. Giacomo Colonna had become bishop of Lombez, in Gascony, and wanted his friend Francesco with him in the new see. Later he recommended him to Cardinal Giovanni Colonna and the rest of his powerful family. So toward the end of 1330, Petrarch entered the service of the Cardinal and the circle of the Cardinal's family, and in his house he came to know some of the most illustrious literary men of the time.

Travels through distant, unknown countries were as dear to Petrarch as a comfortable living place. In 1333 he took a rather long journey to Paris, Ghent, Liège, Aachen, and Cologne. He traveled with the proud consciousness of a Latin, and looked on those cities as little less than barbarous. Then, on horseback and alone, he rode through the Forest of Arden, famous in the legends of King Arthur, came to Lyon and thence to Avignon. The new Pope, Benedict XII, extolled by Petrarch in a poetic epistle exhorting him to return the Holy See to Rome, conferred on him the benefice of a canonry in Lombez, but the poet was not satisfied. A reading of the *Confessions* of Saint Augustine disturbed him deeply. From the top of Mount Ventoux in Provence — Petrarch was one of the first men known to feel the attraction of heights — he felt the vanity of the lives of men and in 1336 determined to give himself to God. A visit to the Holy City at the end of the same year, where he saw his friends the Colonnas again, would have strengthened him in his resolve, were it not that the ruins of ancient Rome seduced him as much as the relics of Christian Rome. On returning to Avignon, he had a small villa built for him in Vaucluse (Valchiusa) at the source of the Sorgue, a tributary of the Rhône, and there, with many interruptions, he lived for fifteen years and composed the greater part of his writings.

Even there vanity harassed him, as love does and more than love. He was now famous and he wanted his celebrity to be formally ratified. On September 1, 1340, he received letters from the Senate in Rome and from the University of Paris inviting him to come and be crowned as a poet, a custom that had fallen into almost complete disuse after the first century of the imperial age. It is extremely probable, if not certain, that Petrarch himself had intrigued in order to be given the high honor. He chose Rome; the idea of being crowned on the tomb of heroes ("on the ashes of the ancient poets" allured him, and he set out for Italy. Before going to Rome, he paid a visit to King Robert of Anjou, in Naples, whom Dante had considered a *"re da sermone"* [king of talk]. To Petrarch, he was one of the greatest princes. In solemn ceremony the king examined him for three days, and wished to crown him in Naples; but when Petrarch held out for Rome, the king gave him a purple robe and sent his dignitaries as escorts on the glorious journey. On Easter Sunday, 1341, in the palace on the Capitoline in Rome, having delivered a speech in praise of poetry before an immense throng, Petrarch was crowned with the laurel by Count Orso dell'-Anguillara, one of the two senators, and declared Roman poet, historian, and citizen. The text of this singular document has been preserved; one looks in vain for an allusion in it to Petrarch's greatness as a poet of the vernacular. The honor awoke in the poet a feeling of deep humility. He went to Saint Peter's and laid his wreath at the altar. Then, with some difficulty, he reached Pisa where, instead of continuing on to Provence he turned aside to Parma, where he had been invited by Azzo da Correggio. On that very day the Correggio forces were driving the garrison of the usurper Mastino della Scala from Parma and resuming possession of the city. Petrarch took up residence at Selvapiana on the Enza. In those solitudes he set to work again, with enthusiasm, on his *Africa,* an epic. But then came the disturbing news of the death of Bishop Giacomo Colonna. He returned to Avignon, where the new Pope Clement VI had just been named.

Petrarch wrote an epistle in verse to him on the duty of returning to Rome, and the Pope conferred on him the benefice of another canonry in the diocese of Pisa. The following year, 1343, a Roman committee of thirteen good men came to Avignon to repeat the same prayer to the Pope. The speaker was Cola di Rienzo, the commoner of Rome, who longed for a government of justice and the restoration of the ancient republic. Petrarch knew and admired him. Then, because King Robert had died, Petrarch went to Naples, with the diplomatic mission of affirming the rights of the Holy See to the kingdom during the minority of the new queen, the famous Giovanna. His welcome to Naples was cordial enough, and his stay was enlivened with outings in the outlying country. But Petrarch was shocked by the corruption of the people, who went so far as to renew the gladiatorial games, during which he saw with his own eyes, a youth pierced by a sword and killed. Even nature showed her disapproval with a frightful hurricane that broke over the gulf. As for his mission, it seems to have ended inconclusively. Perhaps he could hardly believe his good fortune when once more he had reached his friends, one Correggio familiar in Parma.

It was his intention to remain; he even acquired a cottage close to the city. Those were not quiet times however. Azzo da Correggio, sensing that he could not hold the city against Mastino della Scala, sold it to Obizzo d'Este, Lord of Ferrara. The Gonzaga of Mantua, the Visconti of Milan, and the Scaligers of Verona then encircled the city and besieged it, unwilling to let the Ferrarese have it. The poet, having stayed on a good while, with great peril succeeded in fleeing and returning to his beloved Vaucluse, where he probably refused the high office of apostolic secretary, although it is possible that he was not judged fit for that office. In 1347 came news of the revolution of Cola; Petrarch sent a letter to Rienzi and another to the Roman people on the regaining of liberty. He showed no concern for his friends, the Colonna, against whom, along with other patricians, Cola's uprising was aimed. Petrarch hastened toward Rome, to the new Brutus; but when he reached Genova, news of the revolution's ill success reached him. Cola, the tribune, had made himself leader of the rabble, not the defender of liberty. Petrarch sent him a warning letter, and turned aside to Parma. He heard of the slaughter of the Colonna and their adherents by Cola and his bands; and he wrote a letter of regret to Cardinal Giovanni. At Parma, in 1348, the year of the Black Death, news of the Laura's death reached him. He noted the event on the flyleaf of a codex of Vergil, which is still preserved in the Ambrosiana Library of Milan; this he did to keep forever in mind his memory of her death and the fleeting of all earthly things. Some months later, in that same year 1348, the Cardinal also died.

Provence no longer had any attraction for Petrarch, and he decided to make his home, if not his constant residence, in Parma. Only a year later he was in Padua as the guest of a dear friend, Jacopo [James] II of Carrara, the ruler of that city. In 1350 he took a journey to Rome for the Jubilee. He soon left Rome, stopping briefly in Arezzo. In 1351, when he returned to Padua, he learned that his friend Jacopo had died at the hand of an assassin.

Boccaccio, who had made his acquaintance the preceding year, came to invite him to settle in Florence and teach whatever subject he might care to, in the Florentine Studium [College] which the *Signoria* [governing council] wished to found. This offer seemed a compensation for the city's neglect of Petrarch. Petrarch expressed his thanks to Boccaccio, but delayed his answer. Steady work was not compatible with his nature; in any case, the Vaucluse of his youth was calling him back. When he returned there, he found that his former world no longer existed. Soon his thoughts turned again toward Italy, to Naples, at whose court his fellow-countryman, Niccolò Acciaiuoli, was powerful. Now he desired the post of apostolic secretary, but in vain. He had won the enmity of many cardinals, and especially of the new Pope Innocent VI, who believed him to be a sorcerer because of his great love of solitude, of a wandering life, and of ancient culture. In 1353, Petrarch returned to Italy.

He remained in Milan a long time, staying with Archbishop Giovanni Visconti, the adversary of Florence — he, the son of Florentines, and the hater of tyrants! He found life to his liking in that splendid court. He strove to bring about a peace between Genoa and Venice. The two powerful republics reached an accord, not because of the poet's intercession, but because the Venetians were defeated. Meanwhile, Archbishop Giovanni died, the *Signoria* of Milan fell to his three grandnephews — Matteo, Barnabò, and Galeazzo. Petrarch stayed on in their service and celebrated the birth of Marco, Barnabò's son. Later, when the fainthearted emperor, Charles IV of Bohemia, elected king of the Romans in 1346, came into Italy in continuance of the Ghibelline tradition, the poet, who long before this time had exhorted him to come and pacify Italy, sent him an exultant letter. The emperor insisted on his attendance at Mantua; he treated him benevolently and invited him to follow him to Rome. Petrarch was unable to accept, but he endeavored to win the hostile Milanese over to Caesar's cause. Charles IV assumed the Iron Crown in the church of Saint Ambrose in Milan and continued on to Rome. On Easter Sunday he was crowned Emperor. He departed that very evening, satisfied with the title and the money gathered during his journey; Petrarch followed him with letters of blame. Later he was sent to him as ambassador, when the emperor, allied to the Duke of Austria and the king of Hungary, was thinking of destroying the *Signoria* of the Visconti with the aid of Italian lords opposed to that family.

Petrarch was received in Prague with many honors and was honored by Charles IV with the diploma of Count Palatine, but Italy never seemed so fair to him, as then, when he was far away. He returned to Milan, to the service of the Visconti, a service distasteful at times, as when he was obliged to write abusive letters against Friar Jacopo Bussolari of Pavia, who had aroused the city against the Beccaria rule. His by now very dear friend Boccaccio, came to Milan and talked to him about Dante, and afterward sent the *Commedia* in his own handwriting to Petrarch; Petrarch declared he had never before so much as handled a copy. The free Florentine regretted the continuance of his friend in the service of the Visconti tyrant. It may be that the sombre cruelty of Barnabò disturbed or frightened the courtier, but those tyrants relied on him too much to dispense with him. They showed this when they sent him to Paris as their ambassador on the occasion of the matrimonial alliance between the House of France and that of the Visconti. The new outbreak of the plague in 1361, which killed the poet's natural son Giovanni at the age of twenty-four, induced Petrarch to flee to Padua, whence he later went on to Venice. He presented his library (which became the nucleus of the library of Saint Mark) to the Republic, and the Republic presented him with a fine palace on the Riva degli Schiavoni. He lived in Venice for some years with his beloved daughter Francesca and her husband Franceschino da Brossano and their two children — Eletta (named after the poet's mother), and Francesco, who died, to the poet's grief, when barely two years old. He did not lack for honorific missions, nor marks of esteem. Henceforth he was considered the greatest living man of letters. Boccaccio came again to visit him, accompanied by a strange, proud Greek from Calabria, Leontius

Pilatus, whom Boccaccio had called to Florence to read Homer in the *Studium*. Petrarch had already learned the bare elements of Greek from another Calabrian, the monk Barlaam; now he was able to progress a little farther in that language. He received a text of Homer as a gift from Leontius but was never able to understand it. Finally Petrarch yielded to the entreaties of Francesco da Carrara, the son of Jacopo, and settled in Padua. There he received an invitation from the new Pope, Urban V, who had reestablished the Holy See in Rome for a brief time. Petrarch accepted, although he felt his age. Before departing, he made his will (April, 1370), which is still preserved. He requested burial in the church of Sant'Agostino, near his friend Jacopo da Carrara; he left bequests of various possessions dear to him — he left fifty gold florins to Boccacio to buy himself a warm cloak or cassock to wear during the cold nights while studying. When he arrived in Ferrara, he was overcome by syncope and was brought back, very ill, to Padua. From there he had himself carried to Arquà in the Euganean Hills, where he had had a fine house built. But in July, during a night of painfully difficult breathing, Petrarch passed away; legend claims that he was found dead with his head resting on a book.

He was laid to rest in a sarcophagus of red marble, provided by the good offices of his son-in-law, heir to the poet's estate. This monument still stands on the little square of Arquà, in front of the church and bears three Latin distichs, perhaps composed by the poet himself. The last of those lines, "May the soul now weary of life rest in Heaven," expresses the whole character of the man, a wanderer perpetually in search of peace; for Petrarch lived in constant discord between reason and feeling, between the dictates of Christianity and admiration for the men of antiquity: between Saint Augustine and Cicero. In these contradictions are found some of the less attractive aspects of Petrarch's humanity but also the notes of his modernity.

He was not a deep thinker, but a tormented and sick heart. He was an able rhetorician, or a great poet, according to whether he expressed that thought or that heart.

The Latin Writings of Petrarch

The Scholar and the Philosopher

Petrarch is considered to be a precursor of the humanists of the fifteenth century for whom the literature of antiquity was a cult. In his travels he discovered several glorious and forgotten books: Cicero's *Letters to Atticus,* and his *De Gloria,* which later was lost again, and the *Comedies* of Terence. Petrarch, however, did not yet participate in the critical spirit of the humanists, nor was he a new thinker; rather, he was a learned scholar who loved to display his learning, sometimes too ostentatiously.

Ancient history interested him particularly, especially accompanied by reflections, or illuminated by moral aims, as was the custom of his times. He attempted a sort of universal history through biographies entitled *De viris illustribus* [*On Great Men*], which was to go from Romulus to Titus, but he stopped with Caesar. Another work, entitled *Rerum memorandarum libri* [*On Memorable Events*], likewise unfinished, is a collection of examples chosen from Roman and contemporary history intended to demonstrate the power of fortune in human affairs and to warn men against indifference to it.

The transition from these historico-moral writings to writings of practical philosophy is easy. The treatise *De vita solitaria* [*On the Solitary Life*] is devoted to extolling solitude no less necessary to the contemplative life of religious men (such as Moses, Jeremiah, Saint Silvester, Saint Ambrose, Saint Augustine, and that Pope Celestine V whom Dante sets among the cowards) than to the philosophers and thinkers, such as the gymnosophists of India, Anaxagoras, and the two favorite ancient authors of Petrarch, Cicero and Seneca. The dialogues, *De remediis utriusque fortunae* [*On the Remedies for Good and Bad Fortune*] aim at demonstrating that the wise man finds a check to joy and a comfort in sorrows if only he remembers that every joy brings its own sorrows, and that every sorrow brings its own joy. Does glory attract you? Think of the envious ones, whom glory arouses against you. Have you lost a son? Think of how many potential difficulties have disappeared with him. The wretched wisdom that the philosopher preaches here would be, indeed, only the most inhuman apathy. Of more importance are the dialogues *De contemptu mundi* [*On Scorn of the World*], which are imagined to have taken place between Petrarch and Saint Augustine, who experienced the travails of the spirit so well known to the poet. The Saint finally overcame them by his faith. Truth is present during these dialogues, but she does not speak in them. The Saint reads what is in the man's heart and accuses him now of pride, now of avarice, now of loving, too well, women and glory. The man defends himself. Insofar as love is concerned, he feels himself raised up to God by it. It is not clear which one of the two, the man or the Saint, has the best of the argument, and the little book remains a witness to a state of mind painful in its uncertainty and perplexity. Wherefore this work also bore the title *De secreto conflictu curarum mearum* [*On the Inner Battle of my Thoughts*] and more simply that of *Secretum,* as being a confession of the poet spoken more to himself than to others. Certainly Saint Augustine was not wrong in reproving the man for his vainglory; for all his philosophy, Petrarch could never bear the slightest wound to his self-esteem. Thus there is no lack among his writings of lively and aggressive polemics. He launched an *Invectiva in Medicum* [*Against a Doctor*] in a full four books. In doctors he saw empiricists and charlatans and counseled Clement V to free himself from their clutches if he wished to get well. On another occasion, in Venice, he learned that some doubted his worth as a philosopher. So against these detractors he directed the lampoon *De sui ipsius et multorum ignorantia* [*On the Ignorance of Himself and of the Many*]. An anonymous French writer accused him of having counseled Urban V to leave Avignon for Rome. Petrarch responded with the *Apologia contra cuiusdam anonimi Galli calumnias* [*Defense against the Calumnies of an Anonymous Frenchman*]. In its expression of fierce patriotism, this is one of Petrarch's noblest writings.

The Letters

Petrarch felt a need to talk about himself and make himself the center of the world. Hence his very numerous letters which he personally, at least for the most part, selected and arranged in order from the time he was a guest of the Visconti in Milan. He called them *De rebus familiari* [*On Familiar Events*] and spread them out in twenty-four books up to 1361. Friends collected the letters he wrote from then until the time of his death and called them *Seniles* [in old age]. They fill seventeen books. Many others were gathered together, after the preceding collections found no place for them, and were called *Variae* [diverse]. Petrarch sent letters to his brother, to friends (often under classical pseudonyms), also to princes, doges, popes, and the emperor. The intention to, as we would say "make literature" is too apparent. This is a man who is fully aware that the public will read him, and one for whom the letter is a pretext for moral wanderings and descriptive virtuosity.

There is also a group of letters addressed to great men of antiquity — Cicero, Varro, Vergil — of whom Petrarch feels himself to be a contemporary, more so than of his own generation. He does not fail to be pedantic with them also, scolding Cicero, for example, for having preferred the active to the contemplative life and Vergil for having been too immoral in the episode of Dido. There is an important corpus of epistles, called *Epistolae sine titulo* [*Letters without Addresses*] because, in order not to compromise the addressees, he removed the names of the people to whom they were sent. They give a lively account of the scandals of the pontifical court in Avignon — "the new Babylon" — scandals that they deplore with words of fire. Apart from the others is the *Epistola ad posteros* [*Letter to Future Generations*] in which the author gives a brief account of the events of his own life until 1350.

The Latin Poems

Petrarch was a born poet, and his admiration for the ancient world prompted him to a rivalry in Latin, with the Roman poets. *Africa* is Petrarch's principal Latin poem. It sings of the most epic moment in Roman history, the end of the Second Punic War when, to turn the tempest of Hannibal away from Italy, Scipio crosses over to Africa, and the Carthaginian leader also abandons Italy and is defeated at Zama. With the narration of the events leading up to this battle, and with dreams that foretell what is going to happen (expedients common in the classical epic) the poet finds the means to present a summary of the whole history of Rome and the Middle Ages, down to his own coronation on the Capitoline. Though in nine books of hexameters, he perhaps planned to have twelve, like the *Aeneid;* there is a gap between the fourth and fifth books. Petrarch worked on the poem for many years, dedicated it to Robert of Anjou, and ended it with a moving lament on his death. He continued to work on it as long as he lived; he never published it, either because it did not seem perfect to him, or because he did not want a renewal of the criticisms — intolerable to him — that some Tuscans had made of the fragment, full of sadness, that he had given to a friend. The Second Punic War is more poetic in Livy than it is in Petrarch, who could neither detach himself from that historian nor be original. A few poetic passages remain, such as the tragic story of Sophonisbe in the fifth book.

Even more "literary" than the *Africa* is the *Bucolicum carmen* [*Pastoral Poem*], as Petrarch called the collection of his twelve eclogues or shepherds' dialogues. This was a genre very popular with humanist writers, in which, using the names of shepherds and allusions to the pastoral life, the poet draws real persons and events and sometimes his own portrait. Vergil had used this technique in some eclogues. In these disguisings of reality, the Petrarchian eclogues are very obscure and would often be indecipherable but for explanations given in the letters. Among the more meaningful are the second, in praise of the deceased King Robert of Naples, the third, which deals with the two great loves of the poet — woman and poetic glory — the fourth, on the poetic ability of the Italians as superior to that of the French, and the fifth, which develops into a veiled allusion to Cola di Rienzo, restorer of the greatness of Rome. If in the *Bucolicum carmen* Petrarch imitates Vergil, he imitates another great poet of the Augustan Age, Horace, in the *Epistolae poeticae* [*Letters in Verse*]. There are sixty-seven of them, divided into three books. They recount the most diverse events and deal with the most varied subjects with urbanity, grace, and sometimes with true eloquence. Because in them the poet gives himself no airs, and does not attempt to show off, they are more successful than his other works of Latin poetry. Among the most famous of the epistles is the one that narrates one of the poet's many journeys to Italy and hails Italy from the Montgenièvre Pass. In one to Cardinal Colonna he tells of his pleasant quiet life at Vaucluse. In still another, he describes the ceremony of his coronation, the unforgettable day of his life.

The Italian Writings of Petrarch

The Poet of Love

Petrarch was a poet who both expressed his soul and showed the exquisiteness of his art in his Italian poetry. It is mostly about love and was written sparingly principally in his youthful years. It is true that he prized his Latin works highly and feigned great scorn for the Italian verse, but this is not the first time that a poet has mistaken as most beautiful the works that have caused him the most difficulty. At the request of certain distinguished friends, Petrarch later gathered together his rhymes which he called *Rerum vulgarium fragmenta* [*Fragments in the Vulgar Tongue*]. They are preserved, partly in his own handwriting, in a precious manuscript in the Vatican. He added some introductory sonnets, in the first of which he regrets his youthful passions. He kept the poems in approximately their chronological order although he retouched and refined them. The *Canzoniere*, as later editors called this book of Petrarch's, is the most extensive of the fourteenth century and, after the *Commedia*, is the greatest poetical work of that century.

Petrarch's love, like that of the *Dolce stil nuovo* poets, is for a creature who passes amid mankind illuminated by a light from heaven. This love is not reciprocated, or else it is reciprocated more by allurements than by affection. It is a love of yearning and desire. Laura is not an angel, however, as Beatrice was; she is a woman — love of her is not only heavenly beatitude but continual inner travail and melancholy sentiment. Though the poet sometimes declares that in the contemplation of Laura's beauty he is lifted up to the divine beauties, he is also seized by the thought that he was made for something other than being consumed in that passion; he has moments of dismay and remorse, from which with religious fervor he seeks refuge in God. The *Canzoniere* is the ingenuous expression of all those various profound emotions, of all those mental states, sometimes undefined and undefinable, that accompany the basic passion of love. There are brief joys and raptures, as in the sonnet *Stiamo, Amore, a veder la gloria nostra* [*Stay, Love, to See our Glory*]; memories and regrets, as in the *canzone Chiare, fresche e dolci acque* [*Clear Waters, Cool and Sweet*]; soliloquies and meditations, as in *Di pensiero in pensier, di monte in monte* [*From Thought to Thought, from Mount to Mount*]; disconsolate lamentation, as in *Nella stagion che il sol rapido inchina* [*In the Time when the Sun Swiftly Sets*]; despair, as in the sonnet on Laura's death *Oimè il bel viso, oimè il soave sguardo* [*Alas! the Fair Face, Alas! the Gentle Gaze*], and cries of supplication to God, as in various sonnets, and in the *canzone* that closes the *Canzoniere, Vergine bella* [*Beauteous Virgin*]: a confession of Petrarch's wretchedness and inability to lift himself from the earth.

Petrarch's poetry is more sentiment than images; he repeats a small number of themes, varying them and probing them more and more deeply. He requires readers inclined toward meditation. The style of the *Canzoniere* is exquisite, just as the feeling is deep. Familiarity with the classics imbues the verse of Petrarch with a sense of nobility of form that Italian lyrical poetry was to preserve for many centuries. Here there is no plebeian word or phrase, no irregularities; nothing that shows a trace of his maternal dialect; no word that is not still fresh and living today. The softness of the sounds, and the musicality of the rhythms are outstanding, now delicate and light, more often solemn and grave. It is a musicality that expresses in itself what the word cannot always convey. To be sure, the *Canzoniere* is not always free from certain artificialities (like the plays on the word Laura, the overly contrived antitheses, and the protracted allegories), which can be considered an echo of the poetry of the troubadours and self-explanatory for a Provençal poet. Unfortunately the innumerable imitators of Petrarch — as is the wont of all imitators — dwelt on these externals and reproduced and repeated them *ad nauseam* until the word "Petrarchist" came to mean "false and artificial poet." But Petrarch is far above his imitators, and the leading modern critics, beginning with Foscolo, clearly distinguished him from them.

Political Poetry

In the Vatican manuscript some poems on a different subject are interspersed with the poems of love, and they are generally published separately. Leaving out a few things of minor interest, there are three sonnets and three canzoni. The sonnets express the scorn and nausea that the poet feels for the dissolute life of the papal court in Avignon and may, therefore, be classed as abstracts of the *Epistolae sine titulo* discussed above. The poet goes so far in his wrath against the "miserly Babylon," the "shameless whore" as to hope that the Church will fall into the power of a sultan who will execute God's punishment upon her. One of the *canzoni, Italia mia, benchè il parlar sia indarno* [*O Italy, Though it be Vain to Speak*] composed probably during the war around Parma, of which the poet was a witness and in a way a victim, is addressed to the rulers of Italy. The poet urges them to live in harmonious agreement and to withdraw the German soldiery, in which each seigneur stupidly put his faith, from the country. (These were the first mercenary troops.) The poet's words are filled with sadness and discouragement. At the beginning he calls on God to soften the callous hearts; the wretchedness of the most humble inhabitants, who are the real victims of the war, is expressed in terms full of pity. It is a *canzone* trembling with tears, really an elegy, and the most inward and eloquent of the fairly numerous *canzoni* or apostrophes to Italy which later followed this model. Another, *Spirto gentil, che quelle membra reggi*

[*Noble Spirit, Who Dost Raise Thy Arms*], is addressed to "a valiant lord, both shrewd and wise," who has succeeded in winning supreme power in Rome, and by whom Rome expects to be restored to her ancient splendor. Immediately Cola di Rienzo, the tribune in whom the poet reposed such great hopes, comes to mind, but certain passages in the text seem to oppose this interpretation. Some other men were considered, who in the usual manner were thought to be senators of Rome, the two senators holding the highest civil office, old Stefano Colonna, or Bosone of Gubbio. The *canzone* is an evocation of the Roman heroes, now at last happy to see their Rome "beautiful again"; it is a call to the hero to suppress the arrogance of the Roman noble families; it is pervaded by a feeling for the greatness of Rome, still emanating from the city's ruins, from "the ancient walls which he still fears and loves — and the world trembles." In reality it is more oratorical than lyrical. Another one, *O aspettata in ciel beata e bella* [*O Blessed Beauty, Awaited in Heaven*] is more like an oration than a *canzone*. Perhaps it was intended for a sacred orator who would inspire the Italians to cross the sea for one of the many unfortunate expeditions to the Holy Land that followed the age of the Crusades, fervent with faith and hate.

I Trionfi [*The* Triumphs]

Petrarch was determined to try his hand at a vast organic work in Italian that possibly would emulate the *Commedia*. In his mature years, he began to compose *I Trionfi*. It is divided into *capitoli* [chapters] of which the sequence is more probable than certain. In tercets, like those of Dante's *Commedia*, this work tells of a series of visions, of which the first, the "Triumph of Love," is in four *capitoli*. The poet tells how, in spring at Vaucluse, he fell asleep and in a dream saw Love passing by on a triumphal chariot, with uncounted numbers of victims in his train. A friend tells the poet who these are: the most illustrious characters of history or legend, and even ancient deities, including Jupiter; all are slaves of the awesome god. Personages of the Bible are there, heroes and heroines of medieval romances, and ancient poets and troubadours. Petrarch too joins the throng, having first coldly narrated to his friend what he expresses so spontaneously in the *Canzoniere,* the story of his own love. None of these personages speaks, except Massinissa, who tells of his passion for Sophonisbe, a subject that Petrarch had already treated in his *Africa* and which was intended to compete — as far as rhetoric can compete with passion — with the Dantean story of Francesco da Rimini. At Venus' island of Cyprus the procession halts. The second episode is the triumph of a virtue which, at least as exemplified by Laura, is stronger than love — chastity. Laura is the heroine, and her antagonist is Love; Laura entices many celebrated women away from him. They are Greek, Roman, and Hebrew, and include Dido, who is understood to have taken her own life, not for love of Aeneas, but to keep herself pure in the memory of her first, deceased, husband, Sichaeus. The procession of the chaste women ends in the Temple of Modesty in Rome, but Death wins them over. The "Triumph of Death," in two *capitoli,* is a rhetorical evocation of past peoples and heroes. It is an exquisite and celebrated painting of Laura's death, a passing so serene that "Death seemed fair on her fair face." Fame, though, is more powerful than Death. "The Triumph of Fame," more than the other "Triumphs," is a collection of names: there are captains and kings (including Robert of Anjou); famous and storied women; poets and orators and philosophers, the greatest of whom is not Aristotle, as it was for Dante, but Plato. In this "Triumph," the poet who loved glory so much must have felt at home, but he also felt the sadness of Time, whose triumph comes and destroys the names that Fame raised on high and buries peoples and nations in oblivion. The single *capitolo* of the "Triumph of Time" is a lofty elegy on the fleeting of days and the passing of all things, animated by the most moving, evocative, and religious eloquence. From there, it is only a step to the last of the triumphs, the "Triumph of Divinity," which is refuge in God for a frightened humanity and a vision of a stable and eternal world, unlike ours. The memory of Laura blissful in heaven brings the work to a close.

I Trionfi is an expression of all that had lived and still lived in the heart and mind of the poet: love, the sense of glory, terror of death, religiousness. Hence from time to time we still find admirable poetic passages, but his very intention of composing those fragments into an organic whole, his lifeless erudition, and his inability to make a single one of the innumerable personages come alive, make the *Trionfi* far inferior to the *Canzoniere,* even though it contains some of the poet's most beautiful and famous lines. Some of his most vigorous and polished images are to be admired there.

Giovanni Boccaccio: His Life

He was reputedly born in Paris in 1313, the son of Boccaccio di Chellino, a merchant of Florence, and a French mother. Professor Branca now sets his birthplace as Certaldo. Perhaps his maternal French origin may be accounted an influence on the spiritual development of the youth who was to give new life to so much of the satirical spirit of that country in his principal work. Boccaccio derided Certaldo in some famous novellas. He spent his youth in Naples; first, to carry on his father's occupation as a clerk in the branch of a Florentine bank; later, unfitted as he was for commere, as a student of canon law. But the splendid and corrupt Angevin capital drew him into a life of pleasures and love. He fell in love with Maria of the family of the counts of Aquino, natural daughter of old King Robert and the wife of an important personage of the court. Fiammetta was the name by which Boccaccio always deseginated his soon faithless beloved; she was a far cry from the angel Dante adored and the pure lady exalted by Petrarch. In Naples, which for many year was Boccaccio's ideal city (and which supplied him frequent themes and inspiration for his writings) he was not a mere thoughtless young ladies' man. Tradition has it that when he visited the supposed tomb of Vergil near the city, he felt the call of poetry. It is certain that he devoted himself to the reading of the Latin poets, and he was one of the first in Italy to learn the elements of Greek.

Toward 1340 his father called him back to Florence, and Giovanni's gay life came to an end. The republic entrusted him with a number of diplomatic errands, as was customarily the case with its most cultured citizens. He went several times to Ravenna on the Republic's affairs, then under the rule of Ostasio da Polenta. In 1350, in the name of the Captains of the Company of Or San Michele, he went again to Ravenna to bring ten florins to Sister Beatrice, daughter of Dante and nun in the monastery of *Santo Stefano dell'Ulivo* in that city; this is perhaps a proof of the deep love that he then had for Dante. In that same year he saw Petrarch for the first time, when the poet was traveling to Rome for the Jubilee, and he later visited him in Padua and Milan. Thereafter he loved and revered him as his master. He also went to the Tyrol to ask the help of the marquis Louis of Brandenburg against the Visconti, and he went thrice to Avignon.

In 1361 he underwent what today would be called a "religious crisis." A Carthusian from Siena, Gioacchino Ciani, came to him in the name of a deceased hermit, Pietro Petroni, and threatened him with the wrath of God if he did not return to a Christian life. The success of the *Decameron* had stirred up too much scandal. In the clutches of repentance, Boccaccio would perhaps have consigned all his works to the flames had Petrarch not stopped him. From then on he gave himself up to a religious life, even discouraging others from reading his masterpiece. He went again to Naples, on the invitation of his Florentine friend Niccolò, Queen Giovanna's seneschal. But this was no longer the Naples of his youth, and he soon left. In reality he was not greedy for money or glory. He considered it a supreme honor to be allowed to read the *Commedia* aloud in the Church of Santo Stefano di Badia every day except Sunday, beginning in 1373, for one hundred gold florins a year. A little more than a year later, scabies obliged him to stop his readings. Old and ill, he retired to Certaldo, where he died in December of 1375. His home in Certaldo is now a museum.

Boccaccio's Minor Works

The Neapolitan Period

In his early youth, in Naples, Boccaccio produced the *Filocolo,* the *Filostrato,* and the *Teseide. Filocolo* is the amplification of a vague story of love and adventure well known in France and Italy in the Middle Ages: the story of Floire and Blanchefleur. Blanchfleur, orphaned almost at birth, finds shelter at the court of the king of Marmorina [Verona] and grows up as his daughter. Floire, the king's son, falls madly in love with her. The king and queen, do not want their son to marry the girl, who they think is of plebeian origin. They oppose the romance and finally the girl is sold to some merchants as a slave. With a few faithful followers, Floire sets out in the wake of the ship, and he assumes the Greek name of Filocolo which, as the author explains or imagines, means Labor of Love. At last he learns that the ship is sailing to Sicily and sets course for that island. But a tempest holds him and his followers at Naples. Here Floire, or Filocolo, is admitted into the inner circles of the ladies of the nobility, one of whom is Fiammetta. The ladies, as was the custom in the courts, propound thirteen questions of love, interspersed with or demonstrated by little novellas which foreshadow the *Decameron*. After a good five months, Floire and his retainers continue their hunt for Blanchefleur. They touch at Sicily, from Sicily to Rhodes, from Rhodes to Alexandria in Egypt, where the girl is held in a tower. By dint of shrewdness Floire reaches his beloved and makes her his wife by force of arms. The last part of the romance relates the honeymoon of the two lovers, who visit Rome (where Blanchefleur's noble lineage becomes known); converted to Christianity, they finally return to Marmorina. This is the main theme of the story. It is interrupted by accessory elements and digressions in two of which, under the names of Fileno and later Galeone, Boccaccio himself appears, to lament that his Fiammetta has abandoned him. The author was determined to make a show of rhetoric, with the result that he writes an intolerably stilted prose, under which every poetic element of the delicate legend is buried.

Filostrato (a name part Greek, part Latin, which was wrongly interpreted to mean, "conquered by love") is a poem in nine cantos, in *ottava rima* (eight hendecasyllables rhyming *ababaabcc*), the strophe destined to remain for centuries the one proper to narrative poetry. Boccaccio took it from the poetry of the people, and it still has some of the roughness and ingenuous character of the poetry of the masses. The plot is derived from the story of Troy as it had evolved during the Middle Ages; that is, with the addition of amorous and chivalric elements. The heroine is Griseida [in Homer, Briseis], daughter of the priest Calcante. She first accepts the love of Troilus, brother of Hector, then that of the Greek hero Diomede. Learning of this, Troilus goes forth from Troy in search of his rival and dies at the hands of Achilles. In Troilus we see Boccaccio, the jealous and despairing lover of treacherous Fiammetta (Griseida) to whom the poem is dedicated.

Likewise dedicated to Fiammetta is the *Teseide,* a poem in twelve cantos of *ottava rima* that was intended to be the first poem in Italian concerning war. Two Theban youths of royal blood, Arcita and Palemone, prisoners of Theseus in Athens, fall in love with Emilia, the sister of Hippolita, queen of the Amazons. Theseus promises the girl's hand to whomever wins a great tourney in the theater of Athens. Almost all the heroes of the *Iliad,* the *Aeneid,* and the *Thebaid* take part in the tourney. On the day of the test, Arcita unhorses Palemon, but Palemone's patroness Venus sends in the Furies against Arcita whose horse takes fright and shies, throwing his rider to the ground where he is trampled beneath the horse's hoofs. Arcita marries Emilia, but this equestrian incident brings about his death. His last wish is that, when he is no longer living, Palemon will marry the woman who is the prize of all the fighting. This is the finest and most moving point of the poem, that ends with the nuptial ceremonies of the woman and the surviving knight.

The Florentine Period

Boccaccio's second prose opus, the *Elegia di Madonna Fiammetta* [*Elegy of Mistress Fiammetta*] dates from the first years after Boccaccio's return to Florence. It is divided into seven parts, in which Fiammetta narrates the story of her falling in love with Panfilo, that is, with Boccaccio, and bewails his absence. Probably Boccaccio transferred to the woman a desire that existed only in his own imagination. It is a work full of imitations of Ovid (who dealt with the same theme in his Heroides, letters of famous women of antiquity to their lovers) and of hardly bearable rhetoric and prolixity. The delving into feminine psychology is remarkable. From that same period dates another poem in octaves, the *Ninfale Fiesolano* [*Nymph of Fiesole*], which is shorter than those preceding and more beautiful. The poet imagines that in times of remotest antiquity, on the hills of Fiesole, a shepherd by the name of Africo falls in love with Ménsola, a nymph belonging to the chaste Diana, and a child is born to them. For punishment Diana changes the nymph into a torrent that will bear her name and in despair Africo throws himself into the stream, which is thereafter called by his name. So the poet has imagined a mythological origin of the names of the two torrents that rush down from the hill of Fiesole and flow close to Florence. The influence of Ovid's *Metamorphoses* is felt in the basic theme, but Boccaccio also had in mind the legends relating to what Carducci was to call "the mythical peaks of Fiesole." Several passages are ingenuous and moving, such as the amorous laments of Africo.

In the city where the *Commedia* was read, Boccaccio wanted to produce doctrinal and allegorical writings, his most infelicitous as it turned out: *Ninfale d'Ameto* [*Nymphs of Ameto*] and *L'Amorosa Visione* [*Vision of Love*]. Alternating between prose and tercets, the former narrates the loves of the hunter Admetus for the nymph Lia and the six nymphs who dwell with her. They all welcome the youth, and each narrates her story of love. From the song, which each one intones, we understand that they are symbols of the seven virtues with Lia representing Faith. Then, in a column of light, celestial Venus appears, and the nymphs make it possible for the shepherd to bear her aspect. This is an allegory of man, who rises from human senses to God with the aid of the cardinal and theological virtues. In *Amorosa Visione,* in fifty short *capitoli,* the poet visits a castle where in four great allegorical tableaux there appear the Triumphs of Wisdom, Glory, Riches and—longer than the rest—Love. In another room he perceives the great allegorical tableau of Fortune. Then he walks to another door of the castle, which leads to Virtue, but he does not enter. Instead he stops in a garden of beautiful women, almost all historical, among whom he finds, once again Fiammetta. Thus the poem stops short at the point where it would have had to become serious and where it was no longer in tune with the author's spirit.

Boccaccio's Last Writings

The works composed after *Decameron* are animated by a quite different spirit from that of the youthful works. It might be said that in the *Decameron* the author had exhausted all his most vital qualities. A fierce hatred of the sex formerly so loved animates the prose of the *Corbaccio* (perhaps from French *cravache* or Spanish *corbacho*, both of which mean whip. Some think it comes from *corbo*, crow, raven). In this work the author, a widow's lover, is visited in a dream by the spirit of the departed husband, who verbalizes all the evil one can imagine about his former wife and women in general; whereupon the lover escapes from the wrong road on which he was about to get lost. Perhaps for that reason the lively book also has the title of "Labyrinth of Love."

Actually, in his mature years Boccaccio lived engrossed in study and meditation. His greatest devotion in those years was to Dante, whose life he wrote, it is not certain when, under the title of *Trattatello in laude di Dante* [*Little Treatise in Praise of Dante*]. It is one of the oldest and most authoritative existing biographies. Digressions, however, are numerous (for example, on the origin of Florence, against marriage, on the nature of poetry, and so on), and there are many fables. The intention of extolling the poet in contrast to the party which had exiled him is manifest. His commentary of the *Inferno*, which goes as far as Canto XVII, in sixty lessons, is preserved.

Except for the *Eclogae* [*Eclogues*] the fairly numerous Latin works of Boccaccio belong to his mature years. There is far more erudition in them than beauty, and we shall only mention them. We have sixteen *Eclogues*, that allude to events in the life of the author and of his age. Some refer to the last events of the Angevin court, such as the death of King Robert, and to the scandalous reign of Queen Giovanna. Other Latin writings of Boccaccio are learned compilations, to give knowledge about that ancient world, which was just being reborn: a geographical work about that world, *De montibus, silvis, lacubus, fluminibus, stagnis seu paludibus, de nominibus maris liber* [Book on the Mountains, the Forests, Lakes, Rivers, Swamps or Marshes, and on the Names of the Seas]; also, the fifteen books of *De genealogia deorum gentilium* [On the Origin of the Pagan Gods], which were most highly esteemed. They are an organized exposition of the mythological fables which had occupied such an important place in ancient poetry and would be equally important in the new poetry. The nine books of tales, beginning with Adam, which bear the title of *De casibus virorum illustrium* [On Events in the Lives of Illustrious Men], and the feminine biographies (somewhat more mundane) *De claris mulieribus* [About Famous Women], have a moral purpose.

The Decameron

External Data of the *Decameron*

Like others of Boccaccio's works, the one for which he is known bears a name derived from the Greek. *Decameron* (now preferred without the euphonic *e* added by the Tuscans: *Decamerone*) is a genitive plural signifying "of ten days" with "work" or "narration" understood, and more correctly would be *Dekemeron*. The subtitle is "Prince Galeotto." [Galeotto, French Galehaut, who in the Arthurian romance induced Guinevere to kiss Sir Launcelot; cf. Dante, *Inferno*, V, 137. "Galeotto" became synonymous in medieval Italy for "middleman."] The title refers to the composition of the work and the subtitle to its worldliness, which is its fundamental note. It is believed that the book was completed about 1354; it is certain that it was begun after the great plague of 1348, the story of which opens the narration. Boccaccio continued the custom — which went on for several centuries more, and to modern taste would seem pedantic — of enclosing his novellas within a single frame so that the work, for all its variety, achieves a certain organic unity. He imagines, then, in an introduction, that in 1348, the year of the plague, seven noble ladies and three youths met in the Church of Santa Maria Novella. These ladies and youths really lived, the author asserts, but he discreetly calls them by pseudonyms. These ladies are Pampinea, Fiammetta, Filomena, Emilia, Lauretta, Elisa, Neìfile; Panfilo, Filostrato, and Dioneo are the young men. The reader already knows some of these names. To relieve their hearts of the plague's sadness, the ten young people agree to spend some time in a villa not far from the city. There they pass their days in the most enjoyable occupations, and in the hot hours of the afternoon they retreat to a shady spot to tell novellas. Each one tells one novella, ten every day. Before they break up, they name a "chairman" as we might say — that is, the king or the queen, whose duty it is to propose the general theme from which the novellas of the following day will develop. In the evening after supper one of the girls sings a ballad. Then they retire for the night. Out of religious reverence, no novellas are narrated on Friday and Saturday. The stories are told for ten days, making one hundred novellas. After those joyous days, the group goes back to the city. The three young men escort the girls back to Santa Maria Novella and go about their own affairs. At the villa, each day opens with an introduction, in which there is always a description of the dawn, and an account of how the young people pass the time until the hour of the storytelling. At the beginning of the fourth day the author defends himself from accusations of excessive licentiousness, from which it may be deduced that the novellas were made known to the public as they were composed, and the same defence is repeated at the end of the work.

Sources and Spirit of the *Decameron*

The material of the *Decameron* is extremely varied and derived from diverse sources. Sometimes it is a retelling of themes found in older collections of tales; there are echoes of oriental stories and Byzantine romances, and of Roman writers of the decadence. The spirit of mockery of conjugal virtues and aversion to priests and friars in Boccaccio's novellas recall certain keen, witty, and daring stories in verse that were widely disseminated in France after the eleventh century and were called *fabliaux;* however, the Boccaccio's tales are incomparably more refined, subtle, and elegant. Boccaccio frequently tells of historical events of his own time, and very often of things recounted to him by eyewitnesses. Together with the greatest liberty of theme there is a limitation that is obedient to the eurhythmy of the whole book. The storytellers have freedom of choice, but the novellas told on the same day, as we have said, must conform to a common theme. Thus, on the second day, the tales are about those who, after a thousand mishaps and setbacks, finally attain happiness. These are perhaps the most complicated novellas of the book, the tales of intrigue. On the fourth day, loves that end in tragedy are related, and these are the most moving. On the sixth day, there are shrewd witticisms and humor, which were so much a part of the conversation of past generations; on the seventh, the astuteness of wives; on the ninth, jesting which was not always innocent. On the tenth day the tone is more noble; the theme is high-minded loves and noble undertakings.

It should be noted that the novellas change tone according to the character who is narrating. The most innocent are narrated by Neifile, the youngest of the women;

the most daring by Panfilo and Dioneo. There are few tales that do not deal with licentious subjects. The *Decameron* is a book of a society that has lost all its ideals and lives only to enjoy. The asceticism of the preachers was henceforth almost powerless against the invading hedonism. Indeed, the brightest pages of Boccaccio are precisely those aimed at the priests and the monks, who, in his eyes, are as sinful as the others and more hypocritical. Boccaccio's satire is not determined, as is Dante's, by a high religious and moral conscience; vice is portrayed with the pleasure of a participant, not with the scorn of one who has overcome it. Dante and Boccaccio stand for two very different moments in the Italian conscience. The "shameless Florentine women," whose coming was feared by Dante, had come — they were the "gracious ladies" for whom Boccaccio was writing the *Decameron*.

The Art of the *Decameron*

Incapable of sustained effort in long narrations and poems, Boccaccio felt at ease in the novella and could express all the clever devices and contrivances of his art, together with the rich and varied experience of his life; he gave that literary form a breadth and fullness previously unknown. He begins his stories well into the past, sometimes starting with the fathers and forefathers of his characters; or he may begin by recalling important historical facts, to which he can then connect his tale. This contributes to the stories that character of verisimilitude, which the author carefully preserves. Hence in the tales of Boccaccio there is an abundance of all kinds of pertinent details, which help to bring before the reader's eyes the characters and the situations. One might believe that the author had taken part in what he is narrating. He is an unsurpassed master in portraying men and women morally and physically, particularly the types that awaken a sense of comedy and hilarity. The vivacity and spontaneity of the dialogues is masterly, as is his gift of interlacing the strings of a story, and then, with the greatest ease, resolving the complicated, knotty plots; he holds his reader's attention with something new and unexpected, though it is always logical and springs from the premises as unforeseen consequences.

Yet the Boccaccian novella does not completely satisfy modern tastes. Boccaccio savors his narration; he wishes to leave nothing out, for everything interests him. His audience is a public who needs to be diverted and amused and is never wearied or sated. For us the novella is something quite different. We want colorful and dramatic short stories, and the jests and the pranks of those past generations have only a secondary interest for us. For that reason we must set aside our restlessness to enjoy the old storyteller. The introductions to the tales and the accessory parts of the *Decameron* weigh on us especially. These include introductions to the various days, and the Preface to the whole work, including the too famous description of the plague, scrupulously exact, but lacking in pity and humanity.

Something that greatly contributes to keeping modern readers away from the *Decameron* is the elocution especially in the descriptive pages, where Boccaccio continues the stilted style, that has come to be called *boccaccesco* [Boccacian], of the *Filocolo* and the *Fiammetta*. Following a habit that was widespread in the schools of rhetoric, he reproduced in Italian the broad and symmetrical period of Latin prose and in so doing, created a vain and pompous sonority with considerable damage to its clearness and efficacity. Unfortunately that style remained for centuries typical of formal Italian "gala" prose, and was one of the reasons Italian literature was not popular in Italy. But Boccaccio's language is very rich, and his vocabulary is still almost all in use today; the Italian vocabulary, in fact, was derived even more from *Decameron* than from the *Commedia*.

Some Novellas

The liveliest novellas are those that it is not advisable to urge the young to read. Of those that everyone (save hypocrites) may read, the first is very fine, telling the story of a certain Master Ciappelletto of Prato, one of the worst of usurers who, when death comes close in Paris, acquires a reputation as a saint by a false and fervent confession, and for the people becomes Saint Ciappelletto. The second is shrewdly witty: A Jew, uncertain whether or not to embrace Christianity, goes to the court in Rome. He becomes a Christian precisely because of the scandals that he beholds in the court — the church must be the church of the true God if, in spite of its ministers' attempts to ruin it, it still lives. The third, by a little fable told by a Jew to Saladin of Babylon, aims at showing that all religions, or at any rate the three greatest then known (the Christian, Hebrew, and the Mussulman), on condition that they be professed with simplicity and faith, have equal value in the sight of God; a concept of toleration very hardy for those times, although not new. The fifth novella of the second day presents a powerful picture of the Neapolitan life which Boccaccio knew so well. It relates the strange adventures befalling a certain Andreuccio of Perugia in Naples. The fifth novella of the fourth day, about Isabella, whose brothers murder her lover, is deeply moving. She succeeds in exhuming the head of her beloved dead sweetheart and buries it in a pot of basil, where every day she waters it with her tears. When even that pot is taken from her by her suspicious brothers, she dies of a broken heart. Grimly cruel and indicative of an age far more savage than ours, the ninth novella of that same day tells how Guglielmo of Roussillon has his unsuspecting wife eat the disguised heart of her lover. When he reveals the horrible deception to her, she jumps from a window of the dining room to her death. In the ninth novella of the fifth day, there is an example of limitless devotion of a beloved lady. A knight, to win the love of a lady, spends all his wealth trying to please her, until at last he has nothing left but his precious hunting hawk. When the lady visits his home, he, having no other food, roasts and serves her the hawk at dinner. When the lady learns of his abnegation, she marries him. The tenth novella of the sixth day is one of the most famous. The protagonist is Friar Cipolla, the village preacher, an ingenuousness and cunning man, who offers to show his flock the wings of the angel Gabriel. Some jokers remove the feathers from his little box and replace them with coals, but he does not lose his wits upon discovering the substitution; he demonstrates that those are the very coals over which Saint Lawrence was roasted on his gridiron, and with them he makes the sign of the cross over the devout and simple peasant women of Certaldo who are listening to him. The typical simple-minded man is Calandrino, on whom the two painters Bruno and Buffalmacco play the latest jokes. So greatly did the type and the theme please the storyteller, Calandrino is the protagonist of the third and sixth novellas of the eighth day, and of the fifth novella of the ninth day. The first of the three is extremely popular: Credulous Calandrino, believing everything Bruno and Buffalmacco tell him, goes to look for the heliotrope in the bed of the stream Mugnone. The heliotrope is a magic stone that makes its holder invisible. Suddenly the two friends pretend not to see him any more, and he, pleased to have found the stone of invisibility, and loaded down with stones, goes home under the bombardment of his two "friends," who throw stones aimlessly at their "invisible" friend. Petrarch was so taken with the last novella of the *Decameron* that he translated it into Latin: The marquis of Saluzzo has married Griselda, the poor daughter of a countryman. He wants to test her goodness by subjecting her to sorrows and mortifications, against which our modern consciences rebel. He pretends to have her children killed, to take a new wife, and he drives Griselda away from her old father; patient Griselda bears it all. Finally her husband discloses that all this was a test and rewards her patience with the most fervent love and regal honors.

Minor Writers of the Second Half of the Fourteenth Century

Imitators of the Great Writers of the Century

Exiled from Florence, Fazio, of the famous Ghibelline family of the Uberti, lived at the courts of various lords: the Scaligers at Verona, the Visconti at Milan. It appears he died after the year 1367. His major work is the *Dittamondo* (corruption of *Dicta Mundi,* the story of the world), around which he undertakes a journey under the guidance of Solino, an ancient geographer. The pilgrim travels about Italy, Greece, Northern Europe, France, England, Spain, Egypt, and the Holy Land. There are many historical and mythological digressions; the most important is the history of ancient Rome at the beginning of the poem, which remains unfinished. It stops in the middle of Book VI, and the section on Asia is lacking. In the details and the invectives there is much imitation of Dante.

Another writer of the late fourteenth century imitates Dante still more closely. The Dominican Federico Frezzi of Foligno, later bishop of that city, who died at Konstanz [Baden] in 1416 during the Council, is the author of a vast allegorical poem, the *Quadriregio,* which seems to refer to the four kingdoms through which the author contemplatively journeys. The first is the kingdom of the senses. Minerva, the goddess and symbol of wisdom, is then his guide through the multiform kingdom of Satan; this is not in Hell but on earth. Then the pilgrim passes through the kingdom of the mortal sins and finally, the kingdom of the virtues: first the cardinal or human virtues (temperance, fortitude, prudence, justice), then the theological or Christian virtues (faith, hope, and charity). Enoch, Elias, and Saint Paul are respectively his guides. There is great confusion in the architecture of the poem, the distribution of the material. There are four books of heavy allegories and heavy moralizations. The descriptions try to be Dantean, and whole lines are taken directly from Dante; but in spirit and form, the *Quadriregio* belongs to the moral allegorical productions that flourished widely in the schools.

Petrarch had more imitators than Dante. Attempts to create an original lyricism begin toward the end of the fourteenth century and beginning of the fifteenth century, especially at the powerful court of the Visconti at Milan. In this respect, Francesco Vanozzo of the March of Treviso is worthy of consideration, but on the whole, from the fourteenth century on, Petrarch was supreme. Among his close imitators, the Roman Giusto de' Conti is remembered for his canzoniere entitled *La bella mano* [*The Beautiful Hand*], faithfully Petrarchan in style.

Similarly, Boccaccio quickly became a famous model of narrative prose. The novella writers begin the series of so many imitators of the *Decameron*. The first is Master Giovanni Fiorentino, who composed a collection of novellas which he named *Pecorone* [*The Ram*] to indicate his own simplicity and ineptitude in the art: A monk and a nun, in love, tell each other a story every day for twenty-five days, thus creating fifty novellas, which often repeat themes from the *Decameron* and sometimes are taken directly from the chronicles of Villani. The other Boccaccian is Giovanni Sercambi of Lucca, who wrote a chronicle of contemporary events and about one hundred and fifty (or more) novellas, which he does not seem to have named. To escape the plague of 1374, a group of Lucchese gentlemen start on a journey through Italy. Naturally, storytelling is one of their pastimes, and the business of narrating is entrusted to the author himself. He is a very lively but licentious narrator.

This is the place to tell about a singular story of adventures, which is grafted onto historical events: *L'avventuroso Ciciliano* [*The Adventurous Sicilian*], attributed to Bosone of Gubbio, a contemporary and perhaps a friend of Dante, who held, among many offices, that of Roman senator. He died well on in years, in about 1370. In that book is a recounting of how, after the turmoil of the Vespers, which drove the French from Sicily (1282), five barons, adherents of the party of France, discussed quitting the island for ten years to await better times and look for adventure in the outside world. Each of them becomes an important personage, and after many years they meet again in their homeland, where they put together the treasures amassed in their undertakings. It is an inanimate and colorless story, interspersed with frequent orations and harangues (copied from Cicero and Sallust) and descriptions of battles.

Spontaneous Popular Literature

FRANCO SACCHETTI Needless to say, although the three great fourteenth-century authors exerted a powerful influence on the literature of the time, literature also continued on its spontaneous course, developing popular forms, which were to reach full bloom in the fifteenth century. In the second half of the fourteenth century, Franco Sacchetti is the most attractive representative of this unpretentious literature. He was a Florentine merchant who, in the course on his business, traveled a great deal through Italy and Europe and was a keen observer. He held important posts and died around 1400. For the entertainment of groups, he wrote about three hundred novellas, of which only two hundred and seven are extant in complete form. He asserts in his Introduction that he was induced to turn writer by Boccaccio's example, but there is nothing of Boccaccio here. These novellas are not gathered in an organic whole, like those of the *Decameron*. They are short, rapid, and informally dictated with great liveliness. Sensuality is rare. His favorite theme is practical jokes played on simpletons. Some, indeed, take us right into the heart of the customs and usages of the age of the communes and have some slight historical value. Sacchetti did not try his hand only at narrative prose. He wrote many ingenuous poems in the popular manner, such as ballads, madrigals, and *caccie* (poems relating to the hunt). The sonnets and the moral and political *canzoni* are less felicitous, and a poem, intended to be very witty, is without any wit — the *Battaglia delle belle donne di Firenze con le vecchie* [*Battle of the Fair Women of Florence with the Old Women*].

ANTONIO PUCCI The most popular writer was the Florentine Antonio Pucci, a bell-ringer of the commune and then town crier, who died in 1388. He is the poet — if the title is not too solemn — of the things everybody sees; the events and happenings at which he is an enthusiastic spectator. In a *capitolo* he describes *Le proprietà di mercato vecchio* [*The Properties around the Piazza of the Old Market*] where, according to Sacchetti (novella 175) he had next to his house a little garden hardly as big as a bushel basket that was the gathering place of the Florentine populace. In some *Sirventes* [the Provençal name of poems that sang of political events alive in the conscience and memory of the poet and his public], he touches on various woes of his city, and in a *Lament* he imagines that Florence bewails the loss of Lucca. In a little seven-canto poem he recounts the war of Florence against Pisa. For the delight of his public, Pucci wrote a long *Contrasto* in octaves, which presents all the arguments against and in defence of women. He also wrote several stories of chivalry, such as that of *La Reina d'Oriente* [*Queen of the Orient*], and perhaps the *Spagna* [*Spain*]. Finally, in a poem that had been intended to have one hundred cantos (and is called in consequence *Centiloquio*) he reduced to tercets and abridged the *Cronache* [*Chronicles*] of Giovanni Villani, at the same time amplifying the chapter referring to Dante. This shows the increasing importance of the poet in the imagination of Pucci's contemporaries. The *Centiloquio* stops with the ninetieth chapter, that is, in the year 1336.

Religion and Saint Catherine of Siena

The plague, which in 1348 and afterwards visited Italy several times, provoked in the terrified multitudes a craving for repentance to placate divine wrath. Throughout Italy and Europe, the Flagellants multiplied, the cloisters were repopulated, and the life of contemplation gave the sicker, or more delicate, souls new comforts. The book in Latin of *The Imitation of Christ* perhaps belongs to the fourteenth century, and its author is perhaps the Abbot Gersenio, a Dominican of Vercelli. This is the profoundest book of religion after the Gospels, in which many troubled souls found, and still find, peace. Filled with the spirit of Christ, in the second half of the century, a saint appears, Catherine of Siena, who died at the age of thirty-three. She does not belong to literary history but to religious history. As a girl, Catherine entered the order of the Dominican nuns. She experienced raptures and ecstasies; but she was too much an Italian, too much a Tuscan, not to take her combat position in the world. She wished to spread the evangelical spirit of love in her turbulent city of Siena. In the name of her "blessed Christ," she spoke out to the princes, to Queen Giovanna of Naples, and to the popes. It is largely due to her insistence that the Holy See returned to Rome and the scandal of Avignon was ended.

She did not hesitate to approach the most hardened criminals; with her own hands she picked up the head of one or another executed man, who through her had accepted death as an expiation. Her activity and her fervent religiousness is documented by some four hundred *Letters* that, since she could not write, were dictated to her lay sisters. They are warm with spontaneous eloquence, alive with inward movement, effective in phrasing, and rich in language. The Saint also dictated another book, *Della divina dottrina* [*On Divine Doctrine*], in which God himself speaks to his *Diletta* [Beloved]. In it the capital concepts of Christian theory are corroborated, and the decadence of the priesthood is deplored with strong words.

4.

The Fifteenth Century

The Awakening From the Middle Ages

During the Middle Ages, the undervaluing of the earthly life, in which Christian theory and, to a certain extent, Christian practice were summed up well before Dante, had remained more a concept than a fact. Attachment to the active life, characteristic of Western man, was, moreover, far too strong to allow the triumph of a religious concept that would have meant the suppression of history, as it had for so many peoples of the East. The Catholic Church itself preserved its sense of reality, and tolerated, rather than favored, the truly contemplative religious orders. Beginning approximately with the twelfth century, however, special circumstances, which may be considered both causes and effects, brought minds back to a freer and more human sense of life. The feudal regime, which meant the domination of the few and the servitude of the multitudes, began to disintegrate. The Crusades had brought the nations of the Occident into contact with the splendors, thought, and wisdom of the Orient. The rise of the communes gave a soul and a new pride to the people, spreading wealth and well-being. Society thereupon resumed its way from the point where it had been interrupted. The minds returned to that ancient world that signified the exaltation of life in all its forms and the development of man in his integrity. It was not regression, but progress. Later on, the study of antiquity may signify hindrance and stopping, but not then; at that point the ancient world had to reveal all its wisdom. The Latin authors were studied and later the Greeks, though with far more ardor than in the preceding centuries. Men asked them for the new word and the new guidance.

The Renaissance

This spontaneous awakening of the universal consciousness, which was first expressed in the cult of the ancients, is now called the *Rinascimento* [Renaissance]. There were many immediate causes for it or, rather, extrinsic circumstances, that contributed to its development. Toward the end of the fourteenth century and all through the fifteenth century, many *seignories* [despotisms] arose in central and northern Italy. They assumed the protection of writers either as an ostentatious show of magnificence or as an attempt to win public opinion, so necessary for usurpers; moreover, the Renaissance was an aristocratic, cultural movement, which could only take its support from the proximity of thrones. In mid-century, the fall of Constantinople to the Turks caused a considerable number of Greek philosophers and scholars to seek refuge in Italy; this was the beginning, in Italy and all over Europe, of a direct acquaintance with that language and literature. The invention of printing, already in use in the last decades of the fifteenth century, was a powerful aid to the diffusion of knowledge, and the accessibility of those ancient texts that now were being uncovered by industrious researchers. The

Middle Ages were ignorant not only of Greek literature, but also of capital works of Latin literature, including those of the poets Catullus and Lucretius, those of the comic authors and those of the prose writers, almost all of Cicero, and all of Livy. The name of Tacitus was unknown. The widespread wealth in Italy, fruit of the industrial activity of the preceding centuries and the general peace then in effect, especially in the second half of the century, were all conditions favorable to the revival of learning, but contributing factors and timely so-called inventions and discoveries have no value unless they occur in an environment that is ready to receive them. The Renaissance was essentially a necessary moment in the history of the spirit.

The movement pervaded all the activities of the spirit, and first and foremost, art. Throughout the fifteenth and sixteenth centuries, at least in Italy, the relics of ancient art were considered unsurpassable models of beauty. In painting, the Byzantine rigidity disappeared, as did the ingenuous simplicity of Giotto's followers. The painting and the sculpture of the fifteenth and sixteenth centuries are, in the first period, realistic and pleasingly graceful, later an expression of ideal beauty, and finally, the expression of strength and majesty. In architecture, first the Gothic style declines, and then the Christian churches compete in splendor and luminosity with the ancient temples. Saint Peter's — begun in the middle of the fifteenth century and completed at the beginning of the seventeenth century — was originally conceived as the Pantheon superimposed on the Basilica of Constantine. The religiousness of the Church dies away in the fifteenth century, while the severe lines of the old palaces of the despots grow softer, and the palaces of the princes arise strong, elegant, and regal.

The ancient world did not appear merely as beauty, but also as wisdom. New philosophical systems, or new interpretations of the world and of life, are built upon ancient philosophers either newly discovered, or for the first time available in all their integrity. The cult of Platonism or Neoplatonism is widespread in the Renaissance and is particularly strong in Florence; elsewhere, especially in southern Italy, the teachings of the ancient Greek philosophers are adopted, culminating in naturalism and pantheism. Aristotle, removed from the interpretation of the Scholastics and seen in his reality and totality, led to materialistic and atheistic conclusions, particularly at Padua. It should, however, be noted that it would take centuries for the Renaissance to arrive at the formulation of truly new philosophies.

The same may be said for the sciences which, during the Renaissance, hardly free themselves from empiricism and superstitions, but the spirit of investigation, the critical spirit, reveals itself powerfully from the very beginning of the movement. The need arises to review tradition and to deny it any value wherever it is impossible to document it. Therein lies the methodical program of that vast protesting religious revolution that took Germany, England, and a part of Switzerland away from the Church of Rome. In Italy, no contradiction was seen between the new spirit and the ecclesiastical tradition, and at first the Church itself favored and presided over the Renaissance. The historical sense, which means adherence to human reality, developed earlier in Italy than elsewhere: history was born and, as a premise or theorization of history, political observation and science.

Poetry

To come to the point of what is more closely connected to our task, in the Renaissance the production of poetry was varied and plentiful, based on models of all kinds offered by Latin and Greek literature. The Renaissance poets possessed to an eminent degree that sense of form, that sureness and exquisiteness of taste, which thereafter remained an acquired habit in Italian poetry. However, they were artists more than poets. Their age was one geared more to erudition and research than to imagination and sentiment, and besides, in the Renaissance the feeling for religion and chivalry, at least in its ingenuous expression, for austere and chaste love was dead. The great themes of a past age had either disappeared or were alive only on the surface. Italy could no longer produce a Dante or a Petrarch, just as it would have been impossible during the Renaissance in France to create a *Chanson de Roland* or a romance such as *Tristan et Isolt* or in Germany the saga of the *Nibelungen*.

Also, when the liberty of the communes was lost, the poets were left to the protection of the men holding power. This phenomenon is known in histories of literature by the name of *maecenanism,* because Maecenas, a minister of Augustus, won over the souls and the art of the greatest writers for the cause of the empire. It was a saying of the ancients that slaves are only half men, and a poet in the service of a prince can only be half a poet. Liberty is the breath of poetry. The poetry of the Renaissance (and the same may be said for oratory and eloquence) is therefore often a wretched thing, if one looks deeper than appearances: it is abuse or satire against personal enemies or rivals for the favors of the prince; it is a song of unbounded lasciviousness, sometimes in the person of the lord himself, to women loved by him; it is an extravagant enlargement of petty happenings; it is even, in the midst of its substantial moral poverty, a frequent and hypocritical sermon on superior virtues. In the Renaissance, the man and the poet are divided, and literature is separated from life.

Humanism and Humanists

Considered in its literary aspect, the Renaissance takes the name of Humanism. Humanists are learned writers of poetry, history, philosophy, in short, writers of what the Latins called *litterae humanae,* because they have to do with the highest interests of the moral human being. Considering its substance, the Humanist movement occupied three centuries: the fifteenth, sixteenth, and seventeenth. In the fifteenth century it is concerned with erudition; in the sixteenth, art, and in the seventeenth, philosophy and science. Actually, the name of Humanism is given to the first vigorous burst of the literary revival, which, in Italy, coincides approximately with the first half of the fifteenth century. The Humanists, in their enthusiasm for ancient literature, scorned the vernacular and wrote in Latin if they could not write in Greek. Their Latin had little resemblance to the rough, grammatically simple and yet, in its purpose, living Latin, of the Middle Ages; it aimed at the elegance and eloquence of the classical language and was a magnificent and dead Latin.

Today the Humanists are alive only in histories of literature, but in their own time they were very influential. They invaded the upper schools, until then dominated by men of the Church; often they dominated at court, where they obtained political and diplomatic offices. They were subservient toward their protectors and quarrelsome toward their adversaries, or competitors. A great freedom in their habits contributed greatly to the celebrity of many of them, there were many, but for us, a few names and little information must suffice.

Some Humanists

Albertino Mussato of Padua (d. 1329) a contemporary of **Dante**, is generally considered a distant precursor of the Humanists. He wrote two ample histories in Latin and in the style and manner of Titus Livius: *De gestis Henrici VII Caesaris* [*The Deeds of Emperor Henry VII*], and a book about events in Italy following his death, *De gestis Italorum post Henricum VII Caesarem*. He imitated Seneca, in a tragedy about the dreaded Ezzelino da Romano, *Ecerinis,* and the *Tristia* of Ovid in some meditative poems that he called *Soliloquia.*

Petrarch, however, in his enthusiasm for the ancient literatures, and because of his vast poetical and moral production in Latin, is truly the man who initiated Humanism. He launched one of the most important activities of the humanists, searching for lost ancient texts. Petrarch's protracted residence in the halls of the autocrats and his vainglory are typical of the Humanists. Close to Petrarch is one of his great friends, Coluccio Salutati of Stignano in Valdinievole (d. 1406), chancelor of the *Signoria* of Florence. He write Latin poems on scholastic subjects, such as destiny, the Labors of Hercules, the War of Pyrrhus; he also wrote eclogues, and many letters of historical importance.

Florence, where the cultural tradition was more alive than in other parts of Italy, was the first and most felicitous seat of the Humanists. They found there protection and aid in one of the richest and most generous men of Italy or Europe: Cosimo, of the Medici family, who before long was to assume rule over the city. A secretary of the republic, Leonardo Bruni of Arezzo (d. 1444), wrote the history of Florence in Latin, from its origins to 1404, in the republican spirit and without medieval legends; he made use of the Greek he had learned to translate several dialogues of Plato, and the *Ethics* and the *Politics* of Aristotle, into Latin. We also have a biography of Dante that he wrote in Italian. In one of his many letters, he states that the Italian vernacular does not derive from the Latin of the classical authors, but from the speech of the plebeians, an opinion that in modern times was considered to be the most reasonable for resolving the difficult problem of the origin of the Italian language. A Tuscan of Terranova, Poggio Bracciolini (d. 1459), was Pontifical secretary at the Council of Constance, to which he made several lucky trips in search of ancient texts and discovered the *Argonautica* of Valerius Flaccus, some orations of Cicero, the *Institutio oratoria* of Quintilian (which was to become fundamental in the rhetorical theories of the Renaissance), the *Selvae* of Statius, and works of Lucretius and Plautus. One of his books, *Facetiae,* shows the licentiousness of the age. Far more important are his *History of Florence* and his moral dialogues. Giannozzo Manetti (d. 1459) was a Florentine who wrote biographies of Dante, Petrarch, and Boccaccio in Latin.

Later, in mid-century, a famous philosophical academy arose in Florence under Cosimo's patronage; because of the singular cult professed there in favor of Plato and the Neoplatonists, it was called Platonic. An academy, which stood for discussion, was already a step upward from the schools, that rested on authority. Plato, therefore, the father of idealism, stood for opposition to the inanimate formalism of the schools and acceptance of mystical inspirations and intuitions, which later found development in more modern philosophical systems. Platonism could also be considered, as it was by so many Church Fathers, an introduction to Christian theory or perhaps even a reconciling philosophy and dogma. The Florentine Marsilio Ficino (d. 1499), who translated Plato into Latin and sought precisely this reconciliation in his work *Theologia platonica de immortalitate animarum,* was the moving spirit of this academy. Among its members were the extremely learned Giovanni Pico della Mirandola, Cristoforo Landino, interpreter of Dante, and Girolamo Benivieni, the commentator on a *canzone* on love by Cavalcanti, in which he posited the basis of what was called "platonic love." The

Platonic Academy exercised much influence on the arts and poetry. Considering beauty as the expression of things, not in their apparent reality but in their eternal idea. It posited, as a canon of art and poetry, ideal perfection, which later ended in the conventional and the abstract.

Every important city, seat of a seignory, or court had its own Humanists, as well as its college or university. At Venice the increase in Humanism was due principally to two nobles: Francesco, and Ermolao Barbaro, called the Elder, so called to distinguish him from his nephew Ermolao who was also a great man of letters and flourished in the second half of the century. Verona boasted of an enthusiastic Greek scholar Guarino Guarini (d. 1450, in Ferrara); Mantua boasted the father of pedagogy, Vittorino Rambaldoni of Feltre. To the court of the Visconti in Milan came Gasparino Barzizza of Bergamo, the first of the *ciceroniani* or emulators of Cicero, Pier Candido Decembrio of Pavia, who wrote the Life of Filippo Maria Visconti and that of Francesco Sforza; Antonio Loschi of Vicenza, author, among other things, of a treatise of rhetoric, and Maffeo Vegio of Lodi, who was determined to continue the *Aeneid,* which seemed to him to be lacking an ending. He also wrote a poem on Jason's conquest of the Golden Fleece; his little poem that treats of the wretched fate of Astyanax, the son of Hector and Andromache, was more felicitous. In old age, a canon of the Church, he devoted himself to sacred subjects, and in an epic poem, *Antonius,* Saint Anthony of the Thebaid.

At the court of Sigismondo, son of Pandolfo Malatesta and Lord of Rimini, lived the poet Basinio Basini of Parma, the author, among other things, of the *Isottaeus,* letters of a certain Isotta [Isolde] to the lord, her lover, who dedicated a temple to her during her lifetime. In other poems he celebrated the enterprises of Pandolfo Malatesta, wrote about astronomy; spoke of navigation; who knows how many he would have written, had he not died when only thirty-two years old. From Tolentino came Francesco Filelfo (d. 1481), the most accomplished Greek scholar of the early fifteenth century, and one of the most vainglorious, mercenary, and servile men of letters of Italy. He wrote a poem in praise of Francesco Sforza (*Sfortias*) which was to have numbered twenty-four books, but only ten were written; ten books of *Satire,* each one containing ten satires of one hundred lines each; and also ten books of epigrams. In the same proportions he planned ten books of odes, but wrote only five, adding three books of Greek poetry. His fecundity was proportional to his mediocrity. He also wrote prose, oratory and many letters, which reveal his spirit of mendicity and petulance. His son, Giovanni Mario, was also a copious writer, and produced a biography of Dante full of falsity and fantasy.

There were also Humanists in Rome. Indeed, one of the most powerfully critical minds of the age was that of Lorenzo Valla (d. 1457). Enmities aroused against him by his aversion to the methods and the idols of scholasticism made him seek refuge in Naples, at the court of Alfonso the Magnanimous. Later he became apostolic secretary and then professor of rhetoric at the University of Rome. His writings are so many battles: In a long dialogue in three books *De voluptate ac vero bono* [*On Pleasure and the True Good*] he seems to rehabilitate Epicurus, as opposed to medieval tradition which had abased him to the rank of "philosopher of pleasure"; In a little treatise, *De libero arbitrio,* which theologians attempted in vain to suppress, he explains the contradiction between free will and divine omniscience. He established a principle of capital importance: the difference between theology and philosophy was akin to that between faith and reason. In a book on *Dialettica,* he attacks that mechanical formalism to which the art of reasoning had been reduced in the schools. In the dialogue *De professione religiosorum* [*On the Profession of the Monks*], he censures the monastic vows, stating that virtue is affirmed more by fighting out in the world than by retreating from it into solitude. The six books of the *Elegantiae [Elegance* or *Graces]* were texts of the Latin language and served for a long time as the basic work for whomever wishes to write with that Ciceronian good taste which, principally thanks to Valla, came to be considered the ultimate in good writing. Most important of all Valla's contributions is the brief work *De falso credita Constantini donatione [On the Falsely Believed Donation of Constantine]* where he shows the lack of any historical or logical foundation in the legend that the Emperor Constantine, cured of leprosy by Pope Sylvester, had in his gratitude ceded Rome and the provinces of Italy to the Pontiff and had withdrawn to Byzantium. Thus the feigned historical basis for the civil dominion of the Roman Pontiffs was disproved.

Studies in ancient history flourished in Rome, finding their center in an academy founded by a Roman prince, who himself assumed the name of Pomponio Leto. The greatest of these historians was Flavio Biondo (d. 1463) of Forlì, who spent most of his life in Rome as apostolic secretary. From him we have works on Roman archeology: the *Roma instaurata [Founding of Rome]* and *Roma triumphans*; a sort of geography of ancient Italy entitled *Italia illustrata,* and what might be called a *History of the Italian Middle Ages: Historiarum ab inclinatione Romanorum libri XXXI [History of the Decline of the Romans,* 31 books]. The documentation and discussion of the sources of the account make this work one of the first histories written according to a critical method. For freedom of opinion, the *Vite dei Pontefici [Lives of the Popes]* from Saint Peter to Paul II, are also noteworthy; they were written by another historian of the Roman academy, Bartolomeo Sacchi, called "Platina," the Latinization of Piadena, a village in the province of Cremona where he was born.

Before becoming Pope Pius II, Enea Silvio Piccolomini of Siena (d. 1464) devoted himself to the chronicling of contemporary events in his *Commentari* on the Council of Basel, in which he participated as legate and in the *Memorie* [*Memoirs*] of his own life. In a *Cosmographia*, which was intended as a geographical description of the world, he digressed into the historical events of his times, based on his own travels and observations.

The Humanistic movement also enjoyed wide favor at the court of Alfonso, King of Naples. There, numerous men of letters wrote about the undertakings of the Aragonese monarchs, as did Valla and Bartolomeo Fazio of Spezia. The most famous poet, at the beginning of the fifteenth century was Antonio Beccadelli (d. 1471) of Palermo, whence his appellation of Panormita [the ancient name of Palermo was Panormus]. Like so many other Humanists, he saw many cities of Italy: Siena, Bologna, Rome, until Filippo Maria Visconti called him to Milan as his poet and historiographer. Since a poem in his praise was never forthcoming, Filippo grew tired of him, although he had been crowned poet by the Emperor Sigismund. Thereupon he established himself at the court of Naples where he died, old, powerful, and famous. His name is attached to a collection of obscene epigrams that are titled *Hermaphroditus,* and to a species of panegyric of King Alfonso in four books: *De dictis et factis magnanimi Alphonsi* [*Sayings and Deeds of Magnanimous Alfonso*]. He contributed to the spread of literary culture in Naples even more by his activities than by his writings. A group of scholars, poets, and philosophers formed around him, that later became the Pontaniana Academy, from the name of the most important member of the group, Giovanni Pontano (1426–1503).

Other Humanists were active in Sicily, notably Giovanni Aurispa of Noto, who is said to have brought at least three hundred Greek manuscripts from Constantinople to

Italy. Messina became a center of Greek culture, and Constantine Lascaris taught there for a long time. He was a refugee from Constantinople and published the first grammar of the Greek language. Also from Constantinople came one of the few real poets of Humanism: Michele Marullo. A soldier and man of letters, he settled in Florence where his rival in love and glory was Poliziano, who lacerated him in several epigrams. Marullo was drowned in the river Cecina. His *Hymni naturales* are highly inspired and a vigorous exaltation of the gods of mythology. They portray in the most elevated forms the pagan spirit of the age.

Popular Literature of the First Half of the Fifteenth Century

In the first flush of Humanistic culture the humble vernacular fell into an almost universal disregard, at least among the learned. There are few vernacular writers in the first half of the fifteenth century. Widespread, however, in that age, continuing throughout the century and beyond it, was a current of popular production which, by its very nature, could not undergo the influences of Humanism.

A Venetian patrician, Leonardo Giustiniani (d. 1446), left several *strambotti* [rustic love songs] — songs that the lover sings at the window of his fair one — and *canzonetti*, little poems full of grace and naturalness which, set to music by their poet, became popular all over Italy. A Florentine barber, Domenico di Giovanni (d. 1448), became famous for another kind of popular poetry. He was called *Burchiello* because to rhyme *alla burchia,* it is said, means to versify capriciously, carried along by verbal analogies and the rhyme. In effect this is what Burchiello did in burlesque compositions, which perhaps made sense in their own day. To him is owed that amplification and debasement of the sonnet, called the *sonetto caudato,* a sonnet with a caudal appendage of added lines.

The legends of Charlemagne and his Paladins, and also those of the Knights of the Round Table, which had passed from northern Italy into Tuscany, there formed the genesis of two romances in eloquently colored prose. They are among the most popular books in Italian literature: *I Reali di Francia* and *Guerin Meschino*. They were composed by a certain Andrea Magnabotti of Barberino, a notary in Val d'Elsa, who lived in the late fourteenth or early fifteenth century. The subjects of the *Reali di Francia* are the history of the kings of France mythically descended from Constantine, and the birth of Roland [Orlando] to Berthe, the daughter of Charlemagne and Milton d'Aglante, both driven out by Charles, who was opposed to his daughter's marriage to a humble knight. The story ends with the recognition of Roland by Charlemagne. Various minor tales are interspersed through the principal story; among the more moving is that of the loves of Bovo d'Antona [Bueve d'Hantone] and Queen Drusiana. In the other romance, the son of the Duke of Taranto, Guerino, while still an infant, is sold into slavery at Constantinople where he rises to an important position at that court. When insulted as the son of unknown parents, he undertakes to seek out his real father, traveling to the ends of the earth and even descending into Hell, painted with reminiscences of Dante. Finally he discovers his father, an aged prisoner in the Tower of Reggio, frees him, and restores him to his throne. The theme is of the unrecognized and persecuted innocent who is at last revealed and rewarded, a common theme in so many tales of the pious Middle Ages.

Abundant in the same proportions, although contrasted to the sensualism and new paganism of the cultured classes, is the popular religious production in the fifteenth century, of which the fullest and most felicitous expression is found in the *Sacre rappresentazioni* [*Sacred Plays*]. Originating as a development of ecclesiastical rites and of the dialogue which was often an element of the laude, the *sacra rappresentazione* (earlier called a "devotion" or a "mystery") set before the spectators, events of the Bible and the Gospel and the most popular lives of the saints. A messenger in the form of an angel would make the argument of the play known to the audience and explain its moral significance. The play then went on in a rudimentary fashion, presenting in succession, events taking place, sometimes over a period of many years and in places far distant from each other; that is, there was nothing of that which much later was called unity of time and place, and there was no inner development. There could be no drama in the sacred play; drama is a clash of wills, and in the plays there was a sole and undisputed will, that of God. However, the affections, especially the familiar ones, were sometimes well brought out. With sober but eloquent truthfulness, the human element came little by little to stand beside the religious, and later on a vigorous comic element appeared as well. The plays were preferably recited in *ottava rima,* the most popular strophe; the acting was entrusted to confraternities — in Florence those of children — and that contributed a certain element of naturalness and simplicity which was characteristic of the genre. These plays flourished in Italy throughout the fifteenth century. The most beautiful were those seen in Florence, derived from the processions with mystic scenes which were customary on St. John's Day. Many are anonymous. Even some famous writers tried their hands at them, such as Giustiniani, mentioned previously, and Lorenzo d' Medici himself. Feo Belcari, an ascetic Florentine writer, gave perhaps the most ancient *rappresentazione* with his *Abramo ed Isacco* [*Abraham and Isaac*]. Sant'Onofrio, Il

Figliuol Prodigo [*The Prodigal Son*], *Stella* [*Star*], *Sant 'Uliva,* are the names of other plays that became very popular.

In Siena more than anywhere else religious literature flourished, even in the Humanistic Age. San Bernardino degli Albizzeschi, or more simply San Bernardino da Siena, of the Observant Franciscans (d. 1444) has left us the *Prediche volgari* [*Sermons in Vernacular*] which he preached in his city in the Lenten season of 1427. They sparkle with vigor, lively language, and sincerity; they are full of human warmth.

In the fifteenth century there were also many novella writers aiming at a Boccaccian elegance. Masuccio dei Guardati of Salerno stands out above the others with his *Novellino* [*Book of Novellas*]. He lived at the Aragonese court in Naples. In Tuscany, learned men persisted in writing in the vernacular, or in both the vernacular and Latin. Matteo Palmieri, a Florentine, wrote the dialogues *Della Vita Civile* [*On Civil Life*] in imitation of Cicero's *De Officiis* [*On Duty*] and a moral allegorical poem, *La Città di Vita* [*The City of Life*] in one hundred cantos in tercets. The latter is an exterior imitation of Dante's *Commedia,* in which he repeated an ancient, Church-condemned fantasy: the souls of men were originally angels who, in the struggle of Lucifer with God, "were not rebellious, nor were they faithful to God, but they were for themselves," as Dante said (*Inf.* III 38, 39) and that here on earth they must, through trials, become worthy of reward or deserving of punishment.

One of the geniuses of the Renaissance, Leon Battista Alberti, born in Genoa of a Florentine family in exile, spent most of his life in Rome, where he died in 1472. He was a leading architect, and the author of Latin works on architecture, sculpture, and mathematics, and many dialogues on moral themes. He wrote in the vernacular the four books of *Della Famiglia* [*About the Family*]. In them he discusses running the house, matrimony, bringing up children, and friendship; he supports the ethical ideal that happiness consists of the wisdom and calmness of the mind. The latinizing style and the lack of any dramatic movement make Alberti's work unattractive and dull. However, it enjoyed great favor, a faulty summary of it under the name of Agnolo Pandolfini circulated for a long time. Even today the *Vite* [*Lives*] related by the Florentine bookseller *Vespasiano da Bisticci* are of interest; with great sincerity and sprightliness he told all that he knew concerning his most celebrated contemporaries.

The Second Half of the Fifteenth Century: The Group of Tuscan Writers

Toward the middle of the fifteenth century the vernacular once again began to receive due honor. The entirely literary opposition to it had waned, especially in Tuscany, where the literature in Italian had already produced masterpieces. In addition, the essentially democratic spirit of that region (even the Medici were originally a rich family of merchants) would not have tolerated forgetting the popular literature. The vigorous renewal of Italian poetry is owed, in Florence, to Lorenzo the Magnificent.

Lorenzo the Magnificent (d. 1492) belongs to political history. He was a remarkably able diplomat, who succeeded in keeping the various Italian states in equilibrium. His death, in effect, meant the end of peace in Italy, a half-century of war, and ultimately servitude. He was a part-time writer and poet. He wavered between one or another of the literary currents then in vogue and was more productive than gifted. He came to the defense of Italian poetry in a paper that he sent to Frederick of Aragon accompanied by a collection of old poems. For a lady who died young, Simonetta Cattaneo, whom his brother Giuliano loved, he wrote a number of poems in the *Dolce stil nuovo* and added a commentary, as Dante did for the *Vita Nuova*. For another lady, Lucrezia Donati, he composed a canzoniere which is one of the most original of the time. His two *Selve d'Amore* [*Woods of Love*] have been highly praised. They are in *ottava rima*; the principal theme of the first is the memory of falling in love; of the second, longing for the woman far away and jealousy. Plentiful and often redundant images and allegories, like that of Hope, and frequent digressions, like that in the second *Selva* on the fabled age of Saturn are characteristics of the work.

Classical overtones and Humanistic tastes are echoed in the little poem *Ambra*, in *ottava rima*. The poet imagines that Ambra (which was the name of Lorenzo's villa at Poggio a Caiano near Florence) was formerly a nymph loved by Lauro (a name allusive to Lorenzo himself) who was transformed into a rock by Diana. These fantasies are suggested by Ovid and by Boccaccio's *Ninfale fiesolano*. The descriptions, such as that of winter, are the most attractive part of the poem. *Corinto*, in tercets, is the lament of the shepherd of that name for the harshness of the nymph Galatea; it recalls the lament of the Cyclops in an idyll of Theocritus. In the *Altercazione*, the principles of the Platonic Academy are echoed. It is a dialogue between a city resident and a country man. The city man envies the country man and the country man envies the city man. Enter Marsilio Ficino, who teaches that happiness on earth is impossible in any circumstance: on earth there are only imperfect goods and the only happy life is the one which begins after the present one. The poem ends with a fervent prayer to God, which is one of the loftiest things ever written in Italian religious poetry.

The best things that Lorenzo wrote are those in the popular manner. One example is the little poem *Caccia*, in *ottava rima*, which tells about a hunt engaged in by a group of Florentines; it depicts the preparations and progress of the hunt and lets us hear the hunters' dialogues. The author participates in the sport with various illustrious citizens of Florence: one of the Strozzi family, one of the Alamanni. Just as lively is the *Nencia da Barberino,* also in *ottava rima*; although more recent studies attribute its composition to Bernardo Giambullari. In a series of popular *rispetti,* the peasant Vallera makes his declarations of love to Nencia, a girl from Barberino, with a grace touched with realism. In the *Simposio* [*Symposium*] in tercets, also called *I Beoni* [*The Drunkards*] the poet walks with a procession of people leaving the city. A man, Bartolino, of the group explains that they are all on their way to Ponte a Rifredi, for a bit of drinking and points out the leading drinkers. It is a parody of the *Commedia,* or rather, a parody of Petrarch's *Trionfi.* Many coarse expressions abound, which are unpalatable in the guise of Dante and Petrarch.

Lorenzo attached great importance to carnival festivities for lulling the people into serfdom. He introduced carts on which the masked representatives of the different social classes—hermits, craftsmen, and so on rode by—singing songs which alluded to their social stations. Thus were born the *Canti carnascialeschi* [carnival songs], whose basic theme was an invitation to enjoy and forget moral prohibitions. Ambiguous and obscene phrases were abundant in them. Many of them are by Lorenzo, but other writers contributed to the number, and the genre persisted down to the middle of the sixteenth century. The *Trionfo di Bacco e Arianna* [*Triumph of Bacchus and Ariadne*] by Lorenzo is one of the most famous and typical works of the carefree Epicureanism of the time. Also, the singer of the carnival seems also to be the poet of Lent. Lorenzo wrote spiritual laudes, and he composed a Sacred Play, *San Giovanni e Paolo,* in which many things are discussed: the conversion of Constantine's daughter, Constance, who Saint Agnes cured of leprosy; the conversion of Gallicano, Constantine's general and conqueror of the Persians and the Dacians; Constantine's renunciation of the Empire; the death of his sons; the reign of Julian the Apostate and the persecutions of the Christians which he fomented, and in which two youths, John and Paul, former attendants of Constance, were slain. The drama ends with the death of Julian the Apostate, stabbed by the martyr Saint Mercurio. Many scenes express a great tenderness. Julian's character, although barely outlined, is vigorously portrayed in his harshness toward the Christians.

Poliziano [Politian]

Lorenzo is more an occasional than a vocational poet and rarely an artist. The supreme artist of his age who had the greatest sense of beauty, was Lorenzo's protégé and friend, Angiolo Poliziano. He was a Humanist who was able to join to the spontaneity of popular poetry all the nobility of the ancient poetry.

Angiolo Ambrogini was born in 1454 at Montepulciano and from the Latin name of his birthplace *Mons Politianus* he was later called Poliziano [Politician]. He came, financially impoverished, to study in Florence, and while still an adolescent attracted attention by his compositions in Greek and Latin. Lorenzo favored him with his patronage and appointed him teacher of Greek and Latin oratory in the Studio of Florence, and then preceptor of his son Pietro. He died in 1494, two years after his patron's death. His attachment to the Medici after the death of Lorenzo and the resurgence of republican feelings had alienated him from the sympathies of the Florentines. The party of the Pagnoni, under the influence of the unbending Savonarola, leveled many probably unfounded accusations of immorality at him.

Latin Writings

Poliziano left a vast Latin production. Some exquisite elegies are remembered, such as that on the violets given him by his beloved, and another written about Albiera degli Albrizzi, who died young. His translations from the Greek are many, the most important being the second to the fifth books of the *Iliad* in magnificent Vergilian verses. His *Miscellanea* had great importance for philology; in them he sought to correct and rectify, in the name of good sense and good taste, innumerable lines in ancient texts that had been misinterpreted in the Middle Ages. His *Praelectiones* — we would say, "Prolusions" — to his various courses in ancient literature are beautiful in their eloquence rather than deep in their thought. Some are in prose, others in hexameters (and these are titled *Silvae*). The most interesting of them are the introduction to Homer, that on Perseus and the Latin satirical poets; and the one to which he gave the title of *Nutricia,* which from beginning to end is in praise of poetry as the founder and teacher of humanity. In the *Epigrammi,* in Latin as well as Greek, there are frequent adulations of Lorenzo and also frequent invectives against Humanist enemies or rivals: the bickerings of literary men. His letters, in twelve books, are important, as well as the brief account in Latin of the *Congiura dei Pazzi* [*Plot of the Pazzi*], of the attempt, that is, to murder Lorenzo, together with his brothers Giuliano and Giovanni in the church of Santa Reparata. Only Giuliano fell.

The Italian Works

Now only the *Rime* [*Poems*] of Poliziano are read. He began writing in the vernacular in early youth. On the occasion of the festivities held in Mantua in 1471 for the visit of the Duke of Milan, Galeotto Maria Sforza, the eighteen-year-old Poliziano was charged by Cardinal Francesco Gonzaga to compose a theatrical entertainment, which was the *Favola di Orfeo* [*The Fable of Orpheus*]. This was later revised, by whom it is not known with certainty, and divided, in the manner of the tragedies of Seneca, into five acts. The nymph Eurydice, beloved by Orpheus, is bitten by a snake as she flees from the advances of a shepherd in love with her (Aristeo), and she dies. Orpheus descends to the Underworld, and with the beauty and the sadness of his song, he moves the divinities of that region, Pluto and Proserpine, to compassion and obtains their permission for the return of his beloved on the one condition that as he leads her back he shall not turn around to look at her. He cannot resist the urge, and he loses her once more. In vain Orpheus tries the gates of Tartarus again. Then he returns to his native Thrace, where in despair he inveighs against women; whereupon the Bacchantes, the priestesses of Bacchus, angered, tear him to pieces. This is the plot. Poliziano's play is presented in the manner of the sacred plays. Its novelty lies in the fact that, instead of a sacred legend, it is drawn from a classical legend, an indication of the profound change in the spirit of the times. The saint, the hero of the religious age, is replaced by the poet, the hero of the Humanist Age. The action is weak; the poem has the character of an idyll and an elegy rather than that of a drama. Aside from that, there are some exquisitely poetical passages, such as the announcement by a dryad of Eurydice's death, and the solemn and melancholy prayer of Orpheus at the threshold of the Underworld. The *Metamorphoses* of Ovid in the part where the myth of Orpheus is related are an influence in this work.

Giuliano, the youngest brother of Lorenzo, participated in 1475 in one of those tourneys of knights that the Medici, conceivably to conceal their bourgeois origins, frequently arranged. To honor the hero Giuliano, Poliziano composed the *Stanze per la Giostra* [*Stanzas for the Tour-*

nament], which many considered the most perfect art produced in the fifteenth century. The first book tells about Julo (as the name of Giuliano is latinized in remembrance of the Julus of Vergil), a youth averse to love and enthusiastic for the chase in which — painted with great sprightliness and freshness of details — Cupid plans to avenge himself on the youth. He causes a doe to spring up before him, which Julo follows into the wood, where it disappears; instead he finds a beautiful nymph, seated on the grass and busy weaving garlands of flowers. The youth pauses, struck by her divine beauty; Cupid, filled with jubilation, comes to the island of his mother Venus. The ample description of that island closes the first book. In the second, the youth, awakening from a dream in which Glory has revealed herself to him, determines to become famous in some noble undertaking and so to merit the love of the nymph. What this undertaking shall be, the poet does not tell us, but in this manner he has prepared the transition to the tourney. Here, at the forty-sixth strophe of the second book, the poem stops; perhaps because Giuliano died in the Pazzi plot of 1478.

Even if the poem had been completed, the *Stanze* would never have been an organic and close-knit work around a central theme. Its parts are admirable in themselves, but they are fragments: the life of the shepherds, the springtime, the chase, the flowers, the island of Venus, and so on. Poliziano is predominantly a pictorial poet, a painter of scenes. It is not improbable that his "Birth of Venus" inspired Botticelli's painting on the same subject, and that from his Galatea came the Galatea of Raphael in the Farnese palace in Rome. When the poet pictures the nymph with whom Julo fell in love, however, one feels again the freshness and the spiritual quality of the *Dolce stil nuovo* poets. In the *Stanze* the poetic technique reaches its maximum perfection. There is no art or metrical artifice that is unknown to Poliziano. *Ottava rima,* rough and plebeian before him and even in his time, becomes for him a melodic motive and a picture perfect in itself.

In the *Stanze,* Poliziano displays all his classical culture. He imitates Vergil and Theocritus; from Claudianus he takes the description of the island of Venus. At the same time though, he feels all the beauty of popular poetry. He composed a large number of rispetti, either those strung together in long compositions and called *continuati,* or the isolated, single ones called *spicciolati,* and these are the more beautiful. Some of his *canzoni a ballo* [songs for dancing], like the one that celebrates May Day and the one that tells of girls gathering flowers in a meadow, are unfaded and alive with inspiration. Others are graciously frivolous, and still others, gracefully sensuous.

Luigi Pulci

The poet of the Tuscan group who more than any other shows the influence of the popular taste and manner was Luigi Pulci. He was born in Florence in 1432, and it was due to the friendly patronage of Lorenzo the Magnificent that he did not end up as his brother Luca did, in prison for debts. Lorenzo also entrusted several errands to him, in Naples, Bologna, Milan. He died around 1484 in Padua.

Pulci was a prolific poet. He imitated the *Nencia da Barberino* of his patron Lorenzo in the *Beca di Dicomano,* a series of rispetti, which exaggerate the popular manner, but he is famed for his *Morgante.* He took the material of his narrative principally from an anonymous poem of the fourteenth century, perhaps entitled *Orlando.* In twenty-eight cantos, one *Morgante* tells the story of how Orlando, the foremost of the paladins, is banished from France due to the machinations of a traitor, Gano, to whom he had legitimately administered a slap. Gano belongs to the family of the Maganzesi, which in the Carolingian legend is preeminently the family of traitors. Rinaldo belongs to the lineage celebrated for its loyalty and honesty, the Chiaramonte family. Orlando, therefore, goes away to Pagania (which is the name given in Carolingian poems to non-Christian countries). His cousin Rinaldo comes to join him there, indignant because the old and failing Charlemagne, now in his dotage, is letting himself be manipulated by that traitor Gano. A strange giant, Morgante, has made himself Orlando's squire; formerly a rogue, he had been guilty of such activities as disturbing the quiet of a convent. Thanks to his enormous size, he becomes the right arm of the two paladins. His customary weapon is the clapper of a great bell. Later another dubious character, an outstanding master of thievery and fraud named Margutte, offers his services to the paladins; unlike Morgante, he does not become a convert to Christianity; indeed, he does not hesitate to profess a ribald and impudent sort of religious belief. Orlando and Rinaldo perform the most singular feats in Pagania: They dissipate enchantments; they conquer monsters, kings, and queens; they convert the conquered to Christianity. Various daughters of kings, such as Meridiana, fall in love with Orlando. But Charlemagne needs his two paladins to fight the pagans (that is, the Moors) who are threatening France from Spain. A demon, Astarotte, enters Rinaldo's horse, who thus is transported back to France with lightning speed. Orlando also returns. Morgante and Margutte have died before all this: the former from the bite of a small crab at the time of a storm at sea when he went into the water to tow a ship to safety. Marguette had died of laughter at the sight of an ape trying to pull on Morgante's boots. Orlando and the paladins proceed to strike a blow at the pagans in their own domain, Spain, and return triumphant; but the envious Gano then plots dastardly treachery with Marsilio, King of Spain. Charlemagne has already crossed the Pyrenees on his victorious march back to France, at the head of his great army. Orlando and the most illustrious paladins make up the rear guard protecting the army. At the pass of Roncevaux, the pagans ambush the rear guard, as Gano had instructed them. All the paladins, after the most heroic resistance, perish beneath the numbers of the enemy. Seeing that death is close at hand, Orlando, finally humiliated, sounds his horn to call for help. Charlemagne hears the dire sound, returns, and finds all the paladins dead. Then the treachery of Gano is revealed. The miscreant is captured, taken to Paris, judged, and quartered by being dragged by horses.

The poem, like the Carolingian popular poems, lacks organization and unit. The second part, (which derives from another old poem, the "Entry into Spain," or the "Expedition of the Paladins to Spain") is poorly grafted onto the first. Orlando, young at the beginning of the tale, appears old at the end. The themes are those which were considered interesting in the popular epic: trials of strength and courage; wrongs suffered and avenged; punishment of traitors. Love has little part in it. Buffoonery, on the contrary, plays a considerable part; therefore, the poem takes the name of Morgante, who is a minor character in the action, but who brings the most laughter. The scoundrel Margutte, the typical unprejudiced and cynical meddler, is no less grotesque. The clowning invades every part of the story and spoils moments that should be the most serious: Thus the scene of the death of the paladins at Roncevaux, so imposing and great in the most ancient of the French *chansons de geste,* here is deformed. The author is incapable of feeling for the heroic life. However, the *Morgante* does not lack erudite and informative pages; the demon Astarotte, for example, discusses theology with sublety and foretells the discovery of lands beyond the Atlantic. The cultured literary genius of his great friend Poliziano must have had much influence on Pulci, but the rare learned passages add nothing to the merry temper of the poem, and sometimes spoil it. Its value, is in the extraordinary vigor of narration and description. It seems as though the author has seen with his own eyes all that happened in his imagination. Certain syntactical peculiarities contribute to this vigor of presentation. Examples are the frequent use of the present tense and the present perfect, the brief phrases of not more than two lines, and an admirable linguistic ability: an ample vocabulary, a vivid, rapid, deeply felt, and idiomatic language.

Other Figures of the Tuscan Group

In the second half of the fifteenth century Fra Girolamo Savonarola, a Dominican of Ferrara, came from that city to establish himself in Florence in the monastery of San Marco, which Fra Angelico painted with his paradisiacal visions. He is of far more religious and political than literary importance. An ardent preacher, Savonarola felt that he was chosen by God to bring about the restoration of Florence and of the Church. He was the avowed enemy of Lorenzo the Magnificent and foretold the death of the great man and that of Innocent VIII, as well as the invasion of Italy by the French. During the expulsion of the Medici, which followed that event, the Friar became the arbiter of the city and attempted a reform, half democratic, half theocratic. The reform was sternly opposed to luxury and splendor, the great pleasures of the Renaissance. His followers, taking the name of *Piagnoni* [moaners or mourners] increased, but his adversaries, the *Palleschi* (from *palle,* balls, referring to the three balls of the Medici coat-of-arms) who were favored by the Medici, also increased; they accused him of being a rebel against Pope Alexander VI (Borgia). The Pope forbade him to preach, but he continued and appealed to a council against the Pope. The Pope excommunicated him. This marked the beginning of Savonarola's loss of popularity, which increased when he would not or could not undergo the "trial by fire," to prove that he was truly a prophet sent by God. He was hanged and burned in 1498, in Piazza della Signoria in Florence, with two other Dominicans. He was the last heroic and solitary voice of the free and Christian Middle Ages against the new era — a prophet come too late.

A few of his rude religious lyrics have been preserved: a canzone on the ruin of the world; another on the ruin of the Church, and also a love-filled laude praising Christ. His *Sermons* have a religious and political interest; these were saved by one of his faithful auditors. The *Trattato circa il reggimento e governo della città di Firenze* [*Treatise on the Government of the City of Florence*] still exists.

Purely for chronological reasons it is proper at this point to speak of the great Leonardo. Born at Vinci in lower Valdarno, he became a pupil of Verrocchio and a friend of Botticelli in Florence, and assimilated a wide literary and scientific culture. He lived for a long time in Milan at the court of Lodovico il Moro, where in addition to works of art, he undertook to render the Adda navigable. After various wonderings through the cities of Italy, he went to the court of Francis I in France. He died, famous, at Cloux, close by the château of Amboise in Val de Loire. Paintings that are a marvel of beauty and truth (his masterpiece is the *Cenacolo* [*Last Supper*] in Santa Maria delle Grazie in Milan) place him in the ranks of the greatest masters of that art; they are few in number because he was so engrossed in the speculative life and in scientific studies, as is apparent from the numerous manuscripts that he bequeathed to Francesco Melzi. They were later scattered among the various libraries of Europe, especially after the publication at the end of the seventeenth century of some fragments entitled *Trattato della Pittura* [*Treatise on Painting*]. Now, in addition to the Atlantic Codex of the Ambrosiana Library of Milan, which contains very important fragments of his studies in mechanics and mathematics, others of Vinci's codices have been published. A complete edition of all his writings is being attempted with government help. Vinci was an initiator and well-versed in hydraulic studies, the precursor of many modern discoveries; he was a simple but powerful writer on moral and artistic matters.

The Neapolitan Group

Under the tutelage of Panormita, a great Humanist current developed at Naples, in which Pontano held first place. Giovanni or, as it was latinized, Gioviano Pontano, of Cerretto in Umbria, was one of the many men of letters who owed a high political post to his culture. Wielding great influence at the court of Ferdinand I of Aragon, he was the teacher of the king's son, Alfonso. His character was much weaker than his mental ability. Toward the end of the century, when Charles VIII of France invaded Italy, coming as far south as Naples, Ferdinand took refuge in Sicily, and Pontano came forth with eulogies of the new ruler and vituperation for the fallen monarch. But Charles VIII returned to France rather quickly, and Ferdinand regained Naples. Discredited at court, Pontano, in solitude, awaited his death that occurred in 1503. In one of the busiest streets of Naples stands the little temple which he raised to his wife Adriana Sassone, around which are sculptured sayings of wisdom and civic virtue; an odd document for those times.

He wrote exclusively in Latin, a language which he treated with an apt touch and great liberty. He left many works: sprightly dialogues dealing with moral and literary arguments; treatises of philosophy in which, contrary to the tendency of the Florentine Platonic philosophers, he extolled that active life which he lived with such intensity; historical and astronomical works; the poem *Urania*, or *De Stellis* [*On the Stars*], in which every planet is personified into the corresponding deity and the poet expounds the splendid mythological fables which correspond to each divinity. The most felicitous poems are the shortest and least pretentious. Many praise his works dealing with domestic affairs: the elegies *De amore coniugali* [*On Married Love*], which extol his wife; the *Neniae* [*Lullabies*], and the *Tumuli* [*Graves*] written in memory of beloved dead.

Jacopo Sannazaro

Although not so good a poet as Pontano, Sannazaro was a better man. He remained unfailingly faithful to the house of Aragon, especially to Ferdinand's son, Federico, who later inherited the throne. Under the short-lived government of Charles VIII, he protested (albeit in Latin verses) against the heavy taxes with which the French king oppressed the Neapolitans. In the second invasion of the French under Louis XII, he offered his services and the money received from the sale of his castles to Frederick and followed him into exile in France, where they lived until Frederick's death. Then he returned to Naples where he spent the last years of his life in studies and religion until his death in 1530. His tomb is behind the principal altar of the little church of Santa Maria del Parto in Mergellina, which he founded in 1529.

Under the influence of his friend Pontano, Actius Sincerus (as Sannazzaro was called in the academy) wrote much in Latin. His *Eclogae piscatoriae* enjoyed much celebrity in the past: Here the world of the shepherd is replaced by that of fishermen, who take over the world that was until then the domain of pastoral folk; however, the fishermen are no less conventional than the shepherds. He wrote three books of *Elegie* and three of *Epigrammi* (including under that heading any sort of short lyrics). Of the Latin works, a poem in three books on the birth of the

Virgin, *De Partu Virginis,* stands out. He worked on this poem for twenty years and yet, because he judged it still imperfect, it was not published until after his death. The annunciation, the visit of Mary to Saint Elizabeth, and the birth of Jesus at Bethlehem, are the principal parts of the story; they are not portrayed with the simplicity of popular art and poetry—sincerely religious—but are amplified and elevated with epical magnificence; that is, deformed. The parentheses and the digressions compensate, or try to compensate, for the poverty of the fable. Thus in the first book the poet transports us into the Underworld, where the news is spread of the impending birth of Christ, and David prophesies the death of Jesus and his coming to free the souls of the just Jews. In the second book there is a reference to the census that Augustus had imposed on all cities subject to Rome, and for which Mary and Joseph are on their way to Jerusalem to report. This gives an opportunity to describe, with great historical and geographical learning, the regions of the Roman world, in which Greece and Italy held first place. In front of the newborn baby, two shepherds, Egone and Licida (perhaps Pontano and Sannazaro), sing of the new Golden Age which will be begun by Christ (translating freely from the fourth eclogue of Vergil), and later the God of the river Jordan remembers what Proteus once sang to him about the principal miracles of Jesus. By means of such expedients, the whole story of the Gospels is epitomized. In reality the *De Partu Virginis* is more a literary piece than it is poetry. Sometimes exquisite, the beauties are in the details, the comparisons, and in the harmony of the lines. At every step one feels Vergil. In the last lines of the *De Partu,* the poet implies that he has been too audacious and that he is called to the shade of Posillipo and to the peace of his beloved Mergellina. He was more at ease in a poem in minor key, of which the fullest expression is the *Arcadia,* written in the vernacular.

The *Arcadia* is a sort of autobiographical romance in which the author narrates how, to find solace for his spirit afflicted by an unhappy love, he has gone to Arcadia, a region of Greece traditionally sacred to shepherds, and more specifically, to Mount Parthenius. In these surroundings, the poet takes part in the conversations and festivities of the shepherds, listens to their songs; he even ventures to sing one himself. The shepherds are Ergasto, saddened by the recent death of his mother Massilia; Gallizio, in love with the nymph Amaranta; old and wise Opico; and Carino, who like Sannazaro, adores a cruel nymph; there are others. The events of the romance are few and not very interesting for us: that is, the festivities for Pale, the goddess of the shepherds; the description of the wood and of the statute of Pan, to which is joined the myth of his love for the goddess Syrinx, changed into a hollow reed in order to escape him (and with that reed the god made the reed-pipe, whereupon the author digresses to speak of Theocritus and of Vergil, the two great poets of pastoral and georgic poetry); the funeral games in honor of Massilia, in imitation of those celebrated by Aeneas in the *Aeneid* in honor of his father Anchises. The author at first goes incognito among the shepherds. Then he makes himself known and narrates to Carino his own story and that of his ancestors, his unrequited love, and his flight from Naples. But he is unable to forget. A gloomy dream fills him with the darkest forebodings. Awakened by his terror and wandering through the fields, he encounters a nymph who takes him with her through subterranean and mysterious paths, where he beholds the origins of rivers and learns about the giants who are lying, struck by thunder, beneath Etna and Vesuvius. In short, they pass underneath the sea and come out at Sebeto, at Naples, where the tutelary deity tells him that the nymph beloved by the poet is dead. A song between two shepherds on the sorrow of Melibeo (that is, Pontano) for the death of Phyllis (his wife) brings the romance to a close, followed by a prose passage dedicated to the reed pipe of the shepherds, in which the author assumes merit for having been the first in Italy to renew (in the vernacular, of course) pastoral poetry.

The romance includes twelve prose passages, in which the story is told; it is expressed with far more Boccaccian elegance than vigor. After each prose section comes a canto in the style of an eclogue. The canto is sometimes sung by one shepherd, more often by two; sometimes is concerned with the death of a nymph or a shepherd, but more often is a lament for the cruelty of some nymph. In these eclogues the dactylic tercet is preferred, perhaps because it was felt to give the image of the harshness and rudeness of the pastoral poem. It is a difficult meter to tolerate; for one thing, the difficulty of the rhyme scheme forces the poet to employ the crudest Latinisms. Sometimes, however, the lines are more harmonious series of hendecasyllables rhyming in the middle, or the eclogue may be a canzone in the style of Petrarch. The *Arcadia* is essentially a literary product. Therefore, in the literary centuries it enjoyed great vogue, both in Italy and abroad. As for Sannazaro's canzoniere, mention suffices: They simply reproduce the themes and the forms of Petrarchian poetry. His *farse*, [farces] or scenic representations of factual allusions to the history of his time, have some importance for the history of popular poetry.

Court Poets

This is the place to remember some poets, courtiers by trade and by disposition, who flourished in that most propitious of surroundings, the magnificent Neapolitan court and the equally magnificent courts of certain popes. One such was Benedetto Gareth of Barcelona, who presumptiously called himself, in the Greek manner, Cariteo (the favorite of the Charites, the Graces). He lived in Naples and died in 1515. Coldness, strange, linked metaphors or allegories, hyperboles, and antitheses are the characteristics of his rhymes, as they are of the other contemporary court poets. This style was an indication of the absence of any conviction and passion, and a prelude to that literary malady that was *secentismo,* or the manner of the seventeenth century. The special object of his praises was the second wife of Ferdinand II, celebrated under the pseudonym of *Luna.*

No less famous than Cariteo was Serafino Aquilano, a rhymster of the most ingenious and cold witticisms, who was born in Aquila in Abruzzo and who lived for a long time at Rome. He was in the service of Cesare Borgia, and died there in 1500 while still young. His place was taken by Antonio Tebaldi (d. 1537) of Ferrara, called Tebaldeo, who came to the court of Leo X from the court of the Gonzaga at Mantova; he merited inclusion with Dante and Petrarch and the greats of the ancient world in Raphael's Parnassus. He is the rhymer of grotesque images and colossal hyperboles; blood flows from a beauty's nose; the reason is that Cupid missed his mark and hit her in the nose instead of the heart. Francesco Gonzago wept so many tears because of his loves that Mantova has a lake not only outside the walls, as is well known, but one inside as well. However, he also wrote an eloquent chapter on the wretched condition of Italy in that stormy age and a sonnet against Naples, which offered no resistance to the French occupation.

At the courts of Leo X and Clement VII, the two Medicean popes, a warm welcome was extended to Bernardo Accolti of Arezzo, called the Unique Improviser on account of the excellence of his skill, and all Rome flocked to hear him. He died wealthy in 1534.

The Northern Group

Several artists and poets flourished under the patronage of Ludovico il Moro. But Ferrara soon became the center of great poetry, by the influence, chiefly, of Matteo Maria Boiardo, count of Scandiano. He was a very important man at the court of Ercole I, Duke of Este and Lord of Ferrara, in whose name he was governor of Modena and Reggio, where he died in 1494, aged sixty. He was a gentleman and a knight, in the best meaning of the words. He was a great lover of the classics, and he knew Greek, which had been brought to Ferrara by the Veronese Guarino. He translated several things from Greek into Italian, including Herodotus. His own comedy in five acts in praise of poverty is a translation of a dialogue of Lucian, both having the same name, *Timone*. He was a born poet; for him the classical culture was a suggestion to write poetry. We have his canzoniere d'amore entitled *Amorum liber* [*The Book of Loves*], in which there is a feeling for nature and landscape which the reader seeks in vain in the other canzonieri of the time. But the work by which Boiardo lives on in the history of poetry, and which he broke off with the disheartened reference to the "Gauls" who were coming down to "lay waste" to Italy, was cut short by his death; it is a vast poem of chivalry, the *Orlando innamorato*.

The Breton Poems and Boiardo

Because of the feudal origin of the court of Este, the chivalrous traditions were still alive in Ferrara more than in any other region of Italy. This was especially true of the cycle of the Round Table, whose head was the legendary King Arthur, and in which the principal parts were played by Lancelot, Tristan, Paris, the magician Merlin, Guinevere, Isolt and others. These poems, well known in

France and Brittany in a previous age (wherefore they are also called Breton poems), in contrast to the Carolingian epics, which were religious in spirit, sang of adventurous journeys undertaken by knights to please their chosen ladies. In them the fantastic, unexpected, supernatural, and magical played a great part. In medieval France and Germany, such legends produced masterpieces of poetry; it would be enough to recall the romance (which is preserved in its entirety only in the German version of Gottfried von Strassburg) of *Tristan et Isolt*. More delightful and varied than the Carolingian, the poems were the favorites of the aristocratic classes, while the general public persisted in its enthusiasm for the paladins of Charlemagne. Boiardo had the idea of fusing the Breton poems with the Carolingian or, rather, of taking from the Carolingian poems their grandeur of action and most famous characters, developing the whole in accord with the spirit of adventure and love of the Breton romances. The very title of *Orlando innamorato* [*Roland in Love*] shows the transformation of the paladin (formerly represented as unconquered by the passion of love) into the knight, for whom love was the sole or the principal reason of existence. But it must be added that the poet ennobled his story with elements of deeper humanity and more harmonious beauty derived from classical poetry.

The *Orlando innamorato* is divided into three parts and is broken off in canto IX of the third part when the invasion of Charles VIII woke the poet from his joyful dreams. In the last strophe there is an allusion to that unexpected event, which awakened in Italians more astonishment than fear; and there is a promise that is unfulfilled to continue the canto when the tempest is over. Although incomplete and rough in its plebeian constructions and its Lombardisms, the poem was so pleasing that Ariosto chose to continue it with his *Orlando furioso*. In the elegant sixteenth century, however, when the principle of regarding Tuscan as the norm for literary expression was beyond question, Lombard, an uncultured and dialectal language, appeared intolerable. Therefore, Francesco Berni rewrote the poem to conform to the Tuscan idiom. Today people prefer to read it in the original and ingenuous form.

The Material and the Art of the *Orlando innamorato*

It is not easy to give a résumé of the plot of this vast poem, nor is it necessary, especially since the beauty is to be found much more in the individual parts and individual actions of the many characters than in the construction of the work as a unit. The principal theme — the novelty that was to make the poem beloved by the lords and the knights — is the love of the previously austere Orlando, and of others, for the beauteous Angelica, sent by her father Galafrone, king of Cathay (a fabulous country of India) to a *pasqua di rose* [rose festival], an assembly of Christian and pagan warriors held at Paris by Charlemagne. The father's plan was for Angelica to bewitch the most famous warriors of Christ. When her brother Argalía is slain by Ferragut, a heathen warrior, Angelica is left alone and goes through a series of adventures as she is sought after in turn by Orlando, Ranaldo, and by Agricane, King of Tartary, who comes to drag her from the castle of Albraccà where she had at last sought safety. But Agricane dies at the hands of Orlando, who is the most faithful, most pure of heart, and the least compensated of Angelica's adorers. He takes her back to the West, and on the eve of a day of fighting under the walls of Paris between Christians and heathens (in which the Christians have the worst of it), she is entrusted to the care of Namo, Duke of Bavaria, for she is to be given as a prize to the paladin who kills the greatest number of enemies. The expedition to France of Agramante, King of Bizerta, with his allies — among whom are Radamonte, King of Algeria; Mandricardo, Agricane's son; and Marsilio, King of Spain (instigated to treason by the ill-famed

Gano) — is another of the great *gestes* of the poem. To all this may be added the arrival of Gradasso, King of Circassia, as strong as he is willful, bent on winning Durlindana, Orlando's sword, and Baiardo, Ranaldo's horse; and, at the end of the poem, the loves of Ruggero (a pagan king who was fated to become a Christian, despite the enticements of the sorcerer Atlante) for Brandiamante, Ranaldo's sister. The theme is scarcely begun and was to be developed later by Ariosto. These, and numberless minor actions, follow one another, merge, or clash, generating a series of unexpected and marvelous scenes.

The descriptive and pictorial element of the poem is lively; the representations of festivities, battles, and of all that most directly made up the world of the courts of the fifteenth century are fast moving. The characters have little spiritual consistency; the psychology is rudimentary and ingenuous. The absolute lack of religious feeling is striking, and the same is true of the equal sympathy with which the poet portrays the Christian and the heathen warriors. A sense of irony and comedy that comes out here and there in the poem is noteworthy. The dual between Orlando and Agricane for Angelica is, in its roughness, one of the few truly epic pages in Italian narrative poetry (Book I, Chapters XVIII and XIX). Radamante, who has something of the Turnus of Vergil and the Capaneo of Statius, is just as vigorous. Too impatient to wait any longer, he goes ahead of the allies, crosses the Mediterranean alone, conquers a storm, and lands, with the fleet defeated, in France.

5.

The Sixteenth Century

Characteristics of the Century

The sixteenth century is to Italian literature what the century of Augustus is to Latin literature, or the century of Louis XIV to the French. Like those centuries, it also has taken the name of a generous patron of literature and is called the Century of Leo X. In this century the vernacular literature of Italy revived, filled with all the vital elements of the Humanistic culture. It revived richer in critical thought, historical research, and more splendid in form. In the first decades especially, there flourished writers great enough to honor a whole century, such as Machiavelli and Ariosto; but all too soon admiration for the ancient literatures expressed itself in imitation and repetition. The most spontaneous products of the national literature, which could have been further developed, were scornfully neglected and replaced by the genres of classical literature which seemed to correspond to them. Thus the *Sacre rappresentazioni,* disappeared from the Italian scene, instead of developing into the modern theater, as happened in Spain and England. Comedies imitating those of Plautus and Terence became the style, as did tragedies in imitation of Sophocles, Euripides, and Seneca. The "free" poem of chivalry soon died out, and its place was taken by the epic poem in the manner of Homer and Vergil. Imitation resulted in the birth of didactic poetry, and the pastoral fable, which was an amplification of the *Bucolics* of Theocritus and Vergil; similarly, satire in the spirit of Horace was composed, as well as dialogues modeled on Cicero. In lyric poetry, attempts at imitating the Greco-Roman lyric came later; the canon set for the lyric of the sixteenth century was an imitation of Petrarch.

The dogma of imitation therefore became fundamental in the sixteenth century and with it the principle that form exists for its own sake, independently of content. From this concept, beginning with the *Poetics* and *Rhetoric* of Aristotle and having a prevailing character of "art by precept," the first studies of the nature of poetry were undertaken, and investigations into the art of rhetoric multiplied. The personality of the writer diminished as consequent uniformity spread; this is another of the characteristics of sixteenth-century literature, which more and more lost its vivid regional character. Even language in the sixteenth century became uniform all over Italy. It was either modeled on the great fourteenth-century Tuscan authors or it resisted their influence in favor of a more polished and dignified latinized language. Thus the trend was toward that conventionalism against which a great deal of the literature was to react, both in that century and afterward, consciously or not.

Ludovico Ariosto. His Life

Ludovico Ariosto, one of the greatest poets of Italy, was born in 1474 in Reggio Emilia into a patrician family. His father Niccolò was captain of that stronghold in the name of the Duke of Ferrara. Hated for his harsh rule, Niccolò finally established himself with his large family (ten children) in Ferrara. Ludovico was put to the study of law, but he rebelled against all that "nonsense," and his father permitted him to devote himself to literature. He learned Latin and regretted not being able to learn Greek. Of all the ancient poets, it was Horace, the poet of serene epicureanism and keen wisdom, who was his favorite. In 1500, his father died, and he was obliged to put aside his beloved studies, at least for the time being, and devote himself to the administration of the property of his mother's dowry, to find openings for his younger brothers, to experience those miseries and pettiness of life that would later find their principal expression in the *Satires* and would leave an imprint of sometimes bitter irony even on the smiling, fantastic world of the *Furioso*. Later, he became a gentleman-in-waiting in the service of Cardinal Ippolito d'Este, brother of Duke Alfonso I. He was employed in various missions: once to Rome (1509) to seek the help of Pope Julius II, at the time an enemy of Venice, against the Venetians, who shortly thereafter were defeated on the Po. He visited that pope on two other occasions to win him over to the Estense family, allies of Louis XII of France (Ercole was married to Renée, Louis' daughter). For, although earlier favorable to the French against the Venetians who had occupied some Church territories, Julius II later became their great enemy, with the League of Cambrai, which brought about the expulsion of the French from Italy. Ludovico's missions were failures. He went to Rome a third time in 1513, to congratulate the new pontiff Leo X, who, as cardinal, had been his friend. He kissed the foot of the Holy Father, and the Holy Father kissed him on both cheeks; but he allowed the poet, who had expected great things of him, to depart empty-handed The fact is that the Medici (Leo was the son of Lorenzo the Magnificent) hated the Estensi, and the question of priority was long-lasting between the two families. The representative of the Estensi consequently could not have much hope of pleasing that Pope who, however, honored poets much inferior to him. Much more suitable to Ariosto's character was his appointment to what later was called "director of spectacles at the Court," a service that inspired or forced the poet to compose his comedies.

Actually Ariosto was not fitted for service, although he forced himself to do his best to serve. In 1516 he dedicated his *Furioso* to his patron Ippolito, who confined his thanks to asking him where on earth he had dug up all that nonsense. It was impossible to be more coarse and vulgar with such a marvelous artist. A year later, the Cardinal who had been named Bishop of Budapest, wanted his servant to follow him, but the servant refused to follow — the small and uncertain stipend could not make a slave of him. Besides, he had fallen in love with a beautiful woman, the Florentine Alessandra Benucci, the widow of Tito Strozzi; he had seen her in Florence on his way back from the mission to Leo X. In fact, he did not go to Budapest, and the cardinal dropped him from his service.

Then Duke Alfonso took him into his own service and sent him as commissioner to Garfagnana, at that time a wild district in the Apennines between the provinces of Modena and Lucca which, after being fought over for a long time by Lucchesi, Pisans, and Florentines, had surrendered to the Estensi. To govern meant many things: to administer justice; to exact tribute; to keep bandits in check. It is not always true that poets are lacking in practical sense. From his headquarters in Castelnuovo, Ariosto governed honestly and diligently, as can be seen from the numerous letters to the Duke which he wrote at that time and from those of the Duke to Ludovico. He would have done even more, and better, if the Duke, who did not wish to make enemies of these new subjects, had given him greater support. Certainly his heart was always in

Ferrara, and he could hardly believe in his good luck when he was able to return there after the three years of governing that he considered exile. What he wanted was tranquillity; and for love of tranquillity he refused the unsalaried post of resident ambassador in Rome at the court of Clement VII.

He was now in his fifties. The poet, who, thanks to his frugal way of life, had succeeded in laying aside some savings, bought a vineyard in the Mirasole district and built a very simple house there, which is still preserved. On the facade he had a Latin distich set, which expresses all his grief against unprosperous fortune, but also all his nobility of character:

Parva sed apta mihi, sed nulli obnoxia, sed non
Sordida, parta meo sed tamen aere domus.

A little house, but enough for me; not in debt to anyone
Not unclean, and bought with my own money.

Then he married his beloved secretly, so as not to lose certain ecclesiastic income, which, according to the canons, could only be enjoyed by the unmarried. There he remained, reading his Latin classics, cultivating his garden, and correcting his *Furioso* for the third time. The first edition had appeared, in 1516; the second, with improvements in the language and style, in 1521; then, in 1532, the third and definitive edition appeared with new episodes that increased the number of cantos from forty to forty-six. When the *Furioso* was thus completed, Ariosto went to Mantova to present a copy of it to the Emperor Charles V, to whose party the Este dukes had passed when they had abandoned the French; naturally their poet did the same. The Emperor liked to show courtesy to poets and painters: in Venice he stooped once to pick up Titian's brush. It is to be supposed that he accepted the *Furioso* with more graciousness than the Cardinal had shown. Indeed, there was a rumor that the Emperor intended to crown the poet; but the coronation was celebrated by posterity. The poet died one year after that journey, in July 1533.

We find out from the biography written about him by Giambattista Pigna, who was almost a contemporary of his that ingenuousness, goodness, shyness, perplexity and an almost unbelievable absentmindedness were characteristics of the inward Ariosto. He liked frugal living. He delighted in agriculture, but his lack of expertness in that field was great: once he planted capers and then found out they were elder bushes. He was fond of architecture, and he regretted that it was not so easy "to change the buildings as his own verses." We have a portrait of him, attributed to Titian: Large eyes, set well apart; absentminded gaze; high forehead; a countenance, says Carducci in a sonnet, " . . . which still retains the amazement of great dreams" — the visage of a poet. But that poet never gave himself the airs or assumed the pose of an inspired man or a genius; he accepted reality with its prosaism, its demands, and its harshness. Sometimes grumbling a little and sometimes smiling resignedly at the misfortunes and errors of life, he always thought he was a man among men: one of the reasons for the compassion that radiates from his work, sprightly in its fantastic splendor, and rich in human wisdom and experience.

Minor Youthful Writings

Between the ages of twenty and thirty, Ariosto gave good account of his abilities in the Latin poetry so cherished by his fellow citizens; for Latin poets of some ability flourished in Ferrara then, the greatest of them being Ercole Strozzi. Ariosto's first ode is an Alcaic, *ad Philiroen* (written perhaps just when the invasion of Italy by the armies of Charles VIII was imminent) which extols peace and love and is an admonition not to engage in public events; there Ariosto's nature is already visible and so is the temper of the pure artists of the sixteenth century. The elegy *De diversis amoribus* is interesting for what it discloses about the poet; in it he confesses his inconstancy in love. In those poems, indeed, several women are celebrated: a certain Pasiphile (friend of everyone), and a Lydia. There are mordant epigrams, and graceful ones: an epithalamium for the wedding of Alfonso I and Lucrezia Borgia (1502) has been highly praised. Although Bembo, the literary high priest of the time, exhorted him to continue in Latin (even, perhaps to write the *Furioso* in Latin), he preferred the vernacular.

He was already engaged heart and soul in his masterpiece; he had little affection for the scattering of poems that he composed from time to time. He did not collect them, and he never published them. They consist of elegies, *canzoni*, sonnets, madrigals, *capitoli*, and one eclogue. The elegies, in tercets, are at times reminiscent of the Latin elegiac poets, especially Propertius and, like the elegies of the Latins, are ardent autobiographical pages of love. Some refer to his love for Alessandra Benucci (as do most of the *canzoni* and the sonnets). Other elegies celebrate loves of an entirely different sort. In others, there is a vivid analysis of the torment of passion; for example, the tenth, in which the poet tells how, in order to uproot love from his heart, he went to visit the field of the dead after the bloody battle of Ravenna in 1512; but it failed to cure him, and he envied those men lying dead; and the eighteenth (perhaps apocryphal like several others), where the poet expresses the uneasiness of his soul even in the fullness of enjoyment and the perpetual craving for he knows not what: ". . . and if I can crave nothing else, I crave death."

Of the songs, the first, in the manner of Petrarch, is well-known: *Non so s'io potrò mai chiudere in rima* [*I Know Not if I can ever Close in Rhyme*], where he touches on his falling in love in Florence (which happened on Saint John's Day as the Florentines were celebrating the accession of the cardinal Giovanni dei Medici to the pontifical throne, with the name of Leo X). More important (and perhaps apocryphal) is the fifth, in which the shepherd Melibeo, on the lonely banks of the Po, deplores the wrongs of Italy and, more specifically, the bad government of Leo X.

Of the *Capitoli*, compositions in familiar style, in tercets, in which the poet speaks about himself, the first one is interesting. It was written when Ariosto fell ill while in the service of Cardinal Ippolito. In its manner it imitates a very beautiful and delicate elegy of Tibullus. The third capitolo is the beginning, if indeed not the whole first short canto, of a poem on the enterprises of young Obizzo da Este, who involves himself in the war between Philippe le Bel and Edward of England.

The Comedies

The cult for the Roman comic poets (Plautus and Terence) was more alive in Ferrara than elsewhere. From the end of the fifteenth century on, there were in that city frequent performances of ancient comedies, translated into the vernacular. Ariosto gave some thought to performances of original comedies that imitated the Latins, and thus he became the initiator of what came to be called the "regular" comedy. Following the form of the Latin comedy, Ariosto's comedy presents an action that must last only a day or a little more (unity of time) and develop throughout on the same scene, which represents a public place, most often a piazza or square; thus the presence of any or all of the characters is justified. This continuity of scene is called "unity of place." The five acts are preceded by a prologue, that is, by an actor who comes before the audience to call attention to the artistic criteria of the author and often to make a show of wit using ambiguous and indecent language.

It seems that Ariosto wrote his first two comedies in prose; then he rewrote them in hendecasyllabic proparoxytone verse form which he retained for the later comedies; with it he aimed at reproducing the iambic verse of the Latin comedy. He took pleasure — he, the wonderful master of harmony — in creating a verse so dull that it might be taken for prose and might reproduce the dialogue of the lower class.

Characters and themes of Plautine comedy recur in Ariosto's plays: avaricious fathers: prodigal sons; ladies of doubtful virtue; scandals arising from personal resemblances; recognitions that resolve a situation at one stroke, and satirical allusions to the life and corruption of the time. Although the scene of the *Cassaria* takes place in Greece, as in the Latin comedies, when Ariosto was finally able to realize his hope of seeing a fixed stage constructed in a hall of the ducal palace, he insisted on having the scenery represent the main square of Ferrara: a sign that he would certainly base the plots of his productions on the society of Ferrara which lay before his eyes.

But in order that my reader may have a more direct idea of the style and the worth of our comic poet, I shall now give a résumé of the lively plot of the *Cassaria*.*

Crisobolo, an old miser, leaves Sybaris to go to Procida, leaving his house full of merchandise of all kinds in the care of his faithful servant Nebbia. His son Erofilo† is madly in love with the slave Eulalia, who is held by the go-between Lucramo ["fond of lucre"]. On the advice

---

* Note: For Ariosto, as above for Pulci and Boiardo, and as will be the case for the most important writers from the Quattrocento to the Settecento, I have occasionally made use, especially for the résumés of works, of my two little volumes *The Principal Italian Writers from 1500 to 1600* and *The Principal Italians from 1550 to 7100* (Biblioteca dell'Università Popolare Milanese e delle F. I. delle biblioteche popolari). [The publisher has kindly consented, and it is my duty to thank them.]

† The proper names in these comedies, like those in Plautus' comedies and, later on, the French, are often Greek: Erophilus means "lover of love."

of the servant Volpino ["little fox"], Erofilo decides to remove a chest of pure, spun-gold yarn (whence the name of the comedy) and, in the absence of his father, to give it as a pledge to Lucramo for the hundred ducats which is the price he has set on Eulalia. The matter presents little difficulty. Nebbia, the faithful servant, is something of a dolt and it is easy to steal the key of the treasure from him. Trappola, a foreigner who is just about to leave for his own country, dresses up like a great gentleman in Crisobolo's clothing, and carries the chest of gold yarn to the usurer's house to buy Eulalia from him. But they realize that when he returns home, Crisobolo is going to miss the chest. And, indeed, he will get it back. Erophilus will go to the Captain of Justice to report the theft of a chest. That chest must be in Lucramo's house: a man who practices usury is also capable of being a thief. Caridoro ["gift of the Graces"], son of the Captain of Justice, intimate friend of Erophilus and enamoured of another slave likewise held by Lucramo, will help his friend by speaking to his father against the usurer, who will become so frightened that, to avoid the gallows, he will yield the chest gratis. And everything seems to go like a charm: Trappola has already handed the chest to Lucramo and is leading Eulalia to the arms of Erophilus. But now the troubles begin: The sea was too rough and departure for Procida was impossible. Old Crisobolo returns home, and encounters Volpino. Volpino thinks all is lost, but fear sharpens his wits. He bursts out crying and, shouts that Nebbia, that half-wit Nebbia, will be the ruin of his master. After a good deal of suspense, he tells Crisobolo the dreadful news: the chest has been stolen. Fortunately he, Volpino, knows where it is: it is in the house of that miscreant Lucramo. Not a minute is to be lost. Crisobolo must run immediately to the Captain of Justice and have the constable sent without delay to Lucramo's house, where he will find the chest. But Crisobolo has been around too long to have much faith in the operation of justice. He sends for some friends to be his witnesses and accompanied by them enters Lucramo's house; notwithstanding the usurer's cries and accusations and the din, he bravely carries away his chest. But, in front of the door of his house, he finds a stranger dressed in his, Crisobolo's, own clothes. It is Trappola, from whom some servants of Erophilus had snatched Eulalia, thinking he was a foreigner who was departing with the woman beloved by their master. He was now coming to report to Erophilus the fine result of his expedition. He does not know what to say to the questions and threats of the old man. "He's dumb," interjects Volpino. "But why is he wearing my clothes?" Crisobolo keeps on asking. "Nebbia," explains Volpino, "when the chest disappeared, wanted to run away but, not to be recognized, he dressed in the clothes of this mute and gave him yours in return." "But why not his own?" asks Crisobolo, reasonably enough. And Volpino is at a loss for words. The old man smells a rat and causes Trappola to be bound, whereupon he confesses everything. Then he has Volpino tied up with the same rope and drives him into the house to undergo dire punishment. At this moment Erophilus enters, looking for his Volpino: father and son meet face to face and the son receives a paternal tongue-lashing. Now all seems lost. But a certain Fulcius, a servant of Caridoro and worthy colleague of Volpino, appears on the scene, an unexpected savior. He, as a servant in the house of the Captain of Justice, is familiar with the snares of the law. He makes it clear to Crisobolo that Lucramo can complain to the judge and have him taken in as a swindler if he doesn't pay anything; certainly the man who took the chest to Lucramo's house was dressed in Crisobolo's garments. Crisobolo takes fright. "It is necessary," counsels Fulcius, "to pay Lucramo the price of the slave; there's no way out." And only Volpino can deal with the usurer and induce him to be satisfied with two hundred ducats, since nothing less than that will make him keep his mouth shut. "Two hundred ducats?" The old miser protests, then shilly-shallies, and finally yields. Volpino, released from his rope, leaves with the money. Naturally, he redeems both slave girls: one for his young master, the other for Caridoro.

Another comedy, *I suppositi* [*The Exchanged Men*] sketches a series of *quid pro quo,* arising from the exchange of identity which takes place between a Philogonus of Sicily, the real one, and a native of Siena who, by lending himself unawares to the wiles of others, is also taken for Philogonus. The plot is derived from *The Prisoners* of Plautus. The *Lena* (which in Latin means "procuress") has a base woman as principal character, who succeeds in arranging that a youth and a maiden find themselves together; their fathers, since the scandal has occurred and must be repaired, consent to their marriage. The *Negromante* [*Necromancer*] is a trickster who claims skill in the occult sciences; with the help of a scoundrelly servant, Nicchio, he extorts money from blockheads, robs his host's house at night, and engages in scandalous rascalities of all sorts until, exposed, he flees in his doublet. Not, however, before he urges Nicchio to go and steal all he can get from the inn.

Ariosto left the comedy of *Gli Studenti* unfinished; his brother Gabriele completed it with the title *La scolastica.* It turns on the adventures of two students of Ferrara. The portrayal of the student chaos is spirited and detailed; there are some interesting minor characters, such as that of a Dominican friar who, as inquisitor, releases a penitent from a vow on condition of making a gift to the convent.

The Satires

Ariosto wrote seven *Satires* in tercets, a verse form which remained typical of autobiographical and moralizing poetry from the time of Dante and which persisted as characteristic of the satirical genre right down to the Romantic era. He wrote them as occasion offered, and they were published posthumously. He could not have published them without danger during his lifetime since they often touch on real matters and personages and are not harmless generalizations, as was usually the case for the considerable satiric production which followed them. They are in the form of letters to relatives or friends in which the poet's own life is the subject; indeed it is from these *Satires* that the most meaningful information has been derived concerning the poet's life and character. But the poet observer passes from individual events to more general accounts of the life of the times, to moral observations, to witty and shrewd stories and fables in the manner of the *Satires* and, even more, the *Epistles* of Horace which he knew so well. The world of the Latin poet, however, is much more vast and varied and his irony more aristocratic. The *Satires* of Ariosto are rough rather than effective, and the man reveals himself in them as somewhat querulous, narrow and inclined to taking his ease, rather than a deep and calm explorer "of human vices and worth." Nor are all the *Satires* equally meaningful. For example, the first is little more than a very coarse rambling talk about matrimony. Nor is the fifth very important, the one in which the poet recounts his troubled life in Garfagnana. In the second, there is a lively picture of flatterers, the pests of courts. This is addressed to his brother Alessandro, then in the retinue of the cardinal in Hungary; it is here that the poet affirms that his liberty is worth more than the twenty-five scudi that were paid to him every four months — though not always forthcoming — by the Cardinal. In the third, he asks his brother Galazio in Rome to find him a lodging, as he also is coming to that city. Then we have a spiritedly satirical picture of the long wait he will have in the antechamber of some prelate. That is the hard life which is the lot of one who wishes to rise in the world, but under those conditions he personally will never rise. And if, passing from benefice to benefice, from rank to rank, dignity to dignity, one were to become pope, that pope would have to protect his sons and grandsons; he would have to oppress Christian princes to make a place for his bastard offspring, to excommunicate his enemies and to give indulgences to his favorites. He would bring ruin upon Italy; here is a page that is powerful in the manner of Dante, in which horror of the Pontificate of Alexander VI is perhaps still dominant. The seventh satire, written to the literary dean of the age, Cardinal Pietro Bembo, is important. In it he recommends his young son Virginio to be educated under the eye of the great Cardinal and kept away from the too numerous vices of the times: an interesting page, both for what it tells of the youthful life of the poet, and for the history of the usages and evils of the age.

There are also *Cinque canti* [*Five Cantos*], perhaps an episode to be included in the third edition of the *Furioso,* perhaps even the beginning of a new epic poem on the House of Este. In his juvenile years, he wrote a *cicalata* [chatter: name given to dissertations intended partly to show off learning, partly for amusement] entitled *L'Erbolato* [*The Herb Plaster*], in which a seller of simples, medicinal herbs, speaks in praise of the natural life as opposed to the perversions of the civil life and the deceits of medicine.

The *Orlando Furioso:* The Plot of the Poem

The whole of Ariosto is contained in the *Orlando Furioso,* the work to which he devoted himself with seriousness and affection for the better part of his life, as may be seen by the innumerable corrections in his manuscripts and by a comparison of the first edition with the third. Therefore, it may be said that the poem, which seems one of the most spontaneous works of Italian literature, is in reality one of the most meditated and least improvised. Here is the outline of the story:

Boiardo had already brought beneath the walls of Paris, Agramante, king of Africa, other African kings, and Marsilio, king of Spain. [Now, the vicissitudes of that fabulous siege remain as the central vein of Ariosto's poem, as the reference point.] At first the Christians are defeated. Angelica, the woman whom Orlando [Roland] had brought through a thousand perils to France; Angelica whom the Emperor Carlo Magno [Charlemagne] intended to give as a prize to the paladin who would kill the greatest number of infidels, takes to flight when she learns that the Christians are routed. She is followed by Rinaldo [Renaud], whom she hates heartily. He loses track of her; then he is sent by Charlemagne to raise troops in England. Meanwhile, Bradamante appears, fierce fighter and tender woman, lover of Ruggero the pagan (Ariosto continues Boiardo's fiction that the house of Este is descended from them). She is seeking Ruggero, whom the good enchantress Melissa, her protectress, has told her is held prisoner in a castle in the Pyrenees, where the sorcerer Atlante (who has foreseen that Ruggero would turn Christian) is keeping him surrounded by every pleasant thing. Atlante, indeed, was accustomed to collecting in that enchanted castle all the beautiful women he found in those regions. Mounted on a winged horse, a hippogryph, he would swoop down on them with a shield that dazzled and would capture them. As soon as he was discovered, he stunned anyone who dared oppose him.

Bradamante possessed a ring that had belonged to Angelica which defeated all enchantments. With this ring, she defies Atlante and captures him. She does not have the courage to kill him, but she frees Ruggero. The castle has disappeared, but Ruggero mounts the hippogryph and takes the enchanted shield on his arm; the hippogryph soars swiftly, leaving Bradamante desolate, and transporting the young man (in this the will of Atlante is still being obeyed) to the island of the fair Alcina, a seductress who when she was tired of her lovers changed them into trees, springs, animals, and so forth. But good Melissa is mindful once again of her protégée. Assuming the appearance of Atlante himself, she liberates Ruggero; that is to say, she makes him blush for his unworthy love. A wise woman, Logistilla, teaches him how to master the hippogryph, and he rises on high with the idea of returning to France to his Bradamante.

Needless to say, Orlando has also gone into action. Determined to follow Angelica, he departs alone from Paris in search of the woman whom he will never find; he travels the same road as she does but always arrives too late. Angelica, surprised by Corsairs, is carried off to the island of Ebuda where, following a custom of the place, she is to be offered to a marine monster. Orlando heads for Ebuda, but Ruggero has already reached it astride his hippogryph. He frees the girl, stuns the monster with his shield, and pulls Angelica up behind him. When he dismounts to make himself more at ease with her, Angelica takes from his hand the ring that was formerly hers — transmitted by Bradamante to Ruggero — and swallows it. She immediately becomes invisible, for the ring also had that virtue. To cap his misfortune, the hippogryph flees, leaving Ruggero behind. Meanwhile, on the island of Ebuda, another beautiful girl is offered up — unhappy Olympia. Orlando saves her and kills the monster, going into its throat with a skiff and an anchor, then dragging the gasping monster up on the shore. Then he resumes his vain search.

Now the poet transports us to Paris, ringed by besiegers. Charlemagne prays to God, who sends the archangel Michael in search of Silence (which is to guide in the darkness of night, unperceived, the hosts that Rinaldo is leading from England), and Discord, (who shall separate the awesome assailants one from the other). The archangel finds Discord in a most unexpected place, a convent. He finds Fraud there as well, who in turn informs him where he can find Silence; guided by Silence, Rinaldo's hosts reach Paris just as the siege of the city begins. In the assault a gigantic figure stands out: Rodomonte, King of Algiers, who by himself puts Paris to fire and sword until Charlemagne and his paladins succeed in driving him outside the walls. Meanwhile Rinaldo attacks the besiegers from the rear. Then the Emperor sallies forth from the city, and the besiegers become the besieged. By his resistance and his heroic death, Dardinello delays the total slaughter of the Saracens, who take refuge in the trenches. Medoro, an obscure young soldier of Dardinello, emerges with his friend Cloridano, to bury his king. When he is surprised by a troop of Christians, he falls beneath their swords and is left for dead. Angelica, who has escaped from Ruggero's hands with her ring that makes her invisible, has succeeded, meanwhile, safely to traverse a good stretch of territory. She comes upon the dying Medoro and pities him. With the arts she had learned in her native Orient, she heals his wounds; she also falls in love with him, and they spend a few happy days in the dwelling of a shepherd. With him, then, she departs for Barcelona to take a ship to India, to crown him King of Cathay.

Now Orlando, continuing his search, on a hot afternoon reaches the little wood dear to Angelica and Medoro. He sees their names cut into the tree trunks: at the entrance of a cave he reads a long and eloquent inscription that unfortunately he understands. He takes shelter with the shepherd who, thinking it will dissipate Orlando's depression, tells him the story of the lovers and shows him a gem given him by Angelica in payment for lodging: a gem which he, Orlando, had given the girl! That night the paladin does not sleep. The next day he breaks down in a furious madness. Beside himself, naked, he rushes about France, destroying and terrifying. He chances on Angelica as she is about to embark, but does not recognize her, nor she him. Thus, right in the middle of the poem, Angelica disappears forever. Orlando swims across the Strait of Gibraltar and reaches Africa.

Ruggero enters an enchanted palace (which Atlante has brought into being in his determination not to allow the youth to rejoin Bradamante) because he had thought he heard the voice of his dear beloved calling him. He wanders from room to room without finding her. Melissa is aware of the deceit. She comes hurriedly with Bradamante to that palace, warning her that she must immediately kill anyone she meets who looks like Ruggero: only then will the spell be broken. The girl does not dare to strike the specter of the man she loves, and so she too remains a captive in the palace. The paladin Astolfo, one of the former lovers of Alcina and by her changed into a myrtle, then changed back to a man by Melissa, arrives very opportunely. He is the maddest adventurer of the poem. He possesses a book which instructs him in all the charms and enchantments and the ways to defeat them. He also possesses a horn that has a tremendous sound; he blows it, and the castle goes up in smoke. At last Bradamante and Ruggero find each other. But before giving her hand in marriage to Ruggero, she demands that he become a Christian. He would obey her request at once, but he cannot find it in his heart to abandon his king Agramante while the latter is in danger. Bradamante returns to her castle of Montalbano (Montauban), and Ruggero hastens to Agramante's camp. On the way he is accompanied by an Amazon, Marfisa, whom he rather likes. When Bradamante hears about this she burns with jealousy.

The Saracens return to besiege Paris. The archangel Michael once more gets hold of Discord, who was sitting in a chapter of friars convened for the election of a superior. He breaks the shaft of a cross across her shoulders; he wants her back in the Saracen camp. Discord returns there and this time she fulfills her duty quite well. For varied reasons the most formidable pagan warriors come almost to the point of turning their weapons against one another: Gradasso and Ruggero, Marfisa and Mandricardo, Rodomonte and Sacripante. The most unhappy of them is Rodomonte. Convinced that Doralice loves him and that she is dominated by Mandricare against her will, he gives her an ultimatum: to choose between the two. She chooses Mandricare. Rodomonte departs filled with anger against women; he becomes almost as mad as Orlando. He stops near Mompellieri [Montpellier] in an abandoned church by a river. The good Isabella passes that way carrying with her the coffin of her dear Zerbino. Rodomonte falls madly in love with her, but she prefers to be killed rather than yield to his embraces. She has recourse to a falsehood; she tells him that she knows the secret of a liquor that gives invulnerability and she is willing to give it to him if he will promise not to trouble her any further. She squeezes some grass, rubs the juice on her neck, and asks Rodomonte to strike. The uncouth man decapitates her. To expiate his error, he converts the church into a sepulcher for Isabella and builds a narrow bridge over the river. Anyone who passes must battle him, and he will hang the arms of the loser as a trophy owed to the slain girl. He refuses to budge from that place, heedless of Agramante's urging. Bradamante, seeking news of Ruggero, passes over that bridge. An enchanted golden spear gives her the victory. Then Rodomonte goes to hide in shame in a grotto and swears not to take up arms for a year, a month, and a day.

With a band of faithful retainers, Rinaldo has fallen upon the rear of the Saracens and is slaughtering them. Agramante escapes with difficulty and withdraws to Arles in Provence with the few followers he has left. Ruggero is at Arles. Jealous Bradamante comes and challenges him — and lets herself be defeated. Marfisa too has arrived. Bradamante rushes upon her, but a voice from the grave, the voice of Atlante (who had died of sorrow on losing Ruggero to Christianity), makes it known that Marfisa is Ruggero's sister, captured as a child by the pagans. Ruggero embraces his new-found sister, tells her of his love for Bradamante, and narrates the history of his ancestors, beginning with Hector. The outcome is that both Ruggero and Marfisa are Christians by origin; Marfisa wishes to be baptized at once.

The mad Astolfo is the one who contributes most to giving final victory to the Christians. Riding the hippogryph, which had passed from Ruggero to him, he roams France, Spain, Africa, and Ethiopia, where he frees the blind king Senapo from the harpies and, following them with a terrible blast of his horn, drives them down to Hell, whence he ascends the mountain above, the earthly paradise. Here he learns from Saint John the Evangelist, who dwells there, that Orlando has gone mad and that he, Astolfo, is destined to cure him. Upon the chariot of fire of the prophet Elias, he and Saint John rise up to the moon. On the moon is collected everything, good or evil, that becomes lost on the earth, from which only one single thing never departs: madness. The senses of mankind are on the moon. In a large jar, the paladin finds Orlando's and brings them back with him, but not before he has sniffed out and recovered his own. Having redescended upon the earthly paradise, Astolfo plucks an herb, with which he restores sight to Senapo, whom God had blinded for his pride. In his gratitude, Senapo becomes a Christian and gives him men to assail the Kingdom of Agramante and thus force him to abandon France.

But the army has not enough horses. Astolfo makes a fervent prayer to God, rolls stones down the mountainside, and the stones become horses; then he moves to an assault on Bizerta. He also plans to wrest Provence from the Saracens, but he has no fleet. He prays, throws leaves of laurel, palm, and citron trees into the sea, and those leaves become ships. As the fleet is about to raise anchor, a madman appears, devastating the countryside: Orlando. This is the moment. He is bound and made to sniff the jar containing his senses. He is restored to sanity, is ashamed of what he has done, swears to live for the defense of Christianity, and unites with Astolfo in the siege of Bizerta, while the fleet clashes at night with that of Agramante who, defeated, was unfurling his sails to return to Africa. From far off he sees the flames of his burning Bizerta. A duel between Orlando, Oliviero, and Brandimarte for the Christians, and Agramante, Gradasso, and Sobrino for the Saracens, on the island of Lipadusa, puts an end to the war. Orlando kills Agramante and Gradasso; Sobrino is seriously wounded and surrenders. Oliviero is also wounded; and Brandimarte dies, calling for protection of his beloved Fiordiligi. Rinaldo reaches the island too late; he and Orlando transport Brandimarte to Sicily, where he is given a worthy burial.

But what has happened to Ruggero and Bradamante? Duke Amone, the father of Bradamante, will not hear of her marrying Ruggero: he has promised her to Leo, son of Constantine the emperor of Byzantium. Bradamante, as a dutiful daughter, resigns herself to renunciation but succeeds in having Charlemagne decree that only the man who conquers her in a tournament shall marry her (and her father does not dare oppose Charlemagne's will). Under the assumed name of the Knight of the Unicorn, Ruggero, bursting with anger, goes to depose Leo from his throne; but Leo so greatly admires his acts of bravery that the two become great friends. In the name of their friendship Ruggero agrees to fight against Bradamante dressed in the garments and bearing the arms of Leo, to win the lady for him; and he wins. But Leo, learning that the Knight of the Unicorn was Ruggero, the betrothed of Bradamante, refuses to be surpassed by him in courtesy and personally requests the Emperor to give the lady's hand to his friend. At last the wedding is celebrated in the presence of Charlemagne, but not without a disturbance: Rodomonte has left his solitary retreat and appears unexpectedly in the banquet hall to challenge Ruggero as apostate from his proper faith. With the duel of the two warriors and the death of Rodomonte, whose soul flees blaspheming down to Hell, the poem comes to an end.

The Fantasy of Ariosto

Even from this bare outline it is possible to discern Ariosto's great constructive virtue. The *Furioso* is an edifice of great variety and vastness; and yet it is simple. The enormous whole gravitates on three principal themes: The first, which we may call epic and which is the background of the whole tale, is the war between the Christians and the pagans, climaxing in the siege of Paris. The second, the story of Orlando's passion for Angelica, reaches its high point midway in the poem with the count's madness. The third turns on the troubled loves and the conversion of Ruggero, and finally his marriage to Bradamante; from this union the Este family will descend. The three themes merge in a harmonious whole, and the development of one aids the solution of the others. Even the minor actions, many of which we have been unable to mention, are not incidental, but necessary in the unfolding of the story (except for the novellas related by several characters, which serve the purpose of providing diversion and rest); if they were removed, the edifice would collapse and crumble. This sense of symmetry, proportion, and unity (which later would become the fundamental but entirely extrinsic law of narrative poetry), and this capacity to dominate from above the most varied material, is the sign of the classical spirit of Ariosto and differentiates his poem from the preceding romances and especially from the *Morgante*. Nor is the inventive imagination of the poet of minor importance, although it has been shown that the material of the *Furioso* has been derived in very large part from old romances of chivalry and, in no small part, from the Latin poets: Vergil, Lucan, Statius, and perhaps even more, from Ovid. Ariosto transforms the narrations, passages, themes, and similitudes that he draws from other poets; he stamps them with his own impression and makes them conform perfectly to his own fantasy. His originality, that is to say the strength of his artistic personality, seems even augmented, rather than diminished, by this borrowing. Ariosto's representative fantasy or faculty of depicting the world picturesquely is quite marvelous. He is the greatest of the pictorial poets, and it was with justice that he was several times put on the same plane as the painters of his age: with Titian, and even more with Correggio, who came from a neighboring region. Then, too, one of the most individual traits of Ariosto is his sense of the real and the logical. The *Furioso* is full of marvels, enchantments, monsters, and happenings that are beyond the limits of any reality or human experience; but all this world is circumstantiated and determined in such a way as not to seem arbitrary, but real, which, in art, is to seem true. To take just one example: the hippogryph is a fantastic caprice, but the poet portrays it with such brilliance of details that he creates the illusion of its being a real creature.

If Ariosto is a poet of the exterior world and if he feels joy in fusing himself, in a manner of speaking, into the phenomena, the psyche of his characters is still far richer than those of Boiardo. In the *Innamorato*, Orlando is a rather naïve character. In the *Furioso*, he is fiery, a man of passion; connoisseurs think that the moments, the development, and the characteristics of his madness are perfectly true. In the *Innamorato*, Angelica is merely a coquette; in the *Furioso,* she becomes a woman who, through pity for a poor dying soldier, experiences the kind love that gives all and asks for nothing and that causes her to forget that she had been the idol of the most famous Christian and pagan champions. Boiardo's Radamonte is a ferocious and swashbuckling giant; Ariosto's Rodomonte, though cruel and primitive, in the second part of his activity feels remorse for his criminal vulgarity and comes to his end as the defender of his faith against Ruggero, who has abandoned it. While Ariosto's Astolfo retains the eccentric characteristics of Boiardo's character, he is much more urbane and likeable.

Some of the characters are creations of the poet, and they are among the best: Ruggero and Bradamante, for example, are characters that Boiardo had hardly sketched. Ruggero, so much in love with Bradamante, and yet so easily led astray, may appear false to the reader who is not looking for the man but the hero, or who believes that the hero is not a man. Bradamante, in her good and constant affection for Ruggero, in her ingenuousness and her jealousies, in her dual role of unconquered warrior and of timid lover, is one of the most cherished and most real feminine characters in all Italian narrative poetry.

Finally, what is singular in the *Furioso* is that the poet is felt to be present all the time, from the beginning to the end, with his qualities of a gentleman, upright man, and talker, often more salacious and licentious than is considered proper in our modern customs. The poet lives in a constant and agreeable relationship with the reader; he comments on his story, especially in the preludes to each canto, where the recounting offers him a chance for brief digressions concerning the customs of mankind and for the statement of his personal philosophy, in part good-natured, in part resigned. The praises showered on the House of Este, and more especially on the Cardinal, and the many flatteries that Humanism had made obligatory, are tempered by this intrusion of the author, tinged with a confidential attitude that implies the compliment hidden under the hyperbole. However, the presence of the poet reveals itself most especially in a slightly ironic attitude that is difficult to define, in the way that certain profound and complex states of feeling are difficult. Contemplating his world of marvels, the poet is no less conscious of its beauty than of its emptiness. He is also conscious of the prosaic requirements of reality as opposed to the free life, exempt from the law, of the knights. There is in the *Furioso* something of the good sense of Sancho Panza who continually corrects the heroic follies of Don Quixote. A great part of the modernity of the poem lies in that attitude of irony, diffused throughout the story like the salt in sea water.

The Significance of the *Furioso*

The *Furioso* is symbolic of an age in which poetry, great poetry, no longer takes its inspiration from the living world of reality, but lives its own self-contained life segregated from history. The wretched conditions of an Italy, that had become a battlefield of French, German, and Spanish greed, dictate, to be sure, some great-hearted strophes to Ariosto, but the spectacle of the country's ills, which troubles him for a moment, drives him to take refuge in the enchanted lands of his imagination. The great moral, political, and religious problems of the age do not move him at all, and if he has an ideal, it is the restoration of the splendid age of chivalry. Therefore, he curses firearms, which for him represent the death of valor, and the victory of numbers over the individual, of deceit over daring. In this respect the *Furioso* is the antithesis of the *Divine Comedy*, in which reality of every kind presses with such impetus as to become the loftiest passion and poetry. Ariosto's aim is to amuse and divert, purely and simply. As he wrote to the Doge of Venice requesting the privilege of printing the first edition of the *Furioso*, he had labored "for the entertainment and recreation of gentlemen and persons of gentle (noble) mind and ladies"; he had written "for solace and pleasure."

For that reason he was fearful of wearying his public, whose interest he sought always to keep at a high level. To achieve this, he used certain expedients that had no precedent in the classical epic, such as interrupting the narration at the most critical moment and then resuming it much later, meanwhile beginning or returning to a narrative of an entirely different kind on a different tone. He sometimes ends a canto in the middle of the action, inviting his public to come back again later, as was the custom of the old *cantastorie*, the wandering minstrels.

He gave his public great variety and much action. He is the master of images, and the master of style, an entirely unrhetorical style; he shifts with admirable ease from the loftiest tone to the most humble, from a language of splendor to a language that might be mistaken for common prose. But an exquisite feeling of perfection and limits supports his genius. Thus he is abundant but never prolix; spontaneous but never vulgar. He lavished bountiful care on language, as every true poet does. He insisted the definitive edition of the *Furioso* be recast in the Florentine idiom. And through the *Furioso* the Tuscan idiom was becoming more and more accepted even in northern Italy, but not without difficulty. For Ariosto, as for Manzoni later, the Tuscan vocabulary meant precision, richness, and dignity. Those obscure and plebeian modes that were, and are, the delight of professional "Tuscanists" did not get into the *Furioso*, as they did not get into the *Promessi Sposi*.

Niccolò Machiavelli

His Life

Machiavelli was born in Florence in 1469, of a noble but not rich family. From his writings it is possible to ascertain what his education was. He knew Latin and specialized in reading the historians. He was ignorant of Greek and read the Greek historians in Latin translations. He did not receive a complete Humanistic education, but early in life he learned those lessons of practical life which add a singular efficacy to lessons from books.

While still young domestic necessities obliged him to seek employment in the administration of the Commune. In 1494, during the invasion of Charles VIII of France, the Medici were expelled from Florence and a republican form of government was restored, influenced considerably by the democratic and religious ideas of Savonarola. In 1498, young Machiavelli was assigned the post of secretary to the Ten for Liberty and for Peace; the following year he was chosen to head the Second Chancellory, a sort of Ministry of the Interior and War. Thus he acquired that title of "Florentine secretary" by which thereafter he was called.

Those were troubled times. In Florence, although Savonarola was dead, the sects of the Piagnoni and Palleschi, the adversaries and the supporters were more active than ever. Pisa had rebelled and Venice was supporting her. On the other hand, France was aiding Florence in the campaign against Pisa. Because of the lack of discipline and the turbulence of the Swiss and the French, the undertaking collapsed and the army broke up. Machiavelli was present with a commissar of the Republic. It is perhaps at that time that he had the clear idea that a war can be waged effectively only by soldier citizenry. Louis XII was angered by the punishments meted out to some French soldiers. Machiavelli was sent, together with Francesco della Casa, on a mission to calm that powerful monarch (1500). It was not the first mission he had undertaken, nor would it be the last. In 1502, he went to Urbino to the son of Alexander VI, Cesare Borgia (Duke Valentino) who, a gonfalonier of the Church, had seized Imola, Forlì, Cesena, and other cities of Romagna and was casting threatening glances at Tuscany. Shortly afterwards he was sent to quell the rebellious populations of the Valdichiana.

Having become the trusted man of the new "gonfalonier for life," Pier Soderini, to whom the struggle-weary Florentines delegated full powers, Machiavelli was sent once more as ambassador to Cesare Borgia, to whom the republic wished to show its friendship. He was closely associated with the Duke for several months and came to admire and revere the man, who was cruel and dreadful, but of an inflexible will. The secretary sent unperturbed reports on the violent occupation that Borgia made of Sinigaglia, and on the massacre of various lords of that region. Then he decided to carry out, with Soderini's help, his project for a citizen militia. On his initiative, the authority of the Nine for the Militia was created. It was charged with training an army of fifty thousand militiamen, taken from Florence and vicinity. The difficulties of the levee were not a few, nor, in truth, was the efficiency of the new armed forces very great.

Great changes were being readied for Florence. Julius II had formed the Holy League against the French and their adherents in Italy. The League, after the victory of Ravenna, planned to depose Soderini and restore the Medici to power in Florence. The gonfalonier yielded his position to the Cardinal Giuliano dei Medici, who set up a government in Florence, which was republican in appearance only. Machiavelli, who had been a member of the fallen regime, was stripped of his office of secretary and banished for one year to the Florentine territory (1512). In addition, suspected of complicity in the conspiracy in which two lovers of liberty, Agostino Capponi and Pietro Boscoli, died at the hands of the executioner, he was imprisoned, tortured, and finally recognized as innocent. Then, with his wife and four children, he retired to an estate at the Albergaccio, near San Casciano.

His daily life at the Albergaccio is narrated in a famous letter to Francesco Vettori, a Florentine orator in Rome. The former secretary spent the day hunting, conversing with woodsmen, or, often all alone, reading the works of Dante or Petrarch. At the inn, he listened to the news from Florence and played with the customers; but in the evenings he conversed with the ancient historians. He thought and, unable to act, he wrote. Little by little he succeeded in making himself acceptable to the Medici. This was a necessity, since Machiavelli neither was nor wished to be a Cato. He often came to Florence. He became the center of a group of young men of worthy feelings, who met in the Rucellai gardens, and here he read aloud the works that he was composing. In 1520, the Florentine Studio (university) entrusted him with writing the history of the city. He accepted, and in 1525 dedicated the work to Giuliano dei Medici, who two years previously had become pope with the name of Clement VII. After the battle of Pavia, which made Charles V master of Italy, Machiavelli forsaw that sooner or later Florence would be a target of the Emperor's greed, and he devoted himself with zeal to obtaining the office of Secretary for the Fortifications of Florence. But the sack of Rome by the Lansquenets in 1527, during the pontificate of Clement VII, was followed by the downfall of the hated Medicean party. Again the Republic (the last) was proclaimed in Florence, with Niccolò Capponi as gonfalonier. Machiavelli was a candidate for the office of Secretary of the Ten for War, which belonged to him by numerous rights. But the man seemed suspect to the enemies of the

Medici, and the post went to an unknown. The matter grieved him so greatly that he became ill; and in that very year, 1527, he died. Three years later, after a heroic resistance, Florence yielded to the united arms of Charles V and Clement VII, and her servitude began. Only then was it recognized that Machiavelli's had been the last great voice for liberty.

The Secretary was interred without ostentation in Santa Croce, where later Michelangelo, Galileo, Alfieri, Foscolo, and Rossini came to rest. Full understanding of his greatness did not come until the eighteenth century, when under the urging of an English nobleman, a monument was erected to him, bearing the proud inscription: *Tanto nomini nullum par elogium* [For such a great name any eulogy is as nothing].

Literary Works

Machiavelli was a citizen who lived the varied and tumultuous life of his city. Dating probably from his youth are six *canti carnascialeschi* [carnival songs] of which two are noteworthy: the *Chant of the Blessed Spirits,* which is an admonition to civic concord; and the *Chant of the Hermits,* in which there are ironic allusions to the ruin of the world prophesied by Savonarola and his partisans. A very lyrical page is the *Serenata* [*Serenade*] in *ottava rima* where, beseeching love, the lover narrates the history of cruel women of mythology and their ultimate punishment by the gods. The novella of *Belfagor* is also attributed to his juvenile period; in it, reworking an old theme, Machiavelli narrates how most of the damned souls complain of having merited Hell because of their wives. The judges of the Underworld, to ascertain the truth of the matter, send up to the world a demon, Belphagor, who, assuming the shape of a man, is to marry a mortal woman and after ten years to return to the Underworld and give a report on the institution of matrimony. Belphagor establishes himself in

Florence under the name of Roderigo of Castile and, from the numerous competitors for his wealth, marries Lady Onesta Donati. Lady Onesta becomes very proud and insists that her husband enrich her brothers and help her to marry off her sisters. She flaunts herself over all the other women during the holidays of Saint John and she precipitates her husband into debt so deeply that he is forced to flee from Florence with his creditors in pursuit. He finds peace only when he returns to the infernal regions, where life is more attractive than life in this world with a wife. Lastly, the *Primo Decennale* dates from his youth; this is the history of Italy's misfortunes from 1494 to 1504. It is a canto in tercets addressed to the Florentines, whose undertakings form the central part of the narration; it is more a compendium of chronicles than a page of poetry.

The greater part of Machiavelli's writings, literary or otherwise, were composed after 1512, the year so unfortunate for him personally, in which he saw himself separated from his public functions and oppressed by every sort of wretchedness. The *Secondo Decennale* [*Second Decennial*] was written after this date and left unfinished; this deals with events up to the defeat of the Venetians by the forces of the League of Cambrai [Holy League] formed against them by Julius II. After that, there is an odd little poem in tercets, *L'Asino d'Oro* [*Golden Ass*], of which only eight short chapters remain extant. The poet proposes to narrate what happened to him and what he saw when he was changed into an ass by Circe. The initial theme is suggested by the *Metamorphoses* [or *Golden Ass*] of Apuleius, but Machiavelli does not proceed as far as his own transformation. He does not get farther than what might be called the preliminaries to it and his conversations and love affairs with a handmaiden of Circe. Not without importance are the considerations that the author advances in the fifth chapter concering the enlargement and consequent fatal ruin of the states: an order willed by God so that nothing under the sun shall remain fixed and stable, forcing man to keep his energies constantly employed. The satirical allusions of the seventh *capitolo* are numerous and obscure; here the future ass, in a sort of courtyard of Circe's palace, contemplates the many animals who once were famous men, either in politics or literature. The last chapter is noteworthy. Naturally one believes that the ex-lovers of the enchantress want to return to their former condition of men; not so. When questioned regarding the matter, they show how much wiser and happier beasts are than men. The theme derives from a dialogue of the Greek philosopher Plutarch, the *Cricket* (name of the hero) or *Concerning the Intelligence of the Brutes*, in which the wisdom of animals is praised above that of men. The concept of the wretchedness and imperfection of men in comparison to beasts was much used later in skeptical and pessimistic literature.

The minor works of Machiavelli include several *capitols*. One, against *Ingratitude*, probably was written before 1512 and perhaps when some of his adversaries wanted him to be excluded from public office. The author consoles himself with famous examples of popular ingratitude, among them that of Scipio Africanus. The *Capitol di Fortuna* belongs to the years of exile; it is a long allegory on that capricious goddess who presented herself to the political thinker as the adversary of all the measures of wisdom and virtue. The *Capitolo dell' Ambizione* is more important; in it Machiavelli surveys the ruin of the states.

It is supposed that the *Dialogo sulle lingue* [*Dialogue on Languages*] dates from the time of exile. With it the author enters the much-debated question of the time: whether the language of the great writers of the fourteenth century should be called Italian, Tuscan, or Florentine. The central part of the writing is a dialogue between Machiavelli and Dante, in which Dante finally confesses that the "aulic" or courtly language in which he wrote was basically nothing but the Florentine tongue. But among the minor writings of Machiavelli, one deserves particular mention; it is *La Mandragola*.

La Mandragola [*The Mandrake,* or *Mandragora*]

This is one of the most licentious but also most profound and lively comedies of the sixteenth century. It was composed in the early years of the author's exile, when he was kept from active life. The comedy is written with a great sense of truth, in a spirited, colloquial prose. In it there is nothing of the situations dear to the Latin theater which reappear, as we have seen, in the plays of Ariosto and the sixteenth-century writers; rather the spirit of Boccaccio continues in it but with more of a satirical consciousness. The story revolves around the loves of one Callimachus for a certain Lucretia, the wife of a Master Nicia, doctor of laws but somewhat of a blockhead. A potion of mandrake plant, which Lucretia must drink to have children and thus fulfill the desire of her husband, gives the play its title. Lucretia would never consent to violate her conjugal fidelity, but Sostrata, her mother, tries to remove her daughter's scruples, and Friar Timoteo dissipates them completely as Lucretia's confessor. Urged by Callimachus and Master Nicia, he shows by theological arguments addressed to the young woman that the purpose of matrimony is to have children and that all means become legitimate if directed toward that most honest objective. Thus Fra Timoteo becomes the most meaningful character: an expression of supreme hypocrisy and cynical moral indifference. Master Nicia causes laughter but it is impossible not to view with repugnance his contributing to his own personal dishonor.

Far beneath *Mandragola* in importance is *Clizia,* copied from the *Casina* of Plautus. Its theme is the love conceived for Clizia by her guardian, old Nicomachus, and the latter's son, Cleandro who, naturally, is loved by the girl and finally becomes her husband. Two untitled comedies are also attributed to Machiavelli; one in prose, in three acts, has a friar as its hero: Fra Alberigo who is of the same stamp as Fra Timoteo; the other, in verse, rests on ambiguities in names. Machiavelli made a prose translation of the *Andria*, the masterpiece of Terence.

The Great Works of Machiavelli

GENERAL IDEA OF HIS POLITICAL SYSTEM Machiavelli was the first *political* thinker brought forth by Italy and Europe. Not that he was the first to theorize on the nature and the purpose of the state; he was the first to consider politics as a reality and not as an abstraction; that is, as a practice and not as a theory. He derived its principles and their applications from ancient history and still more from contemporary events, of which he was a witness and sometimes a participant. Although, until his time, politics had generally been considered as the translation of the moral law into action, with Machiavelli, politics is separated from moral law; it may coincide with it, and it may also violate it. In that, indeed, is the most striking aspect of his theory, and the most odious; because of this aspect, *Machiavellianism* was for many centuries synonymous with evil and hypocritical politics. In reality the Humanistic Age set the individual above any moral law, and Machiavelli was a man of his age. *Virtue*, as understood by Machiavelli, meant *activity* first and foremost. The superior man has success as his goal. Success consists of knowing how to seize the moment offered by fortune, which continues to be the ultimate ruler of human events. A moral law is felt by Machiavelli, but never expressly formulated. Or rather, he sees it in the state, and in the laws of the state. The man who succeeds in founding the former, and in imposing the latter, by this alone is moral, and he is the more moral if he is capable of subordinating all possible means to that end. After all, the political history of the fifteenth century and the first part of the sixteenth century, where men of violence became great and fraud and treachery were common means to success, trained and educated Machiavelli, and he was a conscience very superior to his age. The state of Machiavelli is regarded more as an object in itself and as an organ of domination, rather than one of usefulness to the majority of men. Problems that concern the material or moral improvement of the multitudes were never formulated by Machiavelli. He was a pessimist who had far more faith in the force and astuteness of leaders than in the heroic soul of peoples. His state is not godless but might be without a spirit. Rather than his state, we prefer, if not that of Dante, the one advocated by Mazzini.

The *"Discorsi Sulla Prima Deca Di Tito Livio"* [*Discourses on the First Ten Books of Livy*]

This is the work in which Machiavelli most amply expounds his political theory and system, and on which he labored the longest: from 1513 to 1521. Antiquity was reputed to be the mistress of all disciplines. But Machiavelli complains:

> in ordering republics, in maintaining States, in governing kingdoms, in organizing the military and in waging war, in judging subjects, in increasing empire, there is not to be found any prince, republic, captain nor citizen who has recourse to the examples of antiquity.

He determines to discover and teach the political wisdom of the ancients.

He starts from the first ten books of Titus Livius, in which the Roman historian tells about the seven fabled kings of Rome and the beginnings of the republic. There is not the least shadow of a doubt about the veracity of

Livy's account (as there was to be no doubt of it for the next three centuries). He undertakes a series of digressions (in the sixteenth century "discourse" still retained its original Latin meaning of "running about, to and fro") on the constitution and government of states, with references to other historians, discovering analogies between ancient narrations and events of his own time. For Machiavelli, men change only in form but in substance remain forever the same. The work is divided into three books, and each book into short chapters, crowded with matter and warm with eloquence aroused by the matter. Very approximately, the first book deals with the constitution or formation of the government; the second, with the waging of war, and the third, with the transformations, revolutions, and decadence of states.

It would be neither easy nor opportune to give a résumé of the work. It must suffice here to take a quick look at some of the main points of Machiavelli's thought. To found a state and also to restore it when it has grown corrupt, the work of a single man is necessary; therefore, Romulus necessarily did away with Remus. That sole ruler must establish laws that constrain the inhabitants to continuous activity, for when abundance exists, states become corrupt more rapidly. To maintain the state, however, a republican government is required, one of such a nature that all social classes, indeed all citizens, be involved in its maintenance, since recognition of usefulness is the only persuasive force for men. Machiavelli, a pessimist in his views of the individual, is convinced that the advantage of the community is that the group sees better than the individual.

Party struggles, though not necessary, are proper because they contribute to the safeguarding of liberty. To avoid degenerating into license or anarchy, however, Machiavelli believes that the parties should have their own organs through which they can express their desires and discharge their anger, and he attaches great importance to the institution of Tribunate of the People.

For Machiavelli everything is subordinate to the well-being and strength of the state, even religion or superstition. However, he is convinced that only religion, with its sanctions of rewards and punishments in another life, can impose observance of laws, and fulfillment of duties so contrary to human selfishness. In the abstract, Machiavelli prefers paganism to the Christian religion, for it was a function of the state, through which the colleges of the priests and the augurs aimed at the triumph of the gods and the power of Rome. Not that Machiavelli scorns the Christian religion, because for him a great failing of the Italians is the lack of religious spirit, not of practices. This lack makes them sceptical and weak; the cause of these evils is the unholy life of the priests. Also, the Italians have another difficulty with the Church, which is:

> the Church "not being powerful enough to hold Italy, nor having granted permission that another hold it, has been the cause that the country has not been able to unite under one head, but has been under several princes and lords, from whom there has arisen so much disunity and weakness that Italy has been brought to the condition of being the prey not only of powerful barbarians but of any who assail her.

Then, discussing military institutions, Machiavelli insists, with considerable heat, on the necessity of the state having its own arms and on the danger resulting from auxiliaries and mercenaries. He thinks that wars should be brief and therefore waged with large armies; then the enemies, for fear of worse, yield. Promptness is another element of success: whosoever is in fear of being assaulted should attack first. Machiavelli is against the idea that money is the sinew of war. He has great faith in personal bravery and discipline; hence he gives little importance to artillery and has little esteem for cavalry as compared to infantry, which, in the last analysis, always wins the battle. He believes, too, that the building of fortresses to hold down subjugated populations constitutes a greater danger than advantage for the dominators. These fortresses are a continuous cause of hatred by the subject populations, offering a pretext for, and a means to easy rebellions.

Concerning ways for extending the state, Machiavelli believes that opening the city to its neighbors by means of commerce is the right way; the way Rome took with Alba was not the best: destruction of the city and absorption of its inhabitants. As for the invasion of foreign territory, that conquest is vain which does not win over the conquered population to the conqueror. This was a result that the Romans achieved by means of colonies; the author devotes a good deal of space to their constitution and usefulness.

The inevitable decadence of states, as of all human things, is dogma for Machiavelli; but because every effect is contained in its cause and every government in its beginnings, decadence is delayed when it is known how to turn back to those beginnings. What we moderns call revolutions — whether they are made by a people or brought about by an individual — are, in effect, a return of the state to its beginnings. Whatever form they may assume, they are inevitable in the life of a state since they represent its need to regenerate. Happy are those states where suitable organs, such as the parliaments in France, constantly recall the public institutions to their beginnings. What is essential is that the revolutions be complete and that no vestige of the old order which has been destroyed shall remain as a threat to the new. It is necessary to follow the example of Brutus, who, when the republic was inaugurated, caused his sons to be condemned to death for plotting in favor of the expelled Tarquin.

In connection with conspiracies, which were frequent

in Machiavelli's time, when the ancient republican spirit was rising against the new usurpers, he examines at length the suitability of this means. He finally judges conspiracies to be insufficient and not to be advocated because it is almost impossible that sooner or later they will not be discovered; in which case, the government becomes more cautious and distrustful of any movement whatsoever. Furthermore, Machiavelli places the safety of the state in expedient measures rather than in violent changes. The wise government is the one that knows how to change in time. And he concludes that a republic needs to make new provisions every day if it is to keep its liberty.

Il Principe [The Prince]

Written in 1513, in the enthusiasm of the composition of the *Discorsi*, *The Prince* is generally considered Machiavelli's fundamental work. In reality, it presented only one side of his political thought, and the princes with which it is concerned have a value more relative than absolute. In twenty-six chapters, the author discusses not princedom in general, but the policies that a new prince should follow to maintain the throne he has acquired by arms or fortune. Machiavelli was thinking not only of the famous tyrants of legend and history (Cyrus, Romulus, Theseus, and the founder of the power of Israel, Moses), but principally of the numerous lords — violent and treacherous men — who had risen to power in the fifteenth and early sixteenth centuries. Already in the *Discorsi* he had taught that the man who founds or resolves to maintain a state must not shrink from any available means. Here the concept that political necessity excludes or may exclude the moral law is stated with still more brutal sincerity. The new prince must take as his model, Cesare Borgia, the duke who had founded a state for himself in Romagna, using the most wicked means and had made provision to maintain it at the death of his father, Pope Alexander VI. The story of Cesare Borgia's successes is narrated with the heat of enthusiasm, and the author deplores that Fortune failed the duke who had done everything to deserve her approval. Like Borgia, the new prince, or usurper, must extinguish at one stroke all vestiges of the old order of things whenever he is unsuccessful in winning them to his cause: a slaughter once in a while is better than remaining ever on guard "with knife in hand." He must win the important men with benefices, or terrify them with torture; he must seek to be acceptable to the new peoples, so that any desire for the fallen seignory is extinguished; he must stand to arms and devote himself exclusively to the art of war. There is nothing which the prince should so carefully guard himself against as contempt. Esteem is in itself a great coefficient of strength. Strength is continually extolled in the book and, what is worse, so are falseness and deceit. To win the love and esteem of the people, it is necessary for the prince *to show himself* religious, humane, and loyal. The people are satisfied with appearances. The prince must know how to be a fox and how to be a lion. Treaties have to be kept; but also they may be violated when it is useful to do so.

These are such wicked maxims that there are those who thought that Machiavelli, so ardently liberty-loving in the *Discorsi,* was employing irony and sarcasm in the *Prince.* They believed that, under the guise of instructing the tyrant on governing his people, Machiavelli was teaching the people how to protect themselves from the arts of the tyrant. That opinion, however, is without followers today. History furnished the types (and could have offered many more) on which Machiavelli — for whom politics was the science and the knowledge of the real — constructed his tyrant. On the other hand it was necessary to place an Italian unity against the formidable national unities which had been or were being formed in France, Spain, and Germany. Credit is due Machiavelli for having been the first to see this need; nor did it seem possible to achieve that unity save through the activity of a prince resolute for any necessity which would bring success in reaching that all-important objective.

The yearning and the design for the unity and independence of Italy are shown in his lamentations over the misfortunes of the fatherland and are stated in the last chapter, *Exhortation to the Liberation of Italy from the Barbarians*. This is a page written with trembling and tears; where Lorenzo di Piero dei Medici, to whom the book is dedicated, is asked to take upon himself the national cause and call on all the peoples of the peninsula to rise up in rebellion, thus at one and the same time founding the princedom and achieving the independence of Italy.

The *Life of Castruccio Castracani*

Written around 1520, this is the story of the famous statesman who, at about the beginning of the fourteenth century, made himself the master of Lucca with the help of Uguccione della Faggiuola (tyrant of Pisa). Then, when his benefactor was driven out of Pisa, Sarzana, and later, Pistoia, he defeated the Florentines and died suddenly, his plan to found a powerful Ghibelline state ending in failure. There is very little history in this biography; it may be considered an exemplification of the theories expounded in *The Prince*. The author had in mind a Greek writing, known to him in a Latin translation: the *Life of Agathocles*, tyrant of Syracuse, narrated by Diodorus.

The Books *On the Art of War*

On the Art of War is the third of Machiavelli's great political works. In it, he studies the possibility of giving Italy what was suggested to him as the supreme necessity by the ruin of its principal states; an army. It consists of dialogues (divided among seven books) which are imagined to be held in Florence in the gardens of the Rucellai family. Machiavelli's ideas are expounded by the protagonist of the dialogues, the famous captain Fabrizio Colonna, a Roman. He proposes the formation of a *battaglione* [battalion] of six thousand infantry, divided into ten *battaglie* [battalions] of six hundred men. He teaches how to train this force rigidly and how to supply it and lead it in campaign, for war is, according to Colona, simplified into battles in the field on a definite day. Personal bravery is considered highly important. Thus, the foot soldier is the backbone of the army; little importance is given to cavalry, little also to artillery, which, to Machiavelli, appeared to be little more than the arrows and stones cast by the ancient archers and slingers to open an attack. The work is of interest to Italians, though, despite the questionable military precepts. In the first book there is lamenting over the mercenary forces, to which a citizen army is compared. Colonna would like to see a citizens' army restored on the model of ancient Rome: not permanent, but always ready, and called up only when circumstances require. The misfortunes of Italy often resound in the eloquent words of the Captain, who, at the end of the dialogues, regrets that the Italian princes, even after the invasion of Charles VIII, have not opened their eyes to their safety and continue playing with men of letters and going ahead with clever diplomatic contrivances and perfidies. For if the poetry, the painting, and the sculpture of the ancient Romans has been born anew, why could there not be a rebirth of the art of war, which is far more important? It is certain that the Italian potentate who first will give serious thought to an army will be the arbiter and dominator of the peninsula, in the same way that Philip of Macedon, "while the rest of Greece lead a life of idleness and listened to poetry recitals," became so powerful, thanks to the military, "that in a few years he was able to occupy the whole of it and leave to his son such a foundation that he, the Prince could make himself ruler of the whole world."

The Minor Political Writings

Machiavelli was a born political writer. Writings connected with his office of secretary begin in 1499, and these are already an expression of his main political ideas. Of special interest are the *Rapporti e ritratti delle cose dell' Alemagna* [*Reports and Pictures of Affairs in Germany*], 1508–1512, and *Ritratti delle cose in Francia* [*Pictures of Matters in France*], 1510. Concerning the Germans, he stresses the wealth due to sobriety and the spirit of liberty; he extols their military system — swift cavalry, strong infantry. He recognizes that the strength of the French nation is due mostly to monarchic unity. As for the French armies, he remarks that they are daring rather than brave, quick to attack, but weak in resistance. He believes the French impulsive, incapable of reflection, insolent when favored by Fortune, very humble in adversity, inconstant, and frivolous.

The *Istorie Fiorentine* [*History of Florence*]

In his "Introduction," Machiavelli notes that historians of Florentine matters who wrote before him gave much space to descriptions of wars but barely mentioned the dissensions, the party struggles, in short, the internal history of the city. This internal history, however, has more importance for him than the external, because it is the cause of it; and since the history of Florence can not be understood without a knowledge of that of Italy, of which it is an inseparable part, he keeps his gaze fixed steadfastly on the history of all Italy. In the opening book, a prelude to the whole work, the author does indeed discourse on the history of Italy, Europe, and, in fact, the Middle Ages; that is to say, from the first invasions of the barbarians to the middle of the fifteenth century. In the second book, he begins the history of Florence itself, covering it from the fabled beginnings down to the famous plague of 1348. With the third and fourth books, he gets as far as 1434, when Cosimo il Vecchio (Old Cosimo) dei Medici returns in glory from the exile to which the opposing faction of the Albizzi had sent him. In these books, the stories of the internal revolutions of Florence attract Machiavelli's attention: in the second book, the struggles between Guelfs and Ghibellines, the revolution of Giano della Bella, the dissensions between Cerchi and Donati; and in the third book, the uprising of the Ciompi. Personages of great will and great mind — those in whom he sees some lineament of his Prince — awaken his interest; such as, King Theodoric, Charlemagne, Corso Donati, Castruccio Castracani, and Gautier de Britenne, Duke of Athens. In the fifth book, he deals very broadly with events of Florentine history, such as the wars with Venice and Milan and the conspiracies that broke out in the most important cities of Italy against the new princes. His sympathies are for the lords, the *condottieri* [military leaders], the conquerors: Piccinino, Braccio da Montone, Francesco Sforza. He comes then to the Medici, their rise to greatness and the death of Lorenzo the Magnificent, whom Machiavelli praises as the wisest of the Italian princes, and whose death was the beginning of the breakdown of the national structure and the misfortunes of the fatherland. Here, at the end of the eighth book, the narration ends. The intention of the author was to reach his own times; either his many undertakings or the impossibility of speaking impartially of his age stopped him.

Machiavelli is the first historian to see events not in themselves, but in their reciprocal dependence, as a development of more general causes; that is to say, the first man to progress from the chronicle to history — history, of which God is no longer the creator, but of which man is the creator, with his free will, insofar as it is granted him by that inexplicable superior will, Fortune. However, if the individualistic concept of history places Machiavelli above preceding historians, and even if he rivals Tacitus in his profound and fruitful exploration of the passions and of human wickedness, he does not succeed in understanding the historical fact in all its fullness and attributes effects too great to causes too small. The great collective events such as the Crusades, elude him; he misses the importance of what we call historical environment, the heroes of which are as much the builders as they are exponents. Then, too, the histories of Machiavelli have slight importance as regards originality of research. In addition to Leonardo Bruni and Poggio Bracciolini, he borrows widely from even the most obscure chroniclers, nor does he concern himself greatly with the truthfulness of the narration. Still, he is a master of political wisdom. Each book, therefore, opens with some general observation or truth, perhaps on the necessity of primitive peoples to emigrate; on the importance of colonies; on the usefulness of factions; on the affinity of license and bondage; or on the necessary decadence of states. The broad and solemn style of the Latin historians is sometimes recognizable in The *History of Florence;* but as in his other works, he is generally a writer remarkable for sobriety, exactness, strength, and movement.

Other Writers of the First Half of the Sixteenth Century. The Historians

Towering above the others, Francesco Guicciardini is worthy of competing with Machiavelli. He was born in Florence in 1483. As a youth, he devoted himself to the study of law. Upon the return of the Medici in 1512, he dedicated himself fully to their cause and received offices and honors from Leo X and Clement VII. After the Medici were driven out for the second time (1527), he was proclaimed a rebel and all his possessions were confiscated. When the Medici returned to Florence after the heroic defense of 1530, he was very faithful to the first duke, Alexander; and after the assassination of the Duke by Lorenzino, he transferred his allegiance to Alexander's successor, Cosimo I. But the Prince neglected him; Guicciardini was too hated by the citizenry. Thereupon, he withdrew to his villa of Arcetri (where he died in 1540). In that bitter solitude, stripped of the ambitions which had troubled him throughout his life, he withdrew into his inner self, relived the years gone by, judged the events of his times with cold impartiality, and wrote his major work, the *Storia d'Italia* [*History of Italy*]. It covers the period 1492–1534: from the death of Lorenzo dei Medici to the death of Clement VII. It is in twenty books, published, like all his other writings, posthumously.

As for material, he continues the *Storie fiorentine* of Machiavelli, but his work is the first example of a national history. Guicciardini is a very precise writer; even the speeches that he puts into the mouths of his personages are reworkings of discourses actually delivered. The causes of events are sought by penetrating research into human interests and greed. Perhaps he does not view matters from a high enough vantage point: the details do not allow him to discern the form, shape, or lines of the whole. A spacious and complex literary technique contributes to making the *Storie* difficult to read. In his book, however, instead of the apathy which many readers find, there is to be seen a sorrowing consciousness of the victory of evil over good, as in Tacitus. The beginning of the work by itself would demonstrate what a lofty and moral vision he had of that tragedy of Italian liberty, which is the subject of his narration.

Among Guicciardini's minor writings, the important ones are the *Storia fiorentina* [*History of Florence*], a concise account of events from the riots of the Ciompi (1378) to the beginning of the sixteenth century; *Considerazioni intorno ai discorsi del Machiavelli sopra la prima Deca di Tito Livio* [*Considerations of the Discourses on the First Ten Books of T. Livius by Machiavelli*], in which he examines various chapters of that work, concluding that Machiavelli had more admiration for the Romans than knowledge of present times. For an understanding of Guicciardini's ethics and that of his times, *I Ricordi politici e civili* [*Political and Civil Memoirs*], some four hundred maxims which the author wrote for his children, are useful. There is too much preaching on selfishness and opportunism but also much knowledge of the wretchedness and ingenuousness of mankind.

Of the many other Florentine historians of the first half of the sixteenth century, let us mention Jacopo Nardi, an opponent of the Medici. After the surrender of 1530, he was banished, and he died in poverty in Venice in 1563. He has left us two comedies, some carnival songs, a translation of Livy's *Histories;* more important is his *Storie di Firenze* [*History of Florence* from 1494 to 1538]. Florence is also the subject of histories by Varchi, Segni, and Adriani. Benedetto Varchi, a man of the people and a lover of his city's freedom, was won over by Cosimo I, who loaded him with honors and wealth. He was consul of the Florentine Academy, which later was to become the Accademia della Crusca. He died in 1565. He was a prolific writer, but his major work is the *Storia Fiorentina* in sixteen books, covering the years 1527–1538. Although penned on the orders of the Duke, he spoke out with a truthfulness that would be more pleasant to read if written in a simpler style. Bernardo Segni (d. 1558) in the *Storie fiorentine dall 'anno 1527 al 1555* [*Florentine History, 1527–1555*] praises with eloquent boldness the last representatives of republican liberty. Giambattista Adriani (d. 1579) was one of the defenders of the city during the memorable siege; later, with many others, he went over to the side of the Medici, who appointed him professor of eloquence (literature) in the university. Continuing Guicciardini, he wrote the twenty-two books of the *Storia de' suoi tempi* [*History of His Times*] down to 1574, which contain much information and veracity.

Pier Francesco Giambullari stands apart from the other Florentine historians (d. 1555). An ecclesiastic and a scholar, he remained aloof from the struggles; therefore, as an historian he did not concern himself with the city or with his own age. He wrote a *Storia dell'Europa* [*European History*] from 887 to 947, in seven books; unfinished, it is of little or no scientific value but possesses great formal elegance. It was formerly much read in the schools. Donato Giannotti, who was very erudite in ancient literatures, a friend of Machiavelli, and a constant opponent of the Medici (d. 1573, Rome), was a man of political rather than historical interests. As an admirer of the free and continuing institutions of Venice, he composed, among other things, the *Libro della Repubblica dei Veneziani* [*Book of the Venetian Republic*].

Outside of Tuscany, the historians of the first part of the sixteenth century preferred the Latin language. One of them was Paolo Giovio (d. 1552) of Como, whose Latinized name is Paulus Jovius. He long resided at the court of Rome under Leo X and Clement VII. His *Historiae sui temporis* [*History of his Times*] was famous; it covers the period from 1494 to 1547, and was dictated in sonorous if not eloquent Latin. There were to have been forty-five books, but several were never written. For Giovio, contemporary history meant, above all, the opportunity to compose panegyrics of the great, and a means to garner, as he did, much wealth. Jacopo Bonfadio of Salò was of a very different temper. He was professor of eloquence at Genova, where he had the task of writing the *Annals* of that republic: he was beheaded in 1550, for reasons about which little is known. His *Annals* go from

528 to 1550; they are exact and veracious, full of moral and political reflections. Many of his very interesting letters, and some Latin verses, which are better than his Italian ones, are still extant.

Among the historians of the sixteenth century, Giorgio Vasari of Arezzo merits a special place. He devoted himself to drawing quite early in life and had Michelangelo as a teacher. He became an artist and architect and produced a large number of works, laboring in many places — in Naples, a long sojourn in Rome, and finally in Florence where he died in 1574. Michelangelo's influence is too prominent in his large paintings; he succeeded better in his architectural works, such as the Uffizi Palace in Florence. But he has, above all, deserved a place in the history of art with *Le vite de' più eccellenti pittori, scultori ed architettori* [*Lives of the Greatest Painters, Sculptors, and Architects*], which range from Cimabue in the twelfth century, down to Vasari himself. Although the author shows some not unjustified partiality for his Tuscans, and although modern criticism has modified and cancelled some of Vasari's judgments, these *Lives* still remain of capital importance, in particular for the art of the Renaissance.

Latin Poets of the First Half of the Sixteenth Century

Much of the Latin literature of the sixteenth century is unquestionably an exercise in scholastic elegance and ostentation of literary culture, but some of those Latin poets are worthy of a consideration that is usually denied them in literary histories. Some of them wrote in Latin with more freedom and spontaneity than in the vernacular, and often their weightiest thoughts and solemn arguments were entrusted to the Latin language.

There are many authors of didactic poems. Marcello Palingenio Stellato, anagram of Pier Angelo Manzolli of

La Stellata in the Ferrarese region, lived in Ferrara as physician to Ercole II. He wrote a poem with the strange title of *Zodiacus humanae vitae* [*Zodiac of Human Life*] in twelve books corresponding to the twelve signs of the zodiac. It smacks of the medieval encyclopedias and, like them, it discusses philosophy, science, and theology in no discernible order, and with frequent invectives against the clergy. Later this resulted in the book's being condemned and the author's bones being disinterred and burned. Aonio Paleario (Antonio della Paglia) of Veroli in Latium, professor of literature first at Siena, then at Lucca and Milan, was arrested as a heretic in 1556, and in 1570 he was condemned to death in Rome, meeting his end with the firmness of the martyrs. He was accused of sympathy with the Protestants, whose principal ideas on the justification of the merits of Christ were the subject of his book in Italian, *Il Beneficio di Cristo* [*The Benefit of Christ*] which was widely read in its time. In his youth he had composed a Latin poem in the manner of Lucretius called *De animarum immortalitate* [*On the Immortality of Souls*] in three books.

The great didactic Latin poet of the age, and one of the greatest of the sixteenth century, was Girolamo Fracastoro (d. 1553) of Verona, a noted medical doctor and scientist. Fracastoro is considered to be a precursor of the Copernican system in astronomy and of many phases of medicine. He studied the nature of poetry, which he distinguished in the Aristotelian manner from history in a Latin dialogue, *Naugerius* (so called from the name of Navagero, the principal interlocutor). Fracastoro was a poet above all. His major work is the three books in hexameters *De morbo gallico* [*On the French Pox*] about the horrible sickness that made its first appearance in Italy around the end of the fifteenth century. First the poet teaches that the course of time brought that malady into the world, as it has brought and will bring other monstrous things throughout the centuries; then he describes the characteristics of it, as exemplified in a Lombard youth. In the second book, the cure is discussed. He imagines that Ilceo, a Syrian youth suffering from the disease, invokes the nymph Callirhoe to cure him. The nymph appears to him in slumber; she tells him there is no remedy among the living, but she counsels him to descend to the Underworld and make sacrifices to the goddess Opi. Ilceo performs the rite. The nymph Lipari guides him through subterranean regions near Aetna, where there is a lake of quicksilver; on immersing himself in it three times, Ilceo is restored to purity and health. In the third book, there is talk of the holy tree, recently imported from America, which is considered an infallible remedy. Syphilus, a shepherd of the island of Ofira, one of the newly discovered lands, scornfully refuses to consider the Sun as a god and the Sun punishes him by sending the sickness upon him. Thereafter, it takes the name of that shepherd and becomes widespread in those regions, later reaching Europe with the returning Spanish conquerors of the New World. But, moved to pity for the sufferers of the dread disease, the gods created the miraculous tree *Hyacus,* with whose praises the poem ends. It is pervaded throughout with a high sense of commiseration for the misfortunes of mortals and for the miseries that beset Italy at the beginning of the sixteenth century; the poet recalls them in moving language at the end of the first book. Fracastoro also wrote epistles in verse to friends, one of which tearfully commemorates the death of the poet's own two sons. When well advanced in years, in obedience to the new winds of religious feeling, he attempted a sacred poem on the biblical legend of Joseph; death did not permit him to carry it beyond the second book.

Much less noteworthy but no less celebrated than Fracastoro, was Marco Girolamo Vida of Cremona, a protégé of Leo X, who commissioned him to write a poem on the life of Christ and furnished the leisure thereto by naming him Prior of San Silvestro, in the pleasant town of Frascati. Clement VII, under whom the poem reached its completion, elected him Bishop of Alba, in Monferrato; there the poet died in 1566. His major work is the poem on the life of Christ, which he called *Christias*. In the manner of the classical poems, he begins right in the middle of the story, starting with the preaching of Jesus, or more exactly, the resurrection of Lazarus, and following the path of the Redeemer up to his death. The earlier events are narrated to Pilate by Saint Joseph and by Saint John the Evangelist, just as the preceding happenings of the story of the *Aeneid* are told by Aeneas at the table of Dido. Thus Vergil is felt in the plan of the poem, as well as in the details and in the elegance of the verses. Before the *Christias*, Vida had written two little poems, one, didactic, *Bombex*, on the silkworm; and the other, for amusement, *Scacchea ludus* on the game of chess. In the latter, he shows his ability to say the most difficult things in a limpid poetical form. He concerned himself with poetry itself in an apposite *Ars poetica* [*Art of Poetry*]. In it he does not discuss the general principles of poetry but, like Horace in the epistle to the Pisoni, he gives precepts illustrated in the poetry itself and, where Horace chooses tragedy, Vida, using his beloved Vergil as a model, discusses the epic poem. His *Art of Poetry* had widespread influence on the literary education of the sixteenth century.

There were many Latin lyric poets; most of them chose to follow the facile manner of Catullus. In quantity and facility Marc' Antonio Flaminio stands out from the others. He was a native of Serravalle in the March of Treviso; while still young, he earned the approbation of Leo X. He spent most of his life in the service of powerful personages, the last of whom was the English Cardinal Reginald Polo (Pole). In his maturity, he had some sympathy for the Protestant reform, which was perhaps the reason that he refused to go as a secretary to the Council of Trent. He died in Rome in 1550. Of his extant work, there are eight books of short Latin poetry (*Carmina*), written at various times and almost all having a character of occasion. Some are tenderly sentimental, such as the one about his own little villa and another on the death of Francesco Sforza; they are all limpid and unclouded. Those of the fourth book are moving; they are written for Hiella, a girl who died of love for the shepherd Iole. The seventh book bears witness to the spirited religious fervor of the author; it contains paraphrases of thirty psalms; the eighth, dedicated to Marguerite, the sister of Henri II, king of France, is made up almost entirely of fervent prayers to Christ and praises of His goodness to mankind. Giovanni Cotta, one of the friends of Flaminio, was a lyric poet of sober eloquence. A native of Verona, he died at the early age of twenty-eight.

Two poets were renowned among the Latin poets of the sixteenth century. One was Nandrea Navagero, a Venetian patrician, and a reviser of texts for the famous Venetian printer Aldo Manuzio. He served first as ambassador of his republic to Charles V in Spain, then later to Francis I in France, where he died in 1529. He left a number of magnificent *orazioni*, an account in Italian of his diplomatic travels in Spain and France, and a small number of Latin poems to which he gave the title *Lusus* [scherzos, playful poems]. They are compositions full of grace and delicacy, especially the shorter ones. Jacopo Sadoleto of Modena came early in his career to Rome, where he enjoyed the favor of Leo X and Clement VII, and died a cardinal in 1547. Over a long period he attempted a work of pacification between Catholics and Protestants, shunning any show of violence. He has left some sixteen books of Latin letters, a treatise in dialogue form in praise of philosophy, and a book on the education of children, *De liberis recte instituendis,* one of the wisest ever written on the subject. In youth, he devoted himself to poetry; among other things, there is his little poem on Curtius, the Roman hero and, more noteworthy, the *Carmen de Laocoonte* [*Song of Laocoön*], which reproduces in all its detail the famous Greek statuary group then recently discovered and which now is admired in the Vatican Museum.

The Principal Men of Letters in the Sixteenth Century

Pietro Bembo of Venice stands out from the others. Studies were his first passion. He accompanied his father, representing the Venetian Republic, to Ferrara where, among others he became acquainted with Ariosto. He fell in love with Lucretia Borgia, the famous wife of Alfonso I, and she returned his love. He then spent a long time at the court of Guidobaldo, Duke of Urbino, one of the most splendid and liberal courts of the time; here his gift for conversation, no less than his poetry, made him celebrated. Giuliano dei Medici was there at the same time and took him to Rome where, with Sadoleto, he was appointed secretary of Leo X. At Rome he had a love affair with a certain lady named Morosina, by whom he had several children. Such conduct did not scandalize Leo X, who bestowed benefices on him and entrusted him with various important missions. After the death of Leo, Bembo retired to Padua, where he devoted himself to art and learning. There he wrote *Le Prose della volgar lingua* [*On Writing in the Vernacular*], which he dedicated later to Clement VII. Soon afterward, the Council of Ten charged him with the task of continuing the history of Venice on which Navagero had been working up to the time of his death. Paul III raised him to the rank of cardinal; then he was ordained a priest, and thereafter lived a life of near-austerity in Rome where he died in 1547. It is enough to mention his Latin works: the *Twelve Books of Venetian History* (from 1487 to 1513), which he himself translated into the vernacular; their subject matter was derived almost entirely from the *Diarii* [*Journals*] of Sanudo. He also wrote dialogues, songs, and epistles. His works in the vernacular were more important. *Gli Asolani* are dialogues that were developed in his villa at Asolo, in the region of Treviso, where the former queen of Cyprus, Caterina Cornaro, had taken up residence in her retirement. In them, love is discussed and extolled as the source of every virtue. This is the theory of platonic love, which was, or pretended to be, the love reigning in the courts and the elegant circles of the century. The *Prose della volgar lingua* are likewise dialogues in which Bembo was one of the first to define the rules of grammar, drawing them from the writings of Boccaccio. He also defended the supremacy of the Florentine or Tuscan speech, an opinion that was shared by many non-Tuscans and commonly accepted. He had little regard for Dante, criticizing his language as rough and uncultured. He praised Petrarch most highly, and he followed closely the phrasing and the manner of Petrarch in his few, but very grammatical *Rime*. In contrast to the clever oddities of the courtly poets of the late fifteenth century, this might seem a return to simplicity and naturalness; in any case, it proclaimed his approval of that Petrarchism which made most of the lyric poets of the fifteenth century so elegant and so cold.

Baldassare Castiglione is, after Machiavelli, the strongest prose writer of the century, but a writer who dealt with matters of much less importance. Born into a noble family in the vicinity of Mantua, he spent his youth in Milan at the court of Ludovico il Moro, where Leonardo da Vinci and Bramante were outstanding among the other authors and artists. On the fall of the duchy of Milan to the French arms, he returned to Mantua whence, in the retinue of his prince, Francesco Gonzaga, he departed for the conquest of Naples in the name of King Louis XII of France. After the defeat of Gonzaga's army at the Garigliano, Castiglione withdrew to Rome where he made the acquaintance of Guidobaldo of Montefeltro, Duke of Urbino, and followed the Duke to that city. Amid the splendors of that court, the most chivalrous of the Renaissance, he conceived his major work, the *Cortegiano* [*Courtier*]. He went on important missions, including one to Henry VII in England. Guidobaldo's successor, Francesco Maria della Rovere, was also very fond of Castiglione and sent him as ambassador to Leo X. He remained in Rome for a long time and became acquainted with the great artists of the time: Raphael (who esteemed his counsel and good taste most highly and painted his portrait), Michelangelo, and Giulio Romano. He died at Toledo in 1529, while on a mission to Madrid in the name of Clement VII.

Il Cortegiano is a series of dialogues, in four books, which it is imagined take place at the court of Urbino in the circle of the Duchess Elisabetta Gonzaga, Guidobaldo's wife. The participants are many noblemen, men of letters, and ladies, such as Francesco Maria della Rovere, Giuliano de'Medici, Pietro Bembo, the Duchess, Princess Emilia Pia. The discussion turns on the ideal, either of the perfect courtier, or perfect lady, the *dama di palazzo*. The courtier must be of noble blood, skilled in arms, sincere, versed in literature and the arts. He is faithful to his prince, but must not obey him in any dishonest matter; he should give him wise counsel and never hide the truth from him. At times the most varied subjects are touched on in literature, art, and love. It is the Code of Law of the Court, written in a candid, noble style, in conscious opposition to that of Boccaccio, as the author states in the Preface, where he affirms that he prefers to appear a Lombard in the eyes of his fellow Lombards, rather than a foreigner to the Tuscans.

The Paduan Sperone Speroni was purely a man of letters: a professor of philosophy in his native city and an authoritative critic. He was the first mentor of Torquato Tasso, but later he became envious of his pupil's glory. He died at an advanced age in 1588. He left many dialogues in the Platonic manner on moral and literary topics: paradoxical rather than profound. He found fault with certain poets; even Vergil, the deity of poetry in the sixteenth century, he did not leave unscathed. One of his own tragedies, *La Canace,* caused considerable stir; his subject, suggested to him by one of the *Heroïdes (Epistulae heroïdum)* of Ovid, was the incestuous loves of the two mythical twins, Canace and Macareus, children of Aeolus. His opponent was Giambattista Giraldi Cintio of Ferrara (d. 1573). The latter wrote an important *Discorso intorno al comporre dei romanzi* [*Discourse Concerning the Composing of Romances*] about those poems of chivalry that still reechoed in Ferrara thanks to the *Orlando furioso.* He defended them against the new heroic poem which was being attempted, counting the chivalric style as superior to the latter in its variety and its capacity for giving pleasure. He also left a mythological poem, *Ercole* [*Hercules*], which narrates the life and deeds of the Theban hero from whom, the author alleged, Ercole II of Este descended; a pastoral drama, *Egle* [*Eagle*], and a hundred novellas *(Ecatommiti),* the source book of Shakespeare's *Othello.* They do not have the licentiousness of Boccaccio, nor do they have the art and the vivacity. From several of these tales the author later drew the subjects of his tragedies, one of which is the *Orbecche,* an extremely cruel play: A king of Persia kills the children of his daughter Orbecche and has their hands and heads served to their mother as she awaited a different kind of present; she in turn stabs her wicked father and herself. Other of his plays were *Altile, Didone* [Dido], and *Cleopatra.* They differ from the other tragedies of the age in their romantic character, and in their imitation of Seneca, rather than the Greek tragic authors.

Giovanni della Casa, scion of a noble Florentine family, continues to enjoy renown. He came as a young man to Rome seeking advancement in the ecclesiastical career, an ambition which did not keep him from enjoying an extremely mundane and sensual life, or from writing, then and later, some chapters on topics better left nameless. Paolo [Paul] III named him Archbishop of Benevento and Papal Nuncio to Venice. He was the instigator of the persecution against Paolo Vergerio, Bishop of Capodistria, who was accused of Lutheranism and forced to flee to Germany, where he made public revelation of the customs and habits of his persecutor. That did not prevent della Casa from aspiring to the cardinal's hat, but his desire was frustrated by the death of his patron Paul III. Paul IV, the persecutor of heretics, rewarded him nevertheless, appointing him Secretary of State, in which employment he died, in 1556.

The well-known work of Della Casa is the *Galateo*, named in honor of the man by whose counsel it was written (Galeazzo Florimonte; in Latin, *Galataeus*). In the book, an old man instructs a youth in "the manners which should be adopted or avoided in general conversation"; that is to say, the manners of a good upbringing. These imply, in short, doing nothing that may reveal a man's innate selfishness and the lower, animal instincts of his nature. The duties of politeness include that of using good language and speaking correctly; in this connection the author seizes the opportunity to censure the language of Dante, which he judges to be too often coarse, and that of Boccaccio, which he thinks is too involute and oratorical. There are many lively pages, especially among those dealing with the types and blemishes common in conversation, such as the man who insists on all the formalities, or the overly shy and modest character, or the eater who delays the serving of the next course. Certainly the book is a document of its age, an age that paid more attention to forms than to substance. The *Rime* of Della Casa have been highly praised; he was esteemed to be a master in the art of writing them. Although he came within the scope of Petrarchian imitation, at times he could rise to expressions of deep passion, couched in terms of a strong style, in solemn harmony.

Bernardo Tasso was a poet, but less a poet than a man of letters. The man who was to be the father of Torquato was born at Venice into a noble family from Bergamo. Almost his entire life was spent in the narrow and difficult status of a courtier, which he was fated to hand down as a wretched heritage to his son. First, he was in the service of Ferrante Sanseverino, prince of Salerno; then in that of Guidobalo II, Duke of Urbino; next in that of Cardinal Luigi d'Este; and finally in the service of Guglielmo Gonzaga of Mantua. He died, while he was podestà of Ostiglia, in 1569; he was mourned by his son Torquato, in whom he early inculcated a love of life and of glory.

We have many of his letters, which he published himself as was the custom of many writers of those and later days; many lyrics of love and sorrow, which in their simplicity and sincerity turn away from the common Petrarchian manner; and there are some graceful mythological poems. But he expected glory to be his from a poem that no one ever reads any more, *Amadigi* [*Amadis*]. The *Amadigi*, a free reworking of an old Spanish romance, tells of the love of Amadis for Oriana; a love ever hindered and frustrated, then at last successful. Endless combats, action more confused than varied, an overdose of the element of marvel, the conventionality of the hero who is the model of all the chivalrous virtues, all this made the vast and serious poem little to the liking of an age that was reading the *Furioso*. *Floridante*, another of Bernardo's poems, with which Torquato helped, is an amplification of an episode of the *Amadigi*.

The Genres: Gian Giorgio Trissino

The literary sixteenth century, as has been mentioned, accepted as a canon the imitation of the Latin and Greek classics. It is therefore understandable that many writers of that age proposed to reproduce in the vernacular the ancient literary *genres* which were still lacking in Italian literature. One of the first to be remembered is Gian Giorgio Trissino of Vicenza. He lived a long time in Rome, where Leo X, Clement VII, and Paul III thought highly of him; then in his villa of Ocricoli near Vicenza, which he beautified in the classical style at the suggestion of his great friend Palladio. He died in Rome in 1550. Trissino represents the tendency to substitute imitation of Greek poetry for the widespread imitation of Latin poetry. Thus, it was in the Greek manner that he wrote his tragedy *Sofonisba* [*Sophonisbe*], which is simple in plot and not without moving passions. It was a tragedy conforming to the strictest rules of time and place, and with choruses — the first so-called *regular* tragedy. In the comedy *I Simillimi* (or *Simillissimi*), he imitates the *Menaechmi* of Plautus while keeping the choruses in the manner of his Greek models. But his great ambition was to give the Italians a heroic epic poem. Among men of letters there was a strong desire to see the grave heroic poem in the manner of the Greeks and Romans take the place of the romances in the manner of the *Orlando Furioso*, and to see the stately epic with a single principal action and few episodes based on an historical or traditional subject replace the fee and episodic poem of chivalry. This new poem was to be the glory of Torquato Tasso, but before him Trissino attempted to create it with his *Italia liberata dai Goti* [*Italy Liberated from the Goths]* in twenty-seven books. He narrated an event that did not find the slightest echo in the minds or souls of the Italians, who did not have the least concern for the liberation of Italy from the Goths a thousand years earlier at the hands of Narses and Belisarius. Moreover, he narrated it with the dryness of a chronicler and archaeologist, copying numerous pages from the Byzantine historian Procopius. But he flattered himself that in achieving an appearance of truth by means of historicity, which is something quite different, and by an abundance of details he had equalled the clearness and effectiveness of his beloved Homer. Certainly, the poem has some beautiful passages, especially those depicting feminine characters, such as Sophia, Cillenia, and Elpidia. It also contains fierce invectives against the degenerate Papacy, and in a series of allegories it seems to aim at the corruption and decadence of Italy. Its dedication to Charles V is not without point, for there were many besides Trissino who yearned for the restoration of the imperial idea and the peace of Italy and the world. However, the *Italia liberata,* which represented twenty years of labor by its author, was no longer read in the time of the younger Tasso. A large part of its unpopularity was due to the unrhymed or blank verse in which the poet wrote it, a verse form that in itself has neither sweetness nor harmony and which may be taken for prose: poetry must, more than anything else, be poetic.

Trissino expected to propagate his literary forms with the aid of numerous critical writings, in addition to his poetical example. He wrote, with equal sufficiency, on the most futile and serious questions. He worked for a long time on the reform of the Italian alphabet, which he thought was deficient in signs distinguishing the short vowels from the long ones, and the institution of the *x* and *z,* previously lacking, are credited to him. He busied himself with *Dubbi grammaticali* [*Grammatical Doubts*] and wrote a *Grammatichetta* [*Brief Grammar*] in the vernacular and one in Latin. With the dialogue called *Castellano*, he took part in the debate on the Italian language, maintaining that it was national not Florentine or Tuscan (which was likewise Castiglione's idea). To strengthen his thesis, he translated Dante's *De vulgari eloquentia* into the vernacular, with the text opposite. This was the first time that the work of Dante made a public appearance. He discussed poetry in his six *Divisioni della poetica* [*Divisions of Poetics*], the first of which contains a diligent study of the most ancient metrical forms of Italian poetry. In the last two, following in the footsteps of Aristotle, the nature of poetry is determined and particular attention is given to tragic and heroic poems.

The Comedy

In the field of the tragedy, Trissino had many imitators, none of whom deserved the name of tragic poet. Tragedy flourishes in places and ages of deeply felt political and moral life, and in the classes of Italian society, there was too much skepticism and critical spirit for the great and ingenuous tragic passions really to live. There was too much effort to substitute effect for power, terror for pity. Seneca, for instance, was raised to a position above the Greek tragedians, especially by the example of Giraldi. On the other hand, comedy was more fortunate and in tune with the epicurean and cynical disposition of the age. Although, if comedy was modeled after the Latin comedians, as we have seen in connection with the plays of Ariosto, it did not always limit itself to themes found in Terence and Plautus.

Angiolo Dovizi of Bibbiena wrote what was perhaps the first example of the classical comedy with his very licentious *Calandria*. There are almost no sixteenth-century writers who did not try their hands at comedy. The most productive writer of comedies was the Florentine *Giovanni Maria Cecchi*, a notary, who died in 1587. He left some fifty plays, many of which long remained unpublished, nor is it certain that all those attributed to him are really his. Some of his plays are *sacre rappresentazioni,* in which, however, as in *Il Figliuol Prodigo* [*Prodigal Son*], he introduced many realistic elements and scenes. Many of his comedies are imitations of Plautus and Terence, such as *I Dissimili* [*The Unlike*]; *Il Martello* [*The Hammer*]; *I Rivali, Gli Incantesimi* [*The Magic Spells*]; *La Moglie* [*The Wife*]; *La Schiava* [*The Slave Girl*]; *La Dote* [*The Dowry*]. Others are original or derived from current events: *Il Donzello* [*The Page*], and *Lo Spirito* [*The Spirit*]. Still others are of Boccaccian derivation, such as *L'Assiuolo* [*The Horned Owl*]. The author's chief merits are a spirited language and dialogue full of movement and action.

Didactic Poems

The didactic poem in vernacular is likewise due to imitation of the ancients. This *genre,* which in the beginning may have resulted from a need to return to the past and tradition, quite soon became a purely literary composition and a facile excuse for those descriptive pieces that always tempt mediocre writers. The Florentine *Giovanni Rucellai* was of the noble family of the Rucellai, in whose gardens Machiavelli was a visitor, and was an intimate of Leo X and Clement VII. Rucellai died in Rome in 1525. He gave the first example of the didactic poem with *Le Api* [*The Bees*], which was some thousand lines of blank verse harmonious in their simplicity and uniformity. He discusses the subject that Vergil adopted in Book IV of the *Georgics,* of which his work is often merely a translation. Two tragedies by him are extant, which are among the earliest of those obedient to the "unities": *Rosmunda,* in which he adapted the famous story of the Lombards to the model of Sophocles' *Antigone;* and *Oreste,* an imitation of Euripides' *Iphigenia in Tauris.*

Another Florentine was more interesting: Luigi Alamanni, a celebrated citizen and friend of Machiavelli and of freedom. A conspirator against the Medici, he went into exile in France, returning to Florence when the Medici were driven out in 1527. On the fall of the Florentine republic, he was again banished and once more took refuge in France, where he won the favor of Francis I and knew the principal poets of that country. He died in the court at Amboise, in 1556. Many of his writings are extant, among them are a tragedy, *Antigone,* which is almost an exact translation of the Sophocles' tragedy; a comedy, *Flora,* written in a special sort of verse form intended to reproduce the iambic meter of the Latin in a more satisfactory manner than was possible with the hendecasyllable; many lyrics and epigrams; and two epic poems. *Giron il Cortese,* dedicated to Henry II King of France, is derived from an old French romance, *Guiron le Courtois* [*Guiron the Courteous*]. It deals with the adventures of that knight, a model of every virtue, one of the Knights of the Round Table. The author displays a broad and competent knowledge of the stories of that Table, as is evidenced also by the dedicatory letter of the poem. The other is the *Avarchide* (Avarcum, or rather Avaricum, was the Latin name of the city of Bourges in France). The siege of Troy becomes the siege of Bourges by the Knights of the Round Table. Every hero and every situation in the *Iliad* has its correspondence in the poem — a perfect example of imitation of the ancients, or rather, plagiarism. But Alamanni is best known for *La Coltivazione* [*Agriculture*], which was published in Paris and dedicated to Francis I. In six books, in the blank verse which thereafter became characteristic of such works, the author discusses everything that has reference to agriculture and the rural life. First he gives general precepts concerning environmental conditions favorable to cultivation; then he talks about mowing, harvesting, the vintage and making of wine, winter occupations, the layout of the rustic dwelling, and gardening. Finally, he makes some remarks derived from practical experience and some from superstition, regarding favorable and unfavorable days and forecasts. There are many episodes such as the praises of Francis I and of France, in Book I; in Book II, those on the happy Golden Age; the eulogy of Bacchus in Book III; and in the fifth, the description of the garden of Fontainebleau. Pity for the misfortunes and poverty of Italy is strongly expressed in the poem; for example, the commiseration for the many Italians forced to live far from their homeland by the frightful conditions of the times, as told in Book IV; and the allusions to the violence and vices of Italian rulers in Book V. Alamanni closely follows parts of Vergil's *Georgics* and often takes material from the ancient treatise of Columella on agriculture. Alamanni's blank verse is still too monotonous and bare.

The Principal Lyric Poets of the Sixteenth Century

The great fame of Petrarch, the example given by that great arbiter of poetry Bembo, together with the elegant life of the courts, prevented the lyric, in the main, from freeing itself from the amorous material and the manner of Petrarch. The sonnets and the songs, the sestinas and the madrigals of numberless versifiers of that age are all bound to the themes and style of Petrarch. There are few attempts to recapture the echos of the Greek and Latin lyric, either in spirit or in meter. Claudio Tolomei of Siena (d. 1555), a distant precursor of Carducci, was one man who tried to reproduce in Italian the rhythms and the strophes of Latin poetry. The following are the names of the most meaningful lyric poets of the century beside those already discussed.

The greatest painter, sculptor, and architect that the age produced, Michelangelo Buonarroti of Florence, who lived almost to the age of ninety (d. 1564 in Rome), was one of the few strongly personal lyric poets of the century. Especially in the last years of his residence in Rome, when the brushes and the chisels were resting, he wrote various *Rime* mostly on love themes, but some of a religious nature. Michelangelo thirsted after Platonism. Art, he says in one of his sonnets, is always inferior to the idea that flashes through the artist's mind. His lines, however, are full of obscurities and harsh expressions. His reader is more aware of his study of his beloved Dante than of Petrarch. Vittoria Colonna was the inspiration for many of his poems.

Productive and impassioned are two adjectives that describe Francesco Maria Molza of Modena who, after an unbridled life in Rome, died in his native city in 1544. He was both a Latin and a vernacular poet. His love lyrics are spirited; his idyll *La Ninfa Tiberina* [*The Tiberine Nymph*] became famous. Giovanni Guidiccioni (d. 1541), a prelate of Lucca, was a noble figure who was rewarded by Paul III with high honors, such as the governorship first of Romagna and then of the Marches. In several sonnets of his canzoniere there are a deep love for Italy and a keen feeling of regret for her lost greatness of times past.

A frigid clarity and artificiality are felt in the many, and at one time celebrated, sonnets of Angelo Di Costanzo, a nobleman of Naples who died in old age in 1591 at Naples. Bernardino Rota (d. 1575), also from Naples, wrote sonnets for his dead wife, with whom he wished to be buried in the temple of Santa Maria Maggiore. Rota is one of the few examples of writers of familiar and intimate poetry. The Baron of Belmonte, Galeazzo Di Tarsia (d. 1553), was a vigorous writer. A sonnet that he wrote when, from the Alps, he again saw Italy is one of the most beautiful of the sixteenth century. From another of his sonnets, Ugo Foscolo took the line that he put into his own *Sepolcri:* "*Se ti fur care le mie chiome e il viso*" [If you loved my hair and my face]. But of all the Neapolitan poets of that age, the most outstanding was Luigi Tansillo (d. 1568), who spent his life in the service of the two viceroys Don Pietro di Toledo and his son, Don Garcia. When he was young, he wrote a little poem, *Il Vendemmiatore* [*The Vintager*], in which it is imagined that in the freedom granted to vintagers in the time of the grape gathering, one of them, taking his place up in a tree, makes the most satirical and salacious remarks. More important is his *Il Podere* [*The Farm*] in three divisions, in tercets. In the guise of a counsel to a friend, the author sings the praises of rural life and quotes, with descriptions, precepts tken from the ancients. In a short poem, *La Bàlia* [*The Wet Nurse*], the author deplores the custom of mothers not nursing their own children. In his latter years, influenced by the religious spirit of the counterreformation, he wrote one of the many penitential poems of the time *Le lacrime di San Pietro* [*Saint Peter's Tears*], in fifteen books. It was so highly admired that the most authoritative French poet of the time, Malherbe, translated it into his own language. The *Rime* of Tansillo were considered by some of his contemporaries to surpass those of Petrarch. Certainly some of his sonnets have a daring imaginativeness, such as those that tell of the sublimeness of his love. Others are striking in their gloomy descriptions of landscapes. While he is skillful in other types of poetry, in the sonnet he is vigorous, concise, and noble.

 A very special place in the lyric poetry of the sixteenth century was earned by some of the women who devoted themselves to literature. Among those most highly regarded is Veronica Gàmbara of Brescia (d. 1550), the wife of Gilberto X, lord of Correggio. Upon the death of her husband, she governed that city with good sense, strength, and kindness. Some of her *Rime* are extant. Somewhat rough in their Petrarchian style, they are concerned with moral or political themes. In some *ottava rima* addressed to Charles V, she deplores the wretched and ever unsatisfied desires of conquest and eulogizes the innocent

Golden Age with a warmth unspoiled by rhetoric. An uncultured, but true poetess was Gàspara Stampa of Padova, who died in Venice in 1554. Hers was a soul created for love and the object of her passion and her poems was Count Collatino of Collalto in the region of Treviso, who tired too soon of that devoted and humble affection. The canzoniere of Stampa is the story and the diary of that passion, and it is perhaps the most fervent, clear, and eloquent feminine love poetry of Italy. Laura Terracina was dexterous and productive, qualities that are customary among Neapolitan poets. But Vittoria Colonna, of Marino near Rome, rises above the other women writers of her age; not so much by her poetic ability as by her feminine dignity and religious inwardness. Left a widow while still young by Ferrante d'Avalos, marquis of Pescara, captain-general of Charles V in Italy, she mourned him for a long time and sought solace in God. Her religious fervor caused her to look sympathetically on the ideas of the Reformation. She lived, now in Ischia, now in Orvieto, but more often in Rome, where she won the veneration of the aged Michelangelo, as mentioned earlier; and in Rome she died in 1547. Her *Rime* tell of the two great passions of her life. Many are for her dead husband, and many of the best tell of her thirst for God and develop in various ways the concept of the goodness of Christ, who has redeemed us by his merits.

Minor Artists and Translators of the Sixteenth Century

Among the men of letters of the sixteenth century, there are some lively writers whose works may be considered more stylistic than artistic. Of these, Annibal Caro of Civitanuova, in the province of Ancona, merits special mention. For many years he was in the service of the powerful Farnese family of Rome, who obtained for him the commendam, with the benefices pertaining to it, of the Order of Saints John and Victor in Montefiascone. Hence his title of *commendatore* [commander]. He died in Rome in 1566. Among his writings, there are the *Rime,* a comedy, *Gli Straccioni* [*The Ragamuffins*]; some lively polemics in verse and in prose against Ludovico Castelvetro, a critic and philosopher of Modena who had dared to censure with great pedantry a canzone of Caro's in praise of the house of France. The polemics led to the killing of a partisan of Caro and an accusation of heresy leveled at Castelvetro, who fled to Switzerland. The many letters of Caro are important to the history of the time; they have undeservedly fallen into contempt on account of the overuse made of them in the schools. But Caro's great work of art is his translation of the *Aeneid,* in blank verse, which for the first time assumes the variety, the flexibility, the quality, and the capacity to render all the aspects of things, affairs, and feeling. In short, all the virtues of which the most aristocratic and erudite of Italian verse forms would have been capable. But the sixteenth century was an age of artists; it demanded of the translator not so much faithfulness to the original, as beauty. He had to show that the Italian language was equal to the refinements, the subtleties, and the daring of the ancient tongues. Most elegant is his translation of the romance of Longus the Sophist: *Daphnis and Chloë.*

In his major work, Angelo Firenzuola of Florence, was a translator in his own way, and in the manner of the times. As a lawyer in the service of the Curia in Rome, he led a very free life in that capital. He was a monk of Vallombrosa and abbot of Vaiano near Prato, more for love of the benefices than of the office. He died midway in the century. Firenzuola's finest work is a free reworking of the previously mentioned Latin romance, the *Metamorphoses,* or *Golden Ass,* of Apuleius, an African writer of the second century. The title of the romance derives from that of the hero, an ass who represents the author himself reduced to that extremity, allegorically, by his love of things of the senses. In his *Asino d'Oro,* Firenzuola speaks of himself and his love affairs in the vein of the Latin tale, with great liveliness of portrayal and much lightness and adornment of language. All of these qualities are no less in evidence in a vast series of fables, each connected to the next, which bear the name of *La prima veste dei discorsi degli animali* [*The First Form of the Sayings of Animals*]. They are taken from an ancient Sanskirt collection (*Panchatantra*) which, through translations into Hebrew, Arabic, and Latin, was widely disseminated during the Middle Ages. It seems that Firenzuola derived his material from a Spanish translation. The moral of the book is an admonition to beware of the innumerable wiles of men who, naturally in the shape of animals are especially clever. Firenzuola's books, *Delle bellezze delle donne* [*On the Beauties of Women*] and *Della perfetta bellezza d'una donna* [*On the Perfect Beauty of a Woman*], derive their importance from stating certain canons of the human form in the plastic arts of the sixteenth century.

The Florentine Giovan Battista Gelli (d. 1563), was also far more important than Firenzuola, keener, more subtle, and simpler for the philosophical content of his works. He was by trade a hosier, but that did not keep him from devoting himself wholeheartedly to studies, on which account he was elected consul of the Florentine Academy and appointed by the ducal government to lecture there on the *Commedia*. His principal writings are *I Capricci del bottaio* [*The Cooper's Whims*] and *Circe*. The former is about the arguments that Giusto, an old cooper, has with his own soul. They are dialogues of moral philosophy based on common sense, and in which the corruption and hypocrisy of the clergy are not spared. The Church banned the book, and its author retracted it. *Circe* stems from Plutarch's dialogue *The Cricket,* as did Machiavelli's *Golden*

Ass previously discussed: Ulysses has obtained from Circe the power to turn back into human form the lovers whom the goddess had transformed into beasts. Each of those beasts, however, refuses Ulysses' gift, teaching that sage what miseries, injustices, and absurdities are the lot of man's life, and how calm, serene, and safe from the ruinous plagues of desire are the animals. Only the last of the beasts with whom the hero speaks, the elephant, who as a man was a philosopher, yields to Ulysses persuasion. There is in these dialogues such a pessimistic vision of life that they sometimes seem to prelude Leopardi.

At this point, mention must be made of some of the numerous novella writers who flourished in the first half of the sixteenth century. The novella output rivalled or even surpassed that of the comedy, which was often a substitute for it. The principal *novelliere* of the century was Matteo Bandello (d. 1561) of Castelnuovo Scrivia near Tortona. When young, he wore the Dominican habit to please his uncle Vincenzo Bandello, who was a general of the Dominican Order. In his uncle's retinue, he visited many cities of Italy, among them Florence and Naples. After the death of his uncle, he took service with a succession of lords, among them a Captain Cesare Fregoso, whose widow, Rangoni, he followed to France. Here he became Bishop of Agen. He wrote over two hundred novellas, composed in various moments of his varied and tumultuous life and made into a collection in his last years. Unlike the Boccaccio, Bandello's novellas are not planned around a central theme; each one stands by itself, with a dedication to some nobleman or lady. Many, and the best ones, are derived from real events. All of them are noteworthy for skill in plotting and dramatic movement. Soon translated into French and from the French into English, they were known to Shakespeare, who based his tragedy of *Romeo and Juliet* on one of them. The same story had been treated in a long novella by Luigi da Porto of Vicenza, who died young in 1529.

Anton Francesceo Grazzini was a spirited novella writer under the pseudonym of Lasca. A Florentine (d. 1584), he was the author of comedies, burlesque poems, and *capitoli*. His novellas, produced toward the middle of the century, are named *Cene* [*Suppers*] because it is imagined that they were narrated at supper on the last three days of Carnival. They were supposed to number thirty; twenty-two of them are extant. The predominant theme is of atrocious, brutal practical jokes played on priests, friars, and men of letters. They form a painting of a society that does not have, and does not want to have, thoughts, and which proposes to laugh and enjoy life. Here is Florence adapting to the new servitude. It was not for nothing that Lasca was faithful to the Medici and with Salviati was the founder of that Accademia della Crusca (crusca: bran; a Florentine literary academy), which the prince was to patronize as a harmless institution to give vent to literature that had become pedantry, and discussions that had become mere chatter.

Among the novella writers of the sixteenth century, a special place belongs to Gianfrancesco Straparola of Caravaggio, who lived in the first part of the century. In his *Piacevoli notti* [*Pleasant Nights*] he gave much space to those fables whose origin is lost in the night of time and which, in the most varied forms, still persist in the rural populations and are the favorite diversion of their children. So it is that we read in his *Piacevoli notti*, in a form that we might prefer to be clearer and simpler, the famous fable of the little bird Belverde and the still more famous one about Cinderella.

Literary Reactionaries and Odd Spirits in the First Half of the Sixteenth Century

Folengo and Macaronic Poetry

Even in the field of literature every exaggeration provokes a reaction. The mania for imitating and classicizing, which was so predominant in the first half of the sixteenth century, raised up some odd spirits who turned that sort of thing into parody and caricature. The brightest of these spirits, and one in whom first class poetical abilities are discernible, was Teofilo Folengo, better known under the pseudonym of Merlin Cocai. Merlin, the name of a sorcerer; Cocai (I think) from Coccaglio, a town of the province of Brescia, whose inhabitants perhaps, in the opinion of those times, were not renowned for excessive intelligence. This Mantuan, (born in Cipada, ancient Andes, the very birthplace of Vergil), was a rather strange sort. Having become a Benedictine monk without any particular desire for that calling, he threw away his habit, not from any impulse of conscience probably, but because he could no longer stand the discipline. Thereafter he entered the service of a series of powerful lords in Venice and Rome, the Orsini among them. It is probably in that time that he assumed the noble surname of Limerno Pitocco (Limerno, anagram of Merlino; Pitocco means either a beggar or a skinflint). Later he returned to religion and went hither and yon, as far as San Martino delle Scale near Palermo; possibly because his superiors thought it imprudent to let him stay too long in any one place. He died in 1544 in the monastery of Santa Croce in Campese, near Bassano Veneto.

He is a master of the poetry to which he gave the appellation of "macaronic." In some parts of northern Italy *macaron* means stupid, dull or silly; perhaps macaronic poetry means the poetry of an ignorant man. Its language is seemingly Latin or, rather, its word-endings are Latin and Latin syntax and meter are roughly used, but the stems of the words are Italian or, mostly, from Lombard dialects. From this combination there results a continuous hilarity in the contrast between the plodding humbleness of the vocable and the sonorous magnificence and the dignity of the Latin much more so than can be heard sometimes in whole solemn Vergilian verses. Manifestly Folengo desired to take a merry vengeance on the countless Latinizing poets of his time by means of his own personal Latin. In that language he wrote a long poem, *Baldus,* which is a mockery of the epic poems and of the romances of chivalry, and to which he returned several times. Baldus is a descendant of Charlemagne. His undertakings and swindlings center on Cipada. His companions, Cingar [Gypsy], Falchettus, and Fracassus [Hawk, and Racket], are huge urchins and rascals. The heroic life is led in the midst of the most plebian people, and it is precisely in the portrayal of this world of peasants, petty merchants, village justices, Sunday fairs and markets, and in the satirical and burlesque depiction of the friars, that Merlin Cocai is most enormously successful. Two other of his macaronic poems are less important: the *Moscheis,* or war between the flies [*mosche*] and the ants, which is reminiscent of the *Batracomiomachia* attributed to Homer; and the *Zanitonella,* or the loves of two rustics, Zoanina and Tonello [Jane and Tony], in which the parody of the pastoral idylls, no less than that of Petrarchian love, is plain. His vernacular writings are extremely bad: the *Orlandino* telling of Orlando's youth, is one of the most slovenly and cynical poems to be found in Italian literature and can hardly be recognized as belonging to the cultured sixteenth century. The *Caos del Triperuno* [*The Chaos of the Three-for-One*], an allusion to the author's three names, a complicated and heavy allegory prevents a clear understanding of whether he is speaking of his conversion to Protestant ideas or of his return to the monastery. Certainly the religious problem worried him more than might have been thought possible. He left an enormous *sacra rappresentazione* which expounded the history of the whole human race and which received the name of *Atto della Pinta* from the church in Palermo where it was presented.

Francesco Berni

Francesco Berni is considered the father of burlesque poetry. Born at Lamporecchio in Tuscany, he spent his entire life, against his wishes, in the service of other men: first at Rome under the Cardinal Bernardo Dovizi of Bibbiena, a relative; then under the latter's nephew, Angelo Dovizi, apostolic protonotary. While in Rome, he witnessed the terrible sack of the city at the hands of the Lanquenets in 1527. Then he was for a long time in the employ of the austere Bishop of Verona, Giammatteo Giberti, whose secretary he was. Finally he found a berth with the Cardinal Ippolito de' Medici, who obtained a canonicate for him in Florence. There he died in 1535, perhaps poisoned by Cardinal Cibo because of his refusal to poison Cardinal Salviati.

The work to which Berni devoted himself with greatest care was the reworking of the *Orlando Innamorato* of Boiardo. In a literary age such as the sixteenth century in which form counted far more than substance, a reworking or a translation might be as highly regarded as an original work; and as such Berni's work was regarded. His *Innamorato* caused the original to be forgotten for several centuries. In the sprightliness of its language and in the gracefulness and naturalness of its style, it vies with Ariosto's work. But the bantering, middle-class spirit of Berni did not feel the epic gravity of Boiardo, and the reworking sometimes seems to be a parody. Berni, moreover, does not fail to make additions to the poem of Boiardo, in which he speaks graciously and at length of himself and his character, and talks about contemporaneous events. Still more celebrated are the *rime* of Berni, which are in farcical style and written without the shadow of an effort. Berni called his style *bernesco,* and in the writings of innumerable imitators it degenerated into a sort of clumsy superficiality. In that style, Berni composed sonnets with long additions (codas or "tails" in the manner of the *sonneto caudato*) concerning persons or events in his life, many *capitoli* and also parodies, especially in the manner of Petrarch's *Trionfi* from which, and from Petrarch's *canzoniere,* whole lines are taken. These *Bernesque* poems deal with the most futile, most cunningly indecent, or the most paradoxical themes, and throughout the sprightly loquacity of the poet appears tireless. Here and there are satirical remarks. The *capitolo* on Fracastoro was very popular; in it Berni wittily tells of an unpleasant night spent in the house of a priest who forced his hospitality upon him.

Pietro Aretino

Because of the cynicism of his life and his writings, the next generation conferred upon Pietro Aretino the title of "infamous." His contemporary, Ariosto, called him "the scourge of princes" (which was, in any case, the title Pietro conferred upon himself) and the "divine Pietro Aretino." A dispassionate examination of sixteenth-century literature shows that Aretino was certainly no better, but neither was he any worse, than many men of letters of his time. He was simply more sincere or more daring. He received no culture in his youth, and he always ridiculed Latinists, Hellenists, and scholars in all sorts of ways. He came to Rome in his youth, where some verses explanatory of certain obscene sketches of the painter Giulio Romano gave him a bad reputation. In Rome he engaged in some love intrigues, in some brawls, and he got some wounds out of it all; but he learned much about court customs, and still more about popular life. He felt safer when he was serving under the famous captain, Giovanni de' Medici, popularly called Giovanni dalle Bande Nere, who died in his arms in the battle of Governolo. After the death of that patron, he settled in Venice where, famous, he lived for some thirty years. He lived in a palace; he squandered money; he was on good terms with the governing powers, which caused a gold medal to be struck off in his honor; he was a friend of artists and writers, among them Titian, who painted his portrait; and from his vantage point in Venice, he judged princes, great and small, exacting payment for both his praise and his silence. He died there in 1556.

Aretino was a prolific writer. Much of his writing was in *capitoli,* obscene *capitoli* and poems which circulated from hand to hand as they left his pen. Some of his extant poetry is on material connected with the romances of chivalry, of which the very title is an infamy. Among his most licentious and liveliest writings are the *Ragionamenti* [*Reasonings* or *Arguments*] or dialogues between low women of Rome, which very often take the form of satire directed against their male friends. His *Letters* and the *Comedies* are less obnoxious. The letters written, or rather, collected in Venice are sprightly, informative, and interesting for the history of customs of his time. The author speaks boastingly of himself, yet reveals his servility toward men holding power. His comedies are among the most original of the sixteenth century and contain little or none of the usual imitation of the Latins: *Il Marescalco* [*Farrier* or *Veterinarian*]; *La Cortigiana* [*The Courtesan*[; *L'Ipocrito* [*The Hypocrite*], which some believe suggested *Tartuffe* to Molière, but an idea now generally rejected. *Il Filosofo* [*The Philosopher*]; *La Talanta* [*Talanta,* name of leading character]. He wrote in prose, and his plots are complicated. The comedies have some very good scenes but fail in overall effect. The lower life of the servant class is especially well presented, also that of others of the lower classes. One of Aretino's tragedies has been highly praised — and also censured: *Orazia.* This is about the legend of the sister of the three Horatii, who weeps at news of the death of her lover, one of the three Curiatii, for which disloyalty she is killed by one of her brothers. The theme would later inspire the great French playwright *Corneille* in his *Hor-*

ace. But passion is lacking in Aretino's version, throughout all those endless dialogues in blank verse and all those allegorical figures. In his last years, scenting the atmosphere of the Catholic reaction, Aretino turned to ascetic literature, writing among other things, *Genesi* [*Genesis*], *Umanità del Cristo* [*Christ's Humanity*], *La Vita di Maria Vergine* [*Life of the Virgin Mary*], *Vita di San Tomaso d'Aquino* [*Life of St. Thomas Aquinas*]. They are, naturally, the least felt of his works: being full of rhetoric, humor, conceits, and bravura.

Anton Francesco Doni

No less famous than Aretino was the Florentine Anton Francesco Doni. Having put off the monkish habit, he settled in Venice, then in Florence, then again in Venice: the city where more than elsewhere the art of typography flourished. Here he was ready to publish the books of other writers and his own, which were humerous. In Venice he quarreled with Aretino, and at him he flung his *Terremoto del Doni fiorentino, colla rovina di un gran colosso bestiale, anticristo della nostra età, opera scritta ad onor di Dio e della Santa Chiesa*, etc. [*The Earthquake of the Florentine Doni, with the Ruin of a Great Bestial Colossus, the Antichrist of our Age, a Work Written to the Honor of God and of Holy Church, etc.*]. He promised to write immediately the following: *Rovina, Baleno, Tuono, Saetta, Vita, Morte, Essequie, Sepolture* [*Ruin, Lightning Flash, Thunder, Arrow, Life, Death, Obsequies, Burial*]. He did nothing about these books, nor about many other books promised and announced; such as an account of his own life, which would certainly have been interesting. Perhaps his death prevented him, striking him down at Monselice, near Padua, in 1574. The title of the pamphlet against Aretino is a sample of the striking titles that Doni affected. One of his works bears the title of *The Gourd: that is to say, Table, or Register of the Idle Gossip, Balderdash,*

Painted Scenery, Chimeras, Castles in Spain, Bits of Wisdom, Whirling and Racking of Brains, Yarns, Opinions, Lies, Weathercocks, Whims, Rigmaroles, Caprices, Nonsense, Ravings, Confusions, Fancies, Chattering, Parables, Jests, Proverbs, Sayings, Jokes, and other About-Turns and Stories. But amidst all of his many eccentricities, Doni has original and daring ideas. In *I Mondi* [*The Worlds*], he anticipates socialist doctrines; in some parts of *La Zucca* [*The Gourd*], he imagines a perfect city. In *I Marmi* [*The Marbles*], dialogues imagined to take place between some idle workers sitting on the marble steps of the cathedral of Florence, literary and moral questions are discussed with an honest good sense, which is worth of lot of philosophy. In *I Pistolotti* [*Tirades;* "purple patches"], he imagines love letters to gentlewomen of the time, especially in Venice: this is a document not to be scorned for the history of customs. In two *Librerie* [Bookstores], he gave information, not always exact, about many works of his contemporaries, which he often criticized harshly. He was the first to write in this *genre*. Doni is a prose writer of great directness, a virtue which is especially evident in the many short novellas that can be dug out from his various writings.

Benvenuto Cellini

This section will conclude with some notes on one of the mos personal and likeable writers not only in the sixteenth century but in all Italian literature, Benvenuto Cellini. This Florentine artist led a varied and strange life. He began by becoming a goldsmith in Florence, but after being condemned for brawls, he fled to Rome where he enjoyed the favor Clement VII. During the siege of 1527, he bravely defended the city from his refuge in Castel Sant'Angelo where the Pope had sought safety; it was his shot, or that of one of his men, which killed the Connétable de Bourbon. He committed two homicides in Rome: he killed the slayer of his brother and later, a Milanese goldsmith, Pompeo dei Capitani, who had succeeded in turning Clement VII against him with the consequent loss of his post as director of the mint. Paul III gave him back this position, but the hostility of the Pope's nephew, Pier Luigi Farnese, was so effective that Benvenuto was arrested and imprisoned in Castel Sant'Angelo, from which he managed to escape. But in the jump from the high wall, he fractured a leg and was recaptured. The intervention of a French cardinal resulted in his freedom, and he thereupon went to France, where he remained for some years in the service of Francis I, at Fontainebleau; he executed for the king some enormous candelabras representing the principal ancient deities. Having offended the king's favorite, Madame d'Etampes, by a certain freedom of language, he thought the time was ripe for him to return to Italy, where he entered the service of Duke Cosimo. Conflict with another of the duke's artists, Baccio Bandinello (or, as he called him, *Buaccio* [Ugly Ox], and financial difficulties saddened those years, which should have been the most glorious of his life. He even thought of becoming a priest. He died in 1571, having passed his seventieth birthday. Little remains of his artistic creation, for the labors he interrupted in his agitated and roving life are more numerous than those he completed. His masterpiece is the Perseus, in bronze, which now stands in the Loggia dei Lanzi: it is a marvel of grace and strength. He was no less an artist with the pen than with the burin and the chisel. His *Life,* dictated in his later years and published without revision at the beginning of the eighteenth century, is outstanding in narrative vigor, in movement and action, and in richness and aptness of language. The syntactical errors, the anacoluthia or lack of grammatical sequence in some of the sentences, frequent in a speaker, increase the warmth of the ingenuous and dramatic story. The telling of the exorcisms in which Cellini took part in Naples, the defense of Rome, the escape from the castle, the mystical visions in his prison cell, the tribulations suffered in France, and the casting of the Perseus, are some of the many admirable passages of the book which has a singular value in the history of art. Art was the sole constant force in the life of Cellini, and he speaks often of the lives and works of the artists of his time: such as his adored Michelangelo.

The End of the Sixteenth Century Humanism Comes to a Standstill in Its Most Vital Elements: The Catholic Restoration

Italian literature in the second half of the sixteenth century is something quite different from what it was in the first decades of the century; not so much in appearances as in its animating spirit. The first thirty-year period closes with the fall of Florence to the united forces of Clement VII and Charles V; less than twenty years later the peace of Castel Cambresis, in 1559, gave the greater part of Italy to Spain. At first this was followed by protest of the Italian conscience, especially in the pages of the historians; then came resignation, indifference, and oblivion. Finally political liberty, awareness of the fatherland, was lacking and with it the oxygen of a truly national literature. The Church, which in the beginning had either favored or tolerated the humanistic movement, now saw in that movement a critical spirit that had strengthened the Protestant revolution and introduced speculative freedom. It set about repairing its position and became the hub of a vast restoration, for which the world was feeling the need after fifty years of political and religious wars.

This restoration was not only religious but moral, philosophical, and political. It started with the Council of Trent between 1545 and 1563, with various interruptions and renewals. Representatives from the Protestant churches were invited to participate, in the hope of finding a mutual agreement concerning the beliefs that were not only disturbing men's spirits but causing Europe to be devastated. The Protestants did not attend, and the Council became merely an examination and affirmation of Catholic discipline and dogmas. It engaged in laudable deliberations that aimed at improving the fallen dignity of the priesthood. To prevent the spread of ideas potentially harmful to the credo and tradition, the Council founded the Congregation of the Index which, with the valid help of the civil authority, would prevent the printing, dissemination, and keeping of condemned books. Besides the books of religious controversy in support of Protestant ideas, all or almost all the historians and philosophers of the humanistic age were placed on the Index, including all of Machiavelli's works. Writings that denied temporal sovereignty to the Papacy, such as Dante's *De Monarchia,* were prohibited, as were those deploring the corruption of the Church, such as Petrarch's *Epistulae sine titulo.* Every possibility for scandalizing the minds of the common people was suppressed.

It is needless to say how greatly freedom of thought and inquiry suffered under the new institution and how free thought from then on found its upholders in Holland, Germany, and Switzerland, countries that had freed themselves from Catholic influence. In Italy and Spain, imprisonment and the stake remained the cures for free thought, the Inquisition having been restored in all its former severity. But the Church felt that severity was no longer enough, and that it was necessary both to win back those classes that humanistic culture had estranged from it and to preserve all that was possible of that culture without damage to the new order of thought and affairs. The Society of Jesus took upon itself the duty of keeping the ruling classes within the faith, forbidding a morality too compliant to mundane demands and too yielding to the sophistries of conscience. The Jesuits aimed principally at the schools, because tomorrow is shaped in the schools. The secondary schools, or as they were then called schools of the humanities, and the universities, after much opposition, fell almost entirely into their power. Humanism lost its vitality and continued on in those schools with a merely apparent splendor. It was oratory, it was erudition, it was technique; it was not poetry, art, or philosophy.

Torquato Tasso

His Life

The poet who best represents the spirit and the art of the restoration in the second half of the sixteenth century, with all that the age could still give or permit that was magnificent and alive, was Torquato Tasso. The son of the prolific poet discussed above, Bernardo, secretary of the Neapolitan Prince Roberto di Sanseverino, Torquato was born at Sorrento in 1544. The contemplative spirit and the philosophic and reasoning spirit of the Southerners was innate in him, just as the musicality and sonority of his poetry are characteristic of the Southern poets. He was educated by the Jesuits in Naples. When the Prince of Sanseverino was exiled from the Kingdom of Naples because of his support of the Neapolitan people, who were opposed to the Inquisition, Bernardo left Naples and his son followed him to Rome. He left his mother, Porzia dei Rossi, behind in Naples: she died there, perhaps poisoned by her brothers who did not want her husband to get her dowry. Torquato accompanied his adored father to Urbino; then he settled in Padua to study jurisprudence. There he knew Scipione Gonzaga and also the grave Sperone Speroni, who guided him into Platonic philosophy without, however, assuaging certain violent religious doubts that Torquato confessed having suffered from childhood. In Padua, with the enthusiasm of his eighteen years, he brought forth his poem of chivalry, *Rinaldo*, which he dedicated to Cardinal Luigi d'Este, brother of Alfonso II, Duke of Ferrara. The Cardinal accepted the dedication and rewarded the poet, admitting him, several years later, to his court in the capacity of gentleman. When he made a visit to his cousin, King Charles IX of France, he took Torquato with him. In France, however, Tasso was too observant and too talkative. It was thought better to send him back to Italy; for he was lacking in that virtue which is most necessary in courtiers and diplomats, and most rare in poets, tact. Then he entered the service of Alfonso II, to whom he had dedicated his *Gerusalemme*. In that court glory was awaiting him; it burst upon him quickly and fully when, in 1573, his pastoral drama *Aminta* was presented. Love was also awaiting him. Legend, which mediocre poets (and great ones like Goethe, in his drama *Torquato Tasso*) made their own, would have it that Tasso fell in love with Eleonora d'Este, the duke's sister, or with another sister, Lucrezia. In truth he wrote poems for both, as earlier he had written some for Eleonora Sanvitali, countess of Scandiano and a lady of the court, and also for Lucrezia Bendidio, a lady of Ferrara. It is probable that Tasso did not love this lady or that, but many fair women, as may be concluded from his many and varied love poems. He loved the elegant feminine intimacies of the courts. His loves were not returned in kind or were rejected, perhaps because they were aimed too high. The theme of the ardent but unsuccessful lover occurs too often in Tasso's production to be a merely literary theme.

His extreme sensitivity, his intense activity and wholehearted anxiety concerning the *Gerusalemme Liberata*, which was already completed two years after the *Aminta*, in 1575, weakened the poet's spirit. He sent single cantos to friends and men of letters; possibly he wanted to create a completely favorable atmosphere for his poem before publishing it. Fully conscious of his poetic worth, he appeared to be seeking counsel, but he expected praise; instead, he often received censure. He thanked his critics, he confuted them, but his pride and his self-confidence were hurt. Besides, he suffered constantly from religious scruples, to such a degree that with his mania for self-accusation and for confession, he became bothersome even to the Inquisition fathers. Tasso's religiousness was the sort of piety that brings no inward comfort, does not overcome sensuality and pride, does not accustom one to accept with serenity good things or, still less, the bad; it was the utterly outward, formal religiousness of the Catholic restoration. These weaknesses and anxieties gradually caused strange manifestations in Tasso: egomania, which made the poet believe that all eyes were fixed on him; a persecution mania, which is a natural concomitant of egomania; inability to exert the will; the inexplicable delay in publishing the *Gerusalemme,* which was eagerly awaited and would have brought the author extraordinary popularity and glory; and generally perplexing behavior. Tasso's life soon became a life without plan or program. He negotiated secretly with the court of the Medici, strongly opposed to the Este family, just when Alfonso appointed him historiographer of his house. One evening, during a conversation with Princess Lucrezia, he had an idea that a servant was spying on him, and he hurled a dagger at the man. He was shut up in the monastery of San Francesco and cared for as mentally ill. He escaped and made his way on foot to Rome, and from Rome to Sorrento (1577) to see his sister Cornelia; he accosted her without revealing his identity and, with the cruelty of the egoist, informed her that Torquato was dead. When she fainted, he felt that she still loved him, and he spent some months with her. The splendor of the courts had become an obsession with him. He went back to Rome, where he persuaded the

Chevalier Gualengo, Alfonso's ambassador to the Pope, to obtain the Duke's pardon in his behalf. Then he returned to Ferrara.

He left Ferrara soon after his arrival there. This time he headed for Turin (1579) and arrived there in such a shabby condition that at the city gates the officials on duty took him for a vagabond and would not let him pass. Fortunately a friend of his, a literary man named Angelo Ingegneri, caught sight of him. He was permitted to enter Turin; he was introduced to the Marquis Filippo d'Este, and presented at court. Duke Carlo Emanuele offered him a place on his staff, with the same remuneration as at Ferrara. By now, however, the life of the poet had become such that he fled Ferrara only to lament it: when he was there, he found the city intolerable; when he was far away, it fascinated him. Once more he went back. Alfsonso II was celebrating his third marriage, this one with Margherita Gonzaga, the daughter of the Duke of Mantova. Obviously, the whole court was occupied with these festivities and had no time to pay much attention to the poet. This seeming indifference drove him into a blinding rage. He burst into invectives against the Duke, and the Duke had him shut up in the asylum of Sant'Anna. He let it be known that he had no wish to punish him, only to cure him. The cure was rather long: seven years, from 1579 to 1586, of a detention very similar to imprisonment.

The reasons that led the Duke to such severity can only be surmised. The opinion that it was a matter of offended honor on the Duke's part is no longer held. One modern scholar has suggested the hypothesis that Tasso, the fervent Catholic, might have disclosed to the Inquisition the heretical currents that perhaps still lurked and spread in Ferrara, which would have been an excellent pretext for the Pope to occupy that city (as he did, in 1598, but for other reasons). The Pope already governed Bologna, and therefore perhaps it was thought wise to keep the poet under surveillance. Perhaps the Duke was not entirely unreasonably offended by the conduct of Tasso who, getting himself welcomed by other courts, came to cast discredit on the Duke, representing himself as a victim. In any case, it is singular that even in that "hospital" Tasso was busy writing and indeed composed his most lucid dialogues, while he believed that he was having visions and that he was in communication with a genii who disarranged his books and robbed him. While the author was incarcerated, his *Gerusalemme* was published (1581) without his knowledge and against his will. The poem aroused violent polemics. A certain Camillo Pellegrini of Capua had the inappropriate idea, in a *Dialogo sulla poesia epica* [*Dialogue on Epic Poetry*] to state his preference for Tasso over Ariosto. He did not understand — and it was only understood much later — that one poet is substantially different from the other one and that each has his own great qualities of beauty. It was the signal for a battle. The Academia della Crusca had just arisen in Florence; its purpose was, in the beginning, and it continued to be, that of separating the flour or meal — in words — from the bran [*crusca*]; that is to say, the Tuscan and pure words from the non-Tuscan and nonpure. Tasso was not a Tuscan, and he had written some strong things against the Tuscans in his dialogues. The Florentines Bastiano De Rossi, under the pseudonym of *Inferrigno,* and Leonardo Salviati, known as *Infarinato,* both founders of the Crusca, together with some others [among whom it is unpleasant to record the then very young Galileo Galilei, whose *Osservazioni* were not to be published until the eighteenth century], set upon both Pellegrini and Tasso; the latter entered the fight by writing a rather sophistical *Apologia* [*Defence*]. But the public, unconcerned with academies, from one end of Italy to the other admired the *Gerusalemme,* and the admiration was the greater the more the critics found fault. One year after that *Apologia,* in 1586, Tasso was released. In vain, powerful princes, among them Emperor Rudolph of Austria and Pope Gregory XIII, had interceded on his behalf. In vain the city of Bergamo, from which the Tasso family came originally, had sent ambassadors to the Duke. Finally Prince Vincenzo Gonzaga overcame all obstacles and carried the poet off with him to Mantua.

There Tasso was received with the greatest honors. To Prince Vincenzo, when the latter acceded to the throne, he dedicated a tragedy he had composed some years previously, *Torrismondo,* an intolerably prolix play more elaborate than beautiful, more narrative and descriptive than dramatic. But henceforth Tasso was no longer Tasso. No matter where he went, he could not find peace or rest. Naturally he never returned to Ferrara. From Mantua he fled to Rome, going by way of Loreto where he was released from a vow in that sanctuary of the Virgin. In Rome he was close to his faithful friend Cardinal Scipione Gonzaga. One day, exhausted from lack of nourishment, he fell down in Via della Pietra and was succored by a confraternity of Bergamasks (natives of Bergamo). He went to Naples and started a suit for the recovery of his mother's dowry. Perhaps he was satiated with depending on others for his living. In any case, he obtained no satisfaction. In Naples he was much honored. The Marquis Giovanni Battista Manso (who was the first to write a biography of the poet) received him as a guest; in gratitude Tasso dedicated to this friend's mother a sacred poem, *Le Sette giornate del mondo creato* [*The Seven Days of the Creation*]. In that noisy city, he preferred the solitude of the monks of Mount Olivet to the more elegant society available to him; he presented to the monks another sacred poem (unfinished) aptly entitled *Monte Oliveto.* It is painful to see how coldly, by this time, the poet was writing verse, from habit, from inertia, in gratitude, or from a sense of obligation.

Grand Duke Ferdinando de'Medici insisted that Torquato stay with him in Florence. Now there was competition among the princes to honor the victim of the lordly Este family. So the poet went to Florence, where he had the joy, if anything could still give him joy, of seeing himself honored by the academicians of the Crusca. Finally the two nephews of Clement VIII, the Cardinals Pietro and Cintio Aldobrandini, insisted that he return to Rome; to the latter he dedicated the tiresome and pedantic reworking of the *Jerusalem Delivered,* the *Gerusalemme Conquistata* [*Jerusalem Conquered*]. He was lodged sumptuously in the Vatican. The Pope weighed the idea of conferring the final honor upon him: coronation on the *Campidoglio* [Capitoline Hill]. It was only just that the Pope should award the highest prize to the greatest poet of the Catholic Restoration; but by now Torquato had become indifferent to this new glory, which had for so many years been his rapt dream. Religion was now his only concern. The ceremony was postponed on account of inclement weather. Meanwhile the poet was overcome by his extreme physical exhaustion. He was transferred to the monastery of Sant'Onofrio on the Janiculum. There he died in April 1595; he was only fifty-one years old, but he seemed a very old man.

The Minor Works of Tasso

Tasso was one of the most prolific writers of his time and, in appearance at least, one of the most diversified. It may be said of him that throughout his lifetime he was a lyric poet, a poet of love, or more particularly, of deference toward women and of gallantry; especially so in his youth and when serving at court. He was also a poet of panegyric and heroic *canzoni* in praise of his Estense masters and of the various lords who sheltered him. In his last years, he was the poet of fervent and melancholy religious poetry. Noteworthy among his many lyrics, and in order of composition, were the original *canzone* to the Montagnola lady in Ferrara; the fragment of an autobiographical canzone to the Duke of Urbino; the canzone written from prison to the Estense princesses and the one to the Madonna of Loreto. In general, however, in the numerous lyrics of Tasso there is little novelty; emotion is limited, and technique, bravura, and artifice often replace inspiration.

Aminta is a cherished youthful fantasy: a love drama in five acts woven over the old pastoral poetry, and written to the most rigid requirements of unity of time and place. Silvia, the heroine, is a shepherdess no less beautiful than she is shy and reluctant. Aminta, a shepherd, is mad about her, but she does not appear even to notice it. The counsels of Daphne, a more practiced shepherdess, that Silvia should yield to love, fall on unheeding ears. Nor are matters advanced when Aminta saves Silvia from the attack of a satyr. She will have nothing to do with shepherds and proposes to become a huntress, not of men, but of wild animals. One day she pursues a wolf into a wood; her arrow misses its mark, striking a tree instead of the beast and, in her flight from it, she leaves her scarf entangled in the branches of a tree. Nerina, on coming into the wood, sees the scarf and sees seven wolves licking the bloody turf; he believes that Silvia has been devoured and carries the news to the shepherds. Aminta, when he hears this, rushes off to end his own life. But Silvia, when she learns of Aminta's violent plan, feels that she loves him. When the old shepherd Ergasto enters to report having seen Aminta cast himself off a cliff, indeed reports having vainly tried to restrain him by clutching his belt only to find that the belt had failed to hold around Aminta's waist, the girl decides to do away with herself. First she wants to give her lover proper burial. Then Elpino comes to announce to the audience that Aminta is not dead. In his fall, he was caught by a clump of grasses, thorns, and branches protruding from the cliff, and so the force of his fall was diminished. The young man, to be sure, had appeared as one dead, but had recovered consciousness. Silvia rewarded his long and despairing love. Making due allowance for the poetic genre, utterly false in itself, the *Aminta* is weak in psychology and artificial in more than one phase, but taken as a whole, it is warm in its sense of love, refreshing in its imagery, and fascinatingly melodious. The sincerity of the poetry also is due to the fact that the poet, behind the transparent curtains of pastoral poetry, sketches the milieu of the court of Ferrara with himself as the spurned lover in the character of Aminta, the favorite poet of the Estensi in the character of the other shepherd Tirsi [Thyrsis], and Speroni in the dark figure of the shepherd Mopso.

Tasso wanted to try his hand at tragedy as well, and he left one, thought out in the first years of his sojourn in Ferrara but completed much later: *Torrismondo,* mentioned above, a tragedy whose basic themes were derived from Sophocles' *Oedipus Rex*. In his last years, he wrote a religious poem in blank verse, *Le Sette Giornate* [*The Seven Days*] which, through continuous moral and theological wanderings, narrates the creation of the world.

The great pride and purpose of Tasso was to give Italy its heroic poem in the manner of the ancients, which would still preserve the lightness and the charms of the knightly romances. While a youth of eighteen, he tried it with his *Rinaldo,* a poem in twelve cantos in *ottava rima,* some of them quite admirable. The theme of the poem was the deeds and the loves of Rinaldo, in love wih beautiful Clarice and tempted by the still more beautiful Floriana. But above all Rinaldo is, like the young author, greedy for glory. While still young, in the happiest years of his inspiration, Tasso composed the *Gerusalemme libe-*

rata [*Jerusalem Delivered*], his masterpiece. He spent many years of his life making corrections on it and then reworking it with the name of *Gerusalemme conquistata* [*Jerusalem Conquered*], an occupation in which he turned himself into a pedant to win the approval of his pedantic friends. Then he imitated Homer still more and dimmed every glimmer of poetry — a veritable suicide. The world punished him by its oblivion to the *Conquistata* in favor of the *Liberata*.

In treatises, such as the one on the heroic poem, and in many *Dialogues* in the Platonic manner, Tasso discussed literary, and moral questions and longed to be considered a philosopher. In those dignified pages, however, there is no boldness of thought, and Tasso's prose writings might rather be considered the credo of the religious, moral, political, and courtly restoration. Much finer, that is to say warmer, in soulful qualities are his many *Letters;* they are interesting material for the outward and inner life of the poet. They cast light on aspects of that troubled soul that are more human and sometimes, for that very reason, less attractive. A long letter to his friend Scipione Gonzaga is noteworthy; in it he tells of the religious doubts that troubled him from his early youth; also noteworthy is one to Maurizio Cattaneo written from his prison of Sant'Anna in which he speaks of devilish visions that disturb him, and heavenly ones that console him. The many letters concerning the correcting of the poem are interesting. Among the most moving is the letter in which, from Sant'Onofrio, he sends word to his friend Antonio Costantino, in Mantua, that death is imminent. Now all utterance of the old man yields to silence, and the poet grows calm in thinking of death and God. But now let us come to a consideration of that *Gerusalemme liberata* which for centuries was considered the most perfect of heroic poems, not only in Italy but in all western Europe.

The Gerusalemme Liberata
The Argument of the Poem

The war of the First Crusade, the great attempt to recapture the sepulcher of Christ from the Turks, had been going on for six years. The Crusaders, under the leadership of Godfrey of Bouillon, had already won Nicaea, Antioch, Damascus, and Ascalon in Asia Minor but had stopped. God decides that the war should be quickly begun anew and fought to the end. Godfrey [Goffredo], to whom an angel announces the divine will, gathers his commanders, inspects his army, and advances on Jerusalem. The king of the city, the cruel Aladino, [Tasso's proper names will usually be used in this exposition] prepares to defend it. On the advice of a renegade Christian, the sorcerer Ismeno, he causes a miraculous image to be stolen from a Christian church and set up in the mosque. It is a statue of the Virgin, which, strangely enough, when placed in that mosque, would protect the city and the Muhammedan religion. But the image is carried away from the mosque by an unknown, but certainly Christian, hand. Aladino, like a new Herod, orders that all the Christians shall be killed: thus the guilty person will surely be punished. Then the saintlike virgin Sophronia, to avert the massacre of her co-religionists, comes forward as the guilty one. Her young lover Olindo also offers himself as guilty of the theft, as he cannot bear to see his beloved perish. It would be pleasing, for the honor of the Christians, that the real thief should reveal himself and face martyrdom. Not knowing whether the guilty person is Sophronia or Olindo, the king condemns them both to the flames. But Clorinda, a female warrior who has come all the way from Persia to defend Jerusalem, arrives at the crucial moment; she takes pity on the two young people and succeeds in obtaining their freedom. Thus they pass from the stake to a wedding and on into exile.

Meanwhile, the Crusaders have reached Emmaus, a days' march from Jerusalem. Two emissaries from the king of Egypt reach Godfrey: Alete and Argante. Alete is an accomplished diplomat, and Argante, a rough man of violence; it is hard to understand why he is engaged on a diplomatic mission. In the name of his king, an ally of Aladino of Jerusalem, Alete tries to persuade the captain not to go ahead with his undertaking: he should rest on his laurels, not provoke the intervention of the king of Egypt. "Our hope is in Christ," responds Godfrey, "and we would all be happy to die for Him." War is declared against the king of Egypt also, to the great joy of Argante who, having become an enemy instead of an emissary, goes straight to Jerusalem, the sooner to get into the fight, leaving Alete to return alone to his king.

The next morning the Crusaders come within sight of Jerusalem; they shout for joy and bewailing their sins, advance on the city. From a tower of the city, Erminia, daughter of the king of Antioch, points out to the king the Christian warriors, especially Tancred, whose prisoner she had been and with whom she had fallen timidly but fervently in love. Tancred rides up to the walls: Clorinda comes out to meet him, but when he has struck off her helmet with a blow of his lance, he recognizes her as the beauty he had once seen cooling her forehead at a fountain; he veers off and goes to attack others. Argante has also sallied forth. Tancred, Rinaldo, and Dudone sweep down on him and Dudone, leader of the unattached knights (free knights, not subject to any lord), dies. Rinaldo rushes up to avenge him, but Godfrey calls back the too daring ones. He gives thought to the problem of carrying on a regular siege of the city and sends soldiers to cut down a forest to get material for constructing siege-works.

Satan, of course, is not asleep. He assembles his subjects and exhorts them to come up out of Hell to lay snares of all sorts for the Christians and ward off the attack. The demons spread out through the world. One of them visits Idraote, a sorcerer and king of Damascus, to suggest to him that he should send his niece, beautiful Armida, to charm and distract as many of the crusaders as she can. Armida appears among the Crusaders and she sets them afire! She experiences no resistance against feminine attractions on the part of the warriors of Christ. When she is in contact with Godfrey, Armida claims to be a victim of her uncle, who has usurped the throne of Damascus, made an attempt on her life, and forced her to flee. She begs to be restored to her native land; ten warriors would be enough for the coup, a mere ten knights. The captain refuses to grant her request; his first obligation is to take Jerusalem. But the Crusaders do not share his opinion, especially the unattached knights. Eustazio [Eustace], although he is Godfrey's brother, swears he will no longer draw his sword unless he is permitted to defend an oppressed virgin. The commander-in-chief has equal good sense and weakness: he yields, but on condition that the ten be chosen from the ranks of the unattached knights. The first order of business is to appoint a commander of those knights to replace the slain Dudone. Rinaldo aspires to the high honor. Another aspirant is Gernando, prince of Norway, who, prodded by one of the devils, publicly insults his rival. Rinaldo simply kills him. Godfrey sends officers to imprison him; Rinaldo would kill the emissaries without compunction, but counseled by Tancred, he goes off to see Bohemond in Antioch, and Godfrey declares Rinaldo banished. Then the unattached warriors draw lots to determine which of them shall be the ten to accompany Armida, but that fair maiden had seduced many more who secretly follow along behind.

Argante can no longer remain inside the walls. He has come out of the city and sent challenges to the Christian knights. Tancred accepts. The two opposing armies stand watching. Clorinda, too, is watching from a high spot. Tancred becomes aware of her and becomes almost paralyzed. Young Ottone rides ahead of Tancred so he is easily unhorsed by Argante, but then Tancred resumes his attack fiercely. Night interrupts the duel, which is to be resumed in the morning, and Tancred, wounded, is helped back to his own side. Erminia, who has followed the action with her eyes and her heart, fears that Tancred is seriously wounded and decides to go and nurse him. In order to pass through the guards, she puts on Clorinda's armor, rides out of the city with a faithful retainer, and sends him to inform Tancred that a lady wishes to visit him. While she waits alone, she is mistaken for Clorinda by some Christian sentinels who had been posted to prevent any supplies from entering Jerusalem, they ride toward her. She flees through a forest all that night and the following day, until, unrecognized, she finds peace and shelter with an old shepherd. Surmising that the woman who had asked for him and who he knows is being pursued is Clorinda, Tancred secretly leaves camp to find her. He is caught and imprisoned in a solitary castle where Armida had already shut up his followers. In the morning, Argante reappears in accordance with the agreement to continue the duel, but Tancred is not there. Argante breaks out in insults against the absent knight, but no one dares to face him. Thereupon Godfrey himself accepts the challenge; so does old Count Raimond of Toulouse and, shamed, many younger warriors. Lots are cast, and chance favors the old count. An invisible angel comes down from heaven to defend him; and to everyone's astonishment, Argante is wounded, while Raimond stands unharmed. Then one of the pagans shoots an arrow at the old warrior. The truce between the two camps is broken and the battle becomes general. The Christians try to force their way into Jerusalem, but the devils stir up a tempest to strike them in the face and force them to retreat.

A survivor brings into camp the news of the heroic death of Sveno and his whole company, who had come from far-away Denmark to help the Crusaders. The survivor brings with him the dead man's sword which, by God's will, is to be given to Rinaldo. With it Rinaldo is to kill the man who killed Sveno; that is to say, Solimano, the defeated King of Nicaea. In the pay of the king of Egypt, he is scouring the country around Jerusalem at the head of a band of Arab robbers, preventing food supplies as well as reinforcements, from reaching the Crusaders. Always invisible, he is impossible to capture as he creates terror. A strong desire grows in the camp for Rinaldo who is far away. Then comes another piece of dire news. Rinaldo's arms have been found and are being brought in. During the night Argillano, influenced by one of the demons, becomes certain that Rinaldo has been slain out of jealousy by Godfrey. He stirs up the camp against their leader, who restores them to a sense of homage and respect merely by showing himself; he condemns Argillano to death. In the night, the former king of Nicaea unexpectedly attacks the crusaders. A panic ensues. Argillano hurries to rehabilitate his name and perishes at the hands of Solimano. The Christians are in flight, for the infernal spirits are with Solimano, but the archangel Michael comes down to help the Christians, and a squad of fifty unknown warriors wins the victory. The band of Arabs is broken at last. Solimano, defeated but not crushed, is miraculously transported by the sorcerer Ismeno into Jerusalem. There a council was being held, and everyone except Argante and Clorinda was in favor of surrender. The appearance of Solimano restores everyone's courage.

Meanwhile, the fifty unknown knights had revealed their identity. They are Tancred and the many whom

Armida had imprisoned in her castle, ordering them to deny Christ. All of them had refused, except Rambaldo. Heavily chained, they had then been sent as a gift to the king of Egypt, but on the way Rinaldo had come up and freed them. So Rinaldo is alive and heading for Antioch. He has discarded his arms, which were broken in that great battle. The desire to have him back increases among the Christians. Godfrey, after a pious procession to Mount Olivet, begins the siege. A formidable assault tower is brought up, object of the anger of the besieged. The rams strike the lower part of the wall. Godfrey fulfills the roles of leader and of soldier, but he is forced to withdraw when an arrow wounds him in the leg. Solimano and Argante sally through a breach that has been opened in the wall. It would go hard with the Christians, if Tancred did not instill new courage in his knights, if Godfrey, miraculously healed, did not reappear upon the field, and if darkness did not fall to force a truce to arms. In the dark, Clorinda and Argante come out to set fire to the conquering tower and are successful in their bold mission. The Crusaders, awakened, press the reckless pair right up to the walls. Solimano opens the gates, forces back the enemy, and welcomes Argante back; but Clorinda, who had turned around to strike back an attacker, is left shut out of the city. Then she pretends to be one of the Christians and rides around the walls looking for another gate. Tancred, who of course does not recognize her, notices her and follows her. He wishes to try his luck against one whom he takes to be a most valorous warrior; after a long duel, he strikes her down. Clorinda, who, before this last undertaking, had learned from a servant that she had been born a Christian, the daughter of Senapo, king of Ethiopia, requests the knight to baptize her as she lies dying. Tancred hastens to perform the pious act, but when he removes her helmet, he recognizes the woman he loves; he too would die of sorrow but for the consolations of the holy hermit Peter, and of Clorinda herself, who appears to him from Heaven where she is now one of the blessed. Now the Christians are obliged to build another tower for the assault. The captain sends men to cut the trees in a forest; but the sorcerer Ismeno has populated it with devils: the soldiers sent there hear shrieks and roars and flee, terrified. Unbelieving, Alcasto penetrates the forest and comes back thoroughly frightened; he has seen a wall of flame, the infernal city, rise up before him. Tancred volunteers to enter the wood, but the trees speak to him in moans; he hears the voice of Clorinda speak to him from one trunk; he too comes back cowed.

The moment is critical, the more so as a great drought oppresses the Christians, who are dying of thirst and hunger. Many desert the camp. However, God sends rain in answer to Godfrey's prayers and also inspires him to send out a party to look for Rinaldo, who alone can overcome the enchanted wood. Carlo, the survivor of Sveno's squad, and old Ubaldo volunteer to seek Rinaldo in Antioch. Peter the Hermit sends them instead to Ascalon, where an old Christian sorcerer informs them that Rinaldo is with Armida in one of the Fortunate Islands in the Atlantic. He teaches them how to overcome the spells laid upon the place and sends them off in the care of a young woman helmsman who looks like Fortune and rapidly takes them across the Mediterranean to the happy island. First frights, then delights of the senses await Carlo and Ubaldo, who are victorious over them all. They discover Rinaldo in a marvelous garden, resting on the bosom of Armida. When she leaves, the two armed warriors come forward. Ubaldo holds out a shining shield to Rinaldo, who sees himself in it and is overcome by shame. The warrior is born again in the softened lover. Ubaldo's admonitions are unnecessary, for Rinaldo wants to depart at once. Armida returns, hopelessly in love with Rinaldo; she urges him to remain or take her with him. He courteously refuses and leaves. Then the girl flies through the air in her chariot, after having sent up in smoke the garden that had been made by magic. From her castle she flies to the army of Egypt, expected soon at Gaza to move against the crusaders. Magnificent in her chariot, she asks to be received among the warriors; they will be the ones to avenge her of the insult inflicted on her by Rinaldo. Fired by her appeal, Adrasto and Tissaferne swear to fight for her, who had never appeared more proud and beautiful.

Rinaldo and the two knights are brought back to the old sorcerer by the girl helmsman; Rinaldo gets new armor, receives the sword of Sveno from Carlo, and the sorcerer foretells the glory of his descendants who become the lords of Este. Then he drives the knights to the Christian camp in an invisible chariot lessening the boredom of the journey (and increasing it in the reader) with the most sycophantic predictions about the future lords of Este and especially about Alfonso II, Tasso's patron. Now the action speeds up. Rinaldo succeeds in freeing the forest from spells, after a fervent prayer at dawn has made him worthy of divine grace. New and more powerful assault machines are built. A dove pursued by a hawk takes refuge in Godfrey's lap, and from a note found attached to its neck he learns that the Egyptian army is on the march. Speed is required. There follows a general assault on the walls of Jerusalem; after a long struggle, victory belongs to the Christians, who invade the city and slaughter the enemy.

Argante still resists, and he challenges Tancred, with whom he has an old score to settle. Tancred goes outside the walls with him, faces him, and kills him; but he has lost so much blood that he falls inanimate. Erminia meanwhile had been surprised in her pastoral retreat by Egyptian knights and had been sent as a gift to the Emireno, the leader of those troops. There she was surprised by

Vafrino, a Christian spy in the Egyptian camp, and had been taken back to Jerusalem. She comes upon Tancred; she believes him to be dead, but with most tender embraces she brings him back to life. On news received from the spy Vafrino, it is easy for Godfrey to face and defeat the Egyptian army, which has now reached Jerusalem. Godfrey kills the Emireno. Solimano, who had shut himself up with Aladino in the fortress of David, sallies forth for a last attack on the Christians and is killed by Rinaldo; while Aladino, remaining in the fortress, is killed by Rinaldo in his exhausting effort to take the stronghold. At last Rinaldo plants the great Christian standard on the summit. Armida was in the camp of the Egyptians. When she sees that all is lost, she considers suicide and indeed is picking out her sharpest arrow. But Rinaldo comes up behind her, dissuades her from her dire idea, and begs her to become a Christian. And she answers: "Here is your handmaid."

Artistry and Meaning of the *"Gerusalemme"*

I have wished to give the plot of the twenty cantos of the *Liberata* with a certain fullness, so that even from this outline the reader may see the organic unity and proportion of the parts and at the same time the simple yet imposing structure of the whole work. For a greater sense of measure and verisimilitude, the heroic poem should be different from the chivalric romance. That the *Gerusalemme* is in spirit a poem of chivalry is of course not very important (love affairs have no less a part in it than fighting). It matters still less that the narration is not historical except for the principal names and events and recreates nothing of the part warlike, partly fanatical and wild ambience of the Crusades, even though historical content and coloring are usually required of the heroic poem. In a work of poetry the poet expresses that which is related to his soul and to the spiritual currents of his times —

and Tasso was truly a man of his times. In the age of the Catholic restoration, when all Christian Europe had drawn together for a final effort against the Turks, terminating in the unfortunately vain victory of Lepanto in 1571, the extolling of the First Crusade, the first great Catholic expedition against those same Turks, was not just the result of research and considerations on a theme rich in literary interest. Thus the *Gerusalemme* is a document of the formalistically and not substantially religious spirit of the Catholic counter-reformation. The religiousness of the poem is altogether external: it reduces to processions, preachings, and acts of contrition; it does not in the least suppress sensuality, although expression of it is more modest, or more hypocritical, than in Ariosto. In his invoking of his muse, whom many take to be the Virgin Mary, the poet ingenuously asks her pardon for having included in his work other pleasures than those purely spiritual, for "the world runs" [*corre il mondo*] to those delights. The poet of restored Catholicism writes for the world, for people, and for the pleasure of the cultured classes who still had in their ears the joyous Epicurean stanzas of the *Furioso*.

Even though they make a great deal of noise, the heroic characters of the poem are weak. Rinaldo passes too easily from avenging fury to lustful love, to forgetfulness of woman and to religiousness. Tancred is too languid in his love. Argante is too blustering, Aladino too ferocious: they are conventional types. Godfrey has his mouth full of words of wisdom and austere precepts, but he is not a character; he is a negative figure. In his indomitable thirst for vengeance on the Christians, Solimano is noble, perhaps because he does not appear much in the action; he is felt rather than seen. The women are more alive than the men except for the female warrior Clorinda, who has nothing feminine about her except her name. She is far inferior to Bradamante, who has nothing of the warrior except her arms and her courage. Erminia is sweet and gentle; Armida burning with passion, although she is too given to declamation. Often Tasso tries for an effect, as is apparent in the famous council of the demons. Sometimes he has the virtues of a magnificent orator, more than those of a poet. He speaks as though from a stage and declaims more than he speaks. His style is always lofty and magnificent; he likes to see only the most striking and showy aspect of things. Epithets and pairs of verbs and adjectives of similar meanings abound; his thought is never expressed with the precision and clarity of Ariosto. Some quality — passion, warmth, or softness — unusual in the poetry of the sixteenth century flows through Tasso's strophes. Underneath the characters and behind the heroic situations, the poet appears with his loves, his travails, and his weary desire for peace and rest. There is something autobiographical about the *Gerusalemme;* it is less and more than a work of pure art. It speaks to the heart and feeling. Therefore, it rapidly became popular and caused the *Furioso* to be forgotten, though the latter has considerably more artistic merit. The full sonority of the Tasso stanzas — which rather quickly fatigues the refined ears of today's moderns — contributed in large part to the success of the poem in an age when nothing of poetry was left alive but the sound; an age in which, in fact, the first works of music were being created. In that fascinating wave, the many stylistic artifices and devices passed almost unnoticed: the witty remarks, the plays on words, which later would rage in the poetry of the seventeenth century.

Other Writers of the Second Half of the Sixteenth Century

Poets

Tasso's *Aminta* found many imitators: the poetry, filled with conventionalities, lasciviousness and music, was what was most fitting to the Italian soul of the time of the Restoration and servitude. Giambattista Guarino (d. 1612) was highly successful in that genre; he was a courtier, like Tasso in the service of Duke Alfonso II. Then when Ferrara fell to the Pope, he was in the service of the Grand Duke of Tuscany. His tragicomedy, *Il Pastor fido* [*The Faithful Shepherd*], does not have the simplicity of line of the *Aminta*; it is complicated by motifs taken from the Sophocle's *Oedipus*. The characters speak a lofty language and there is an inopportune abundance of moral maxims and aphorisms. For all that, the voluptuous morality that pervades everything and the soft sweetness of the verses made the *Pastor fido* highly pleasing, and it was soon translated and imitated in all the civilized languages.

Less famous than Guarino was Bernardino Baldi (d. 1617) of Urbino, a former mathematics teacher to Don Ferrante Gonzaga, lord of Guastalla. Baldi served as abbot of that church and finally became a servitor of his natural lord, Francesco Maria della Rovere. Among his numerous works a didactic poem in four books of blank verse was well known: *La Nautica* [*Art of Navigation*]. In the fourth book, the fable concerning the invention of the compass is pleasing, and his brief account of the voyage of Columbus with its praises of Italy at the end has a certain interest. His *Eglogue* [*Eclogues*], also in blank verse, are sprightly in their lively and unconventional treatment of the joys and healthfulness of the pastoral and rural life. [He was also the first scholar to attempt an explanation of the Eugubine Tables.]

Another didactic poem worthy of mention is *La Caccia* [*The Hunt*] in five cantos in *ottava rima*, by Erasmo, lord of the castle of Valvasone in Friuli, where he died in 1593. The treatment of the theme, as often happens in didactic poetry, allows for many episodes: the portrayal of the first men forced to defend themselves from wild beasts (which was the origin of the hunt); the description of the various races of dogs; the story of Terone, a hunter torn to pieces by a wild boar (because he went hunting without having performed the proper religious rites); the adventure of the wonderful deer encountered and pursued by King Arthur. But Valvasone is more significant as a poet of the Catholic Restoration. He left behind the *Angeleide* in three cantos telling of the battle between the angels who rebelled and the angels who remained faithful and of the consequent fall of Lucifer. He also wrote the *Lagrime della Maddalena* [*The Tears of Mary Magdalene*], which narrates the story of the famous sinner who was redeemed by Christ and who, learning of his death, withdrew to mourn him in solitude. These were fairly frequent themes in the religiousness of the time. There were many poems on the battle between the archangel Michael and Lucifer, in which the defeat of heresy was symbolized and in which not only does the God triumph but so does authority. *Lacrime* [*Tears*] then and later, were so numerous as to constitute a special genre of poetry. It is sufficient to mention the *Lacrime della Vergine* [*Tears of the Virgin Mary*] and the *Lacrime di Cristo* both by Tasso and the *Lacrime di San Pietro* by Tansillo, mentioned above.

There is little personality and much of the academic in all these poets. There were some original spirits however, especially in that field which by its very nature is least academic, namely, comedy. Toward the end of the sixteenth century, comedy was already deviating from classical imitation and portraying popular life complete with its dialect and its customs. Already Angelo Beolco, called *Il Ruzzante* [the Romper], of Padova (d. 1542) had employed the Venetian idiom in his comedies. Andrea Calmo of Venice (d. 1571) followed his example; he was an acute observer of men and customs not only in his clownish comedies and farces, but also in his letters, which document the licentious and tumultuous life of sixteenth-century Venice.

Historians and Political Writers

In the second half of the sixteenth century, history loses the writers' passionate participation in the events and becomes erudition, or art. The noble tradition of the Florentine historians terminates in the works of a translator, Bernardo Davanzati, a noble by birth and a merchant by profession (d. 1606). He decided to translate Tacitus, the Latin historian who, with sovereign art and bitter knowledge of life, portrayed the dissolution of Roman power and was much read and meditated by the historical and political writers of the sixteenth and seventeenth centuries. Davanzati preserved the brevity of the original, but at a price: obscurities, anacolutha, and vigorous plebeian Tuscan phrases, which deform rather than translate the noblest of historians.

The old living and industrious spirit of the Tuscan people revealed itself in the Florentine Filippo Sassetti who, charged with supplying *spezie* [spices, including drugs; cf. *speziale:* apothecary], undertook a voyage to the East Indies, where he lived for five years. He considered going to China and from there to the West Indies, since he had the passion of the explorer, but death prevented him, for he died in the full maturity of his years at Goa, in 1588. Many of Sassetti's *Lettres* are extant: to relatives, diplomats, to the Grand Duke, to the Cardinal Ferdinando dei Medici. In a joking vein he relates many interesting things, especially about India. He discusses the industries and religion of those countries, as well as the language, which he, with an intuition touched with genius, did not hesitate to recognize as related to the European languages. There exists also, from the pen of Sassetti, a rough *Vita di Francesco Ferruccio* [*Life of Francesco Ferrucio*], the last heroic defender of the liberty of Florence.

In Naples, history was cultivated by Angelo di Costanzo, mentioned above among the lyric poets. His

Storia del Regno di Napoli [*History of the Kingdom of Naples*] in twenty books, from the death of Emperor Frederick II in 1250 down to 1486, is minutely detailed, honest, and elegant, but lifeless. Its dedication, to Filippo II, King of Spain and Naples, shows that the spirit of the historian was not very proud. As a poet, he was a Petrarchist colder than the others, wherefore Foscolo called his sonnets "rhymed syllogisms." A contemporary and fellow citizen of Costanzo was Camillo Porzio of Naples (d. 1580) who left a history, in three books, of the *Congiura dei baroni del regno di Napoli contro il re Ferdinando I* [*The Conspiracy of the Barons of the Kingdom of Naples Against King Ferdinand I*]. Its pages are full of strength and humaneness, especially those that deal with the punishment inflicted upon the rebels.

In Venice, Paolo Paruta was an illustrious historian who held high offices in his Republic (d. 1598). As official historiographer, he wrote in Italian the history of the Venetians from 1513 to 1551; to that he added the history of the war in Cyprus from 1570 to 1572. The inexact narrative is a continuous occasion for expressing moral and political remarks and teachings. For Paruta is a political writer rather than a historian, and he reveals himself as such in the work in three dialogues, *Della perfezione della vita politica* [*On Perfection in Political Life*] in praise of the active life over the contemplative life. In the two books *Dei Discorsi politici* [*On Political Speeches*], the main interest is in his reflections on the causes of the greatness of the Romans, which the politician attributes above all to the military education of that people and to its diplomatic capability. On the whole, Paruta's political system was that approved by his time and realized in the government of Venice: an intelligent aristocracy with the people serving as the instrument of its objectives. His noteworthy autobiography, or *Soliloquio*, was composed late in life.

Giovanni Botero (d. 1617) of Bene Vagienna in the province of Cuneo, a very pious man, was a Jesuit in his youth, then secretary to Saint Carlo Borromeo and to Cardinal Federico Borromeo, and finally tutor of the sons of Duke Carlo Emanuele. Of his many writings, the most famous is *Della ragion di Stato* [*On Reason Of State*] in ten books. It deals with a subject related to that of Machiavelli's *Principe,* though in a wider range. The prevailing spirit is Christian: war against the Turks should be the principal program of the Catholic states.

Giordano Bruno

The nature of this book does not permit the inclusion of numerous Italian writers who, in the second half of the sixteenth century because of sympathy for the Reformation or the fervor of a more inward religiousness, suffered exile, persecution, or torture. However, we cannot pass by without mentioning one of the fathers of modern philosophy, Giordano Bruno, born at Nola in 1548. He was a Dominican in early life. In 1576 he was accused of heresy, and he fled. Then, his own master, he became a teacher of philosophy [ca. 1577] in Geneva, Toulouse, Paris, London, and elsewhere, until, having been accused of heresy and refusing to abjure his ideas, he was burned at the stake at Rome, in 1600. He wrote *Il Candelaio* [*The Candle Maker*], a comedy in five very long acts, containing too many realistic scenes and numerous obscenities. The characters are very lifelike: the pedant Marfurio, who latinizes as he speaks; the necromancing trickster Scaramurè; and the alchemist Bartolomeo. Bruno, though, was born to be a philosopher, and all his writings are philosophical, both in Latin and the vernacular. As was the custom of the times, their titles are quite odd: *La Cena delle Ceneri* [*The Supper Of The Ashes*]; *Lo Spaccio della bestia trionfante* [*The Shop Of The Triumphant*

Beast]; *La Cabala del cavallo pegaseo* [*The Intrigue Of The Winged Horse*]; *Degli eroici furori* [*On Heroic Rages*]; and so on. Perhaps his most significant work is *De la causa principio ed uno* [English tr., 1950; *The Infinite In Giordano Bruno*].

Here are some of the ideas of this thinker, who was a genius turbid in thought yet one of the warmest, least temperate, least gracious, and most seventeenth-century-like writer that the late sixteenth century produced.

First and foremost, Bruno is an intolerant adversary of Aristotle's method; he preferred the ancient naturalist philosophers, like Parmenides who found wide sympathy in the humanistic age. As regards cognition, he is one of the first to attribute great importance to those faculties that are not properly the logical faculties: intuition, imagination, and inward ecstasy. In the theory of Copernicus, whose tenets he accepted, he finds confirmation of his own system of pantheism (God is all, all is God). The universe reveals itself to him as infinite in its unity, and because it is infinite, the universe itself is God. God pervades all creatures; rather, they are but a radiation, a spark emanating from Him. Such concepts as good and evil, beauty and ugliness, life and death, and, in short, all those which to us seem to be antitheses and contradictions, have no reason for being except the limitations of our minds. In reality, all things are divine; they are all equal, because they are all an expression of God; they all are God. One who is able to penetrate beyond phenomena, to find and sense the eternally equal, the absolutely perfect, God, and is beyond all perturbation, agitation, or sorrow, is aware of his indestructible greatness, indeed, of his divinity. He does not fear misfortune and considers death a return to the original source of being, or a transmigration to other forms of life.

This is not inert contemplative mysticism. Man reaches such inward grace after long travail, by continuous renunciation; he reaches it by cognition, which is won by freeing oneself from the illusions of the senses and from general opinions. Knowledge, the discovery of verity, is the highest function and the purest joy of man; it is his sacrosanct right. No religious credo can set itself against the search for truth; this would be the same as opposing God, who is truth itself; it would be a denial of the pilgrim's right to rest in his own shelter. Certainly, religions have a value in that by symbols, and popularly, they too speak of God; that is to say, of truth. They are sensible, popular philosophies, which lead to a higher philosophy that transcends the senses. The philosopher is not opposed to religions: he is outside them; beyond them. The religion of the wise man is the adoration of God through the countless forms of nature, in which He is revealed. All nature appears sacred to his eyes; it is transformed, evolves, is raised continually in fulfillment of the will of He who pervades it and animates it and is the absolute Being, always the same, always different. The modern theories of evolution seem to be implied in the pantheism of Bruno. The great German poet Goethe, a precursor of those theories, was likewise an ardent pantheist. However, still other modern spiritual principles and attitudes derive from the system of Bruno: tolerance of all religions, which all, in their various ways, aim at exalting one or another attribute of the divine, even though none succeeds in exalting all of them and understanding them; liberty of search and investigation; the relativity of all assertions.

6.

The Seventeenth Century

General Character of the Century, Especially in the First Half

The seventeenth century was a great century in the field of the plastic arts, even though ostentation and daring accomplished more than beauty and eurhythmy. Sacred music was brought to perfection and profane music was begun. In the field of literature (poetry, eloquence), the seventeenth century, especially its first half, represents, not a stasis — for its literary production is enormous — but a degeneration. Effect triumphed over taste, so that later on the expression "seventeenth-century style" became a synonym for presumptuous and ridiculous style. The poets of that age are to be looked for in France, England, Spain. In the seventeenth century, Italy does not have a single great and real poet among the thousands of versifiers who considered themselves and proclaimed themselves to be poets. In truth, both private and public life was too poor in substance for poetry to flourish, for poetry draws its sap and its inspiration from life. Formalism reigned supreme in life, so poetry too could be only form: rhetoric, compliments, gallantry, playfulness — an ornament of life, not the profound expression of it. In that lack of all inner warmth, a word finally became an end in itself. A word was worked on elaborately, as something that stood up by itself: the aim was to secure *elegance*, which in that age consisted of speaking as differently as possible from the common usage. Moreover, even Spain, whose domination of Italy was not just political, and England followed that style, which in those countries was called gongorism and euphuism respectively. In Italy it was called secentism or, after its foremost poet, marinism.

Speaking in metaphors, a linking of one metaphor with another (allegory) in such a way that the second is born from the first and so on; a multitude of antitheses to put the idea into greater relief; a rattling off of the most violent and unexpected hyperboles; a phrase put together as a play of symmetry and of correspondences: these are some of the extrinsic symptoms of that malady of secentism or marinism. Most prevalent was the abuse of those ingenious little flighty ideas, or puns, seized on at every opportunity that were called *concetti* [conceits] or *acutezze* [wit]. The most profound characteristic is the lack of any passion, the completely cerebral travail done in all coldness. One gets the impression, which after a while becomes exasperating, of having to put up with some sort of juggler or histrion, some virtuoso who does not let you glimpse his soul but wants to demonstrate his ability and make you raise your eyebrows in astonishment. In fact, the poetics of the seventeenth century is summed up in the verbs "to astonish," and "to amaze."

G. B. Marini

His Life

In that false manner, innumerable versifiers drew applause, among them Claudio Achillini of Bologna, Gerolamo Preti of Ferrara, and the Sicilian Giuseppe Artale (the wildest of them all). However, the man who became most famous was Giovanni Battista Marini, born in Naples in 1569. While still very young he knew and loved Tasso, and tried to emulate him. In his ingenuous pride he even thought he had outdone Tasso. But the spirituality and the life of Marini were too different and inferior for his poetry to equal that of Tasso. Tasso was a "wandering pilgrim" and Marini an adventurer; Tasso was a man of melancholy, Marini a dissipated epicurean. Imprisoned for his part in the rape of a nun, condemned again for falsification of documents (although for the purpose of getting a friend out of jail), Marini fled to Rome. Here he found a place in the service of Cardinal Pietro Aldobrandini who took Marini with him first to Ravenna where Pietro was archbishop then to Turin where he went as papal legate. Carlo Emanuele I became the patron of the already famous poet and conferred the cross of San Maurizio upon him; hence the title of *cavaliere,* which thereafter Marini always paraded. From this, or *also* from this, arose the jealous anger of another poet, the Duke's secretary, Gaspare Murtola of Genoa, author of a very mediocre poem, *Il Mondo creato* [*The Creation*]. Marini answered Murtola's libel the *Compendio della vita del cavalier Marino* [*Résumé of the Life of the Cavalier Marino*] with the *Murtoleide, fischiate* [*Exploits of Murtola: Boos!*]. Murtola came back with the *Marineide, risate* [*Exploits of Marini: Laughs!*] but that did not satisfy him. Murtola lay in wait for his adversary and treacherously fired a pistol at him; the shot failed of its mark but hit a favorite of the Duke. Murtola was condemned to death, but the sentence was changed to exile on the intercession of Marini himself, either out of generosity or as a fine gesture. Certainly, the attempt can not have aroused much emotion in the poet. Later in his *Adone,* he described it with rhetorical apathy. But safe in

Rome, Murtola continued to annoy him. He found a youthful poem of Marino, *La Cuccagna* [*Cockaigne*], and insinuated that certain satirical stanzas in it alluded to the Duke of Savoy. The latter jailed the poet for a while, on whom previously he had conferred the title of *cavaliere*. Marini fared better in France, where he was invited by the wife of Henry IV, Queen Marguérite de France. His great patroness was Marguérite's successor, Queen Maria de' Medici. For her he completed the *Adone,* which she presented to Louis III. In France the poet received money and honors and became the favorite of the court salons. But he became homesick for Italy, and the desire to enjoy a full and heady glory in that country seized him — Italy, where his *Adone* had become the subject matter of spirited polemics that had finally made him still more famous. In Turin and in Rome his arrival was a triumph. A public statue was erected to him in Naples, but he died there shortly after his return, in 1625.

The Adone [Adonis]

Marini's output was vast: endless lyrics, collected under pompous names such as *La Lira* [*The Lyre*], *La Zampogna* [*The Shepherd's Pipe*], *La Galleria;* and narrative poems, like *La strage degli Innocenti* [*Slaughter of the Innocents*]. From his letters it is clear with what conscientiousness and ardor he devoted himself to his art, which was truly the one and only worship of his life. However, his major work, and the one that best reveals the literary and moral trends of the century, is the *Adone,* written, as the author informs his critics, "conforming to current custom and to the taste of the century." It therefore dies with the death of that taste. *Adone* is a poem in twenty cantos, like the *Gerusalemme,* but the cantos are two to four times as long as those of Tasso: an enormous poem made out of practically nothing. An adversary of the poet called it a giant with the skeleton of a dwarf; a series of tableaux, narrations, and descriptions, which stand by themselves, but are connected to one another by the slenderest of threads. Here is the story. At one time or another Venus had spanked her petulant little Cupid who, to avenge the thrashing, makes her fall in love with the very handsome young son of Myrrah, the shepherd Adonis, whom a storm had cast up on the shore of Cyprus, the island of the goddess. Venus takes Adonis to here palace, that is filled with beautiful and delightful things. There the youth hears the novella of Psyche as narrated by Cupid, himself the lover of Psyche who is persecuted by Venus. There too he attends magnificent theatrical entertainments with beautiful scenery and based on mythological themes, which are reminiscent of the intermezzos that were customary in the seventeenth-century theaters. There, in separate rooms, Adonis satisfies each of the senses one after another. Then Adonis and Venus make their way through a marvelous garden full of surprises and singularities to the fountain of Apollo, the god of poetry; here, in the person of Fileno [Philenus], the poet narrates the events of his life. Carved or engraved into the marbles of the fountain are the escutcheons of illustrious Italian families, patrons of the arts and of poetry, such as Savoia, Estensi, Gonzaga, and Medici; the poet finds means to extol them all. Conspicuous above them all, the shield of the House of France stands out. Various swans symbolize the most excellent Tuscan poets, and Dante is placed on a level with della Casa; the owl and the magpie are Stigliani and Sarrocchi, a poet and poetess inimical to the author. Guided by Mercury, Adonis and Venus then mount to the third heaven. During this aerial journey, Mercury speaks at long length of almost all the human knowledge of the seventeenth century: philosophy, astronomy, astrology, notwithstanding the fact that he effusively praises Galileo and the telescope. Then he devotes his eloquence to the wars of France, extolling them in hyperboles. In the third heaven, which is that of

Venus, are heard the praises of the beautiful Italian and foreign women, and particularly of the Queen of France, Maria de' Medici. Now Mars, the official lover of Venus, enters the scene. On the advice of Venus herself, Adonis flees and reaches the enchanted land of Falsirena, who falls madly in love with him. He resists her advances and abandons her, she has him followed and imprisoned. Mercury frees him. Changed into a bird, Adonis finally returns to Venus, after a thousand mistakes. She has finally been definitely left alone by Mars. After having won a beauty contest, Adonis is elected king of Cyprus. He goes on a hunt. Implacable Mars and austere Diana plot against him. A wild boar gores him and kills him. The news is brought to Venus who, drawn by Triton, arrives and weeps in despair over the corpse. Other goddesses come to console her and tell of the unhappy loves of Hyacinth, Leander, and other young men known to mythology. Adonis is buried with much ceremony. The Adonisian games, originated by Venus, bring the action of the poem to a close. Warriors take part in them and symbolize the reigning houses of the poet's time. The poem closes with the glorification by Apollo of that wretched crime, the massacre of the Huguenots.

In the whole interminable poem, there is not one psychological situation, not one verity, and not one human character. Venus is not a character, still less that lover-boy, that paramour, that Adonis, too many times repugnant in his effeminacy. The merit of the *Adone* lies in the oriental richness of the descriptions, a richness that makes for heaviness. Brilliant though the descriptions are, they are never anything but an inferior poetical product. But descriptive poetry was liked in an age of luxury, splendor, and show like the seventeenth century, by a society that saw mirrored in the *Adone* its gardens, its palaces, its magnificence, no less than its own artistic and doctrinal preferences. Needless to say, no spirituality flows through the *Adone:* an unwholesome, sluggish sensuality that is never illuminated by a smile pervades and penetrates it throughout. In homage to the hypocrisy of the time, Marini premised each canto with an allegory, which was intended to give the poem a moral meaning. Indeed he protests how "immoderate pleasure ends in sorrow." Naturally no one can place any credence in the morality of the *Adone,* which is the bacchanal of all the joys of material life. Nor through its few hostile attitudes to Spain does the poem give voice to any Italian national consciousness or conscience; those attitudes consist of sympathy for and homage to France and Louis XIII to whom the poem is dedicated. As for the expression of the poem, there is in Marini all the worst of his age's taste; but leaving out of consideration that taste — if such a thing is possible — he is a poet of marvelous facility and fluency of speech, master, as few have ever been, of the language and all the musical expedients of verse.

Other Poets of the First Half of the Seventeenth Century

Marinism raged throughout the first half of the century. Even in that age, however, nobler or more serious poets can be found, among whom Gabriello Chiabrera was one of the finest. He died, old and honored, in 1638. Urban VIII personally composed the epitaph for his tomb; in it he calls him a rival of Columbus, for having discovered new poetic worlds. These new worlds are *canzoni* in the manner of Pindar, the poet of Thebes. Pindar celebrated the Greek public games to which such great national importance was attributed, and from them the poet was uplifted in rapid flight to sing the glories and the myths of the Hellenic cities. Chiabrera proposed to do as much for Italy or, rather, he wanted to and did extol her princes and lords, great, small, and minimum. Out of this there came a poetry simulating enthusiasm, rich in metrical daring and images, and completely external. However, like

Marini, Chiabrera believed that "poetry must cause the eyebrows to be raised." The other poetic worlds discovered by Chiabrera are the little odes — too mannered and affected — which reproduce the slender themes and meters of Anacreon, the Greek poet who seduces one into forgetfulness, arouses one to enjoyment, and who found far more correspondence than Pindar in the substantially sensual and futile life of the Italian seventeenth century.

Less sensational and deeper than Chiabrera was Fulvio Testi of Ferrara, a courtier of the Este rulers in Modena, he ended up in 1646 as a prisoner in that fortress and was perhaps executed there for unknown reasons of state. He achieved wealth and honors, but his soul was not satisfied with those vanities; therefore, in many of his poems there is scorn for the courts and the power of the world, glorification of the simple and tranquil life, and a looking down sternly from above upon the corruption of the times. There recur frequent reminiscences of the great Latin lyricist, Horace.

Meanwhile, the pastoral drama continued with the passionate *Filli in Sciro* [*Phyllis in Skyros*] of Guidobaldo Bonarelli della Rovere of Urbino (d. 1608). Ottavio Rinuccini of Florence (d. 1621), started a new genre, the melodrama; i.e., drama with music, a derivation from the pastoral, although the world of the shepherds was soon replaced by the world of myths and heroes. Of his works, *Dafne, Euridice,* and *Arianna* are still extant, with music by Peri and Monteverde. The music, which was intended to reproduce that of the Greek theater, was like that which is now called *recitativo,* except that it became richer and more animated in the choral parts, which then became arias.

A dramatic poet of a very individual sort was the Florentine Giambattista Andreini, a member of the theatrical company of the *Fedeli* [Faithful], one of the many such companies that then were being formed in Italy and travelling all over Europe. He died a little after the mid-point of the century. He left behind him comedies and tragicomedies, and a sacred play, *Adamo,* which narrates the creation of Adam and Eve, the temptation, the fall, and the explusion from paradise: a vast canvas, a painting in which the rebel, Lucifer, has the most important and active role. The overly sententious and rhetorical style, declamation instead of action, detract from the basic potential of this drama, which at one time was held to have inspired Milton's *Paradise Lost;* this opinion is now abandoned.

Alessandro Tassoni

Good common sense rose in revolt against Marinistic poetry and all the seventeenth century falsifications. Common sense found utterance in the odd personality of Alessandro Tassoni, born at Modena in 1565. He went to Rome in his youth in the service of the Cardinal Ascanio Colonna, who took him with him to Spain. Tassoni saw with his own eyes what the Spain of Philip III was like and felt himself more and more animated by a hatred of that government against which he would later write some fierce orations, the *Filippiche* [*Philippics*], which are now definitively recognized as his. After many struggles with envious enemies and perhaps the opposition of the Spanish government, he went over to the service of the Cardinal Maurizio of Savoy, first in Turin, then in Rome, until the Cardinal, who did not want trouble with Spain, let him go. It is said that the pretext for his dismissal was his having made a horoscope in which it was stated that the Cardinal was a big hypocrite. Tassoni retired to his little villa in Trastevere, where he had his portrait painted with a fig in his hand, implying the benefit he had gained from his services in the courts. Then he went back into service (how many men of the seventeenth century, otherwise free, were servants!), this time in the service of Cardinal Ludovisi, and finally that of his natural sovereign, Francesco I, duke of Modena. He died in that city in 1635, but not without having shown something of his oddness even in his testament: among other bequests, he left to the church where he was to be buried ten gold scudi "without any obligation whatsoever, as I do not think I deserve any compensation for such a small sum; I am leaving it mainly because I can't take it with me."

La Secchia Rapita [*The Stolen Bucket*, or *The Rape of the Bucket*]

Tassoni's fame started with the ten books of his *Pensieri diversi* [*A Variety of Thoughts*], which flow in great part from physical arguments and disparage the Aristotelian method which derives from metaphysical and absolute principles. Several of those *Thoughts* deal with literary questions, and the tenth book stirs up the problem that later became very acute in France: whether the ancients were superior to the moderns. Tasso is in favor of the moderns. His *Considerazioni sopra le Rime del Petrarca* [*Reflections on Petrarch's Poetry*] are hostile to Petrarch but are not as profound as they are sharp. Indeed, they are more pedantic than sharp; for they never go beyond the word, nor penetrate to that inner world where alone it is possible to understand and evaluate a work of art. But the classic work of Tassoni is *La Secchia Rapita* [*The Rape of the Bucket*]: a heroicomical poem in twelve cantos which, in a solemn and heroic manner, deals with a most futile and exhilarating subject.

In the thirteenth century, the Modenese defeated the Bolognese at Zappolino, carrying off a bucket as a trophy. Tassoni builds up his poem on this historical event, imagining that a tremendous war breaks out between the two cities. All the Italian potentates, including the Pope, take part in the hostilities: some for the Petronians (as the Bolognese are called from their patron saint Petronius); some for the Modenese or Gemignanians (so named for their Saint Gemignano); even the gods, meeting in an amusing council, participate. The Emperor Frederick II sends his son Enzo to aid the Modenese; he is captured by the men of Bologna, while the Modenese retain possession of the memorable bucket.

To some, it seemed that the poem was a satirical account of the communal struggles which, for so many centuries, kept Italy in turmoil; but that is too modern an interpretation. Perhaps the *Secchia* is a mockery of the seventeenth century mania for writing heroic poems in imitation of the *Gerusalemme,* of which several hundred appeared in that century. More probably the work has no other purpose than to amuse its readers, especially with its portrayal of characters in which his contemporaries recognized one or another of the enemies (or even friends) of the poet: in the Count of Culagna, arrogant, timid, a dandy, and deceived by his wife, it was easy to discern Brusantini rising to combat the *Considerazioni sul Petrarca.* The poem is a bit boring and a bit heavy, abounding it seems to us more in puns and coarseness than in wit; but it is written rather cleverly, with great immediacy and verity. It won immense success and had many imitators in Italy and abroad. In their fundamental theme, it is possible to make comparisons and parallels between the *La Secchia Rapita* and *Le Lutrin* of Boileau in France and Alexander Pope's *The Rape of the Lock* in England.

Other Comic Poets

Tassoni was not alone. Especially in Tuscany, where the tradition was now ages old, the comic poets, helped by a language that had all the freedom and the spontaneity of a dialect, flourished throughout the seventeenth century. One of the most successful was Francesco Bracciolini of Pistoia (d. 1645) with *Lo Scherno degli Dei* [*The Mockery of the Gods*], which was a satire (in truth, out of time) of the ancient divinities ill-treated in poems; the author was deeply religious, as he revealed in another poem, *La Croce riconquistata* [*The Cross Recovered*]. A very sprightly piece was the *Malmantile riacquistato* [*Malmantile Recovered* — Malmantile, the name of a castle] by the Florentine Lorenzo Lippi (d. 1664), a painter noteworthy for his truthful and realistic art. He kept these qualities in his poem, which is full of plebeian phrases and Florentine witticisms; this work won plaudits and commentaries from scholars and academicians. On the contrary, Gian Battista Lalli of Norcia made himself famous with his *Eneide travestita* [*Travesty on the Aeneid*], a parody in *ottava rima* of the divine poem: a caprice in the worst taste, yet one which had great success in Italy and in France.

In the category of the comic poets, we find Michelangelo Buonarroti the Younger of Florence (d. 1646), the son of a brother of the illustrious artist. He left a comedy in *ottava rima, Tancia,* in which he does not so much portray the loves of the peasants as their language. The author was a member of the Crusca and, to better serve that academy by gathering quantities of Tuscan words and phrases taken from life for his vocabulary, he wrote the endless *Fiera* [*The Fair*]: five comedies in one, built around a fair, which forms the basis for making diverse characters of every social class perform and, above all, speak.

Historical Writers of the First Half of the Seventeenth Century

Paolo Sarpi

Contemporaries of too many time-wasting poets, a few austere spirits looked into the depths of reality. They continue with even a more bitter knowledge of life the manner of the historical writers of the sixteenth century, but in a form no less noble while more spirited and immediate. Paolo Sarpi in particular deserves such praise. A Venetian, born in 1552, he was a Servite friar, an adviser of the republic, and a valiant defender of its rights against the encroachments of the pontifical authority. An attempt was made to kill the troublesome monk, but he was only wounded. After a life of austerity and study he died in 1623. Sarpi was a voluminous writer, but perhaps he would never have published anything on his own initiative. Philosophy and the natural sciences attracted him chiefly, especially in the years before the republic had absorbed him for its own needs. He was perhaps the first to demonstrate, or to divine, the law of the circulation of the blood. When finally he became involved in the struggle between the Venetian state and the Roman curia, he had need of probing deeply into ecclesiastical history. He specialized in the origin of the *benefices,* which originally were legacies of Christians to their bishops to provide for the support of the clergy but, principally, to be administered for the benefit of Christ's poor. Instead, they had become the scandalous wealth of the ministers of the altar, giving rise, little by little, to a series of juridical abuses. Sarpi also devoted considerable attention to the privilege of the right of asylum, by which a delinquent, who took refuge in a church, convent, or other sacred place, escaped justice; it was also easy for him to demonstrate that, although the sacred places might be a refuge for an innocent victim of persecution, in a vast number of cases they protected delinquents and the temples of God were converted into robbers' dens.

Without his knowledge, and under the anagram of *Pietro Soave Polano,* his major work, *La Storia del concilio trentino* [*The History of the Council of Trent*], was published in London in 1619 and quickly became famous. It dealt with a subject of extreme importance. As mentioned above, the Council of Trent was the starting point of the Catholic Restoration. It was the review and the discussion of dogmas, but also the sanctioning of abuses and of privileges that had become inveterate in the centuries. Sometimes they were interests of every kind which, in the dis-guise of religion, opposed every real reform of the Church. Sarpi drilled deeply into these interests: he observed that in comparison with the lengthy preambles by which they were preceded, the decrees of the Council were very weak things. He saw that in those preambles it was necessary to affirm the general principles of Catholic theology, necessary to safeguard the interests of the various categories of churchmen represented in the Council. He profited by his acquaintance with several prelates who were taking part in that assembly, and especially the familiarity that he enjoyed in Rome with Cardinal Gonzaga, who had the task of drafting the decrees for the Council. Serious, rapid, and without literary pretensions, Sarpi's history is pregnant with content, piercing in its penetration into all the secret places of the human heart, and it may be read, even today, with pleasure. The Church condemned the work. The Cardinal Sforza Pallavicino, a most learned Jesuit, wrote from a Catholic viewpoint his *Storia del concilio di Trento*, which follows, or pursues, step by step, that of Sarpi. The history of Pallavicino is very fully documented, but far more external than that of Sarpi and too ornate and elegant in style to appear sincere.

Other Historians

Cardinal Sforza Pallavicino, a Roman (d. 1667) besides the *Storia* just mentioned, left a treatise *Del bene* [*On the Good*], a book, *Della perfezione cristiana* [*On Christian Perfection*], and an essay, *Dello stile* [*On Style*], not without importance in the history of aesthetics. He was more a scholar than a writer. The same may be said of Guido Bentivoglio of Ferrara (d. 1644), who was papal nuncio in Flanders and in France while the last religious struggles were still aflame. He wrote a *Storia della guerra nelle Fiandre* [*History of the War in Flanders*], an account of the insurrection and the heroic acts on the Flemish side and the bloody repressions on the side of the Spanish and the Austrians a magnificent drama, but one that did not have the power to arouse the emotions of the narrator. Enrico Caterino Davila of Padua (d. 1631) was an historian of an altogether different temper. He served with Henry IV in France and was governor, in the name of the republic, of several border cities. His *Storia delle guerre civili in Francia* [*History of the Civil Wars in France*] in fifteen books is the richly detailed account of the wars, religious in origin, that finally carried Henry IV to the throne. Davila often narrates things he witnessed personally, or that he heard directly from participants in events; his accounts, therefore, has all the life and drama of participation: the characters speak and move before the very eyes of the reader. Davila has been accused of too great a tenderness for the court of France — but can there be a historian without passion and attachment?

To the names of the historical writers, we shall add that of Raimondo Montecuccoli of Modena, illustrious captain of the Emperor in the Thirty Years War, (d. 1680 in Linz with the title of Prince). He left military works, particularly the *Aforismi* and *Commentari,* long forgotten and brought back to light and usefulness by Foscolo, who showed how great was the military wisdom of Italians even in the centuries of servitude. The captain reveals himself as a master of his trade, inhumane and unscrupulous. He writes with epigraphical concision and strength.

Critics

Criticism, the judgment of works of art, was in the sixteenth century still entirely faithful to the Aristotelian tradition, but became freer in the seventeenth century. Even in its heavy erudition, the criticism aims at contradicting the judgments of the school and at paradox, as is characteristic of so many manifestations of the intellectual life of the seventeenth century. The writings of Traiano

Boccalini are still read with pleasure. He was adverse to the Spanish monarchy, refusing to become its historiographer, and was probably slain by its hired assassins at Venice in 1613. The most popular of his works is the *Ragguagli di Parnaso* [*Reports from Parnassus*]. Apollo on Parnassus, the mountain of the Muses, holds court and parliament. As occasion offers, he passes severe judgment on both literary writers and Aristotelian critics and on the wicked Spanish government besides. This last is struck more directly and right on the mark in another work that is like a sequel to the *Ragguagli: La Pietra del paragone politico* [*The Political Touchstone*]. In that book, not only the tyranny and the evil of the Spanish monarchy is shown, but also its weakness.

The opinions of Benedetto Fioretti of Pistoia (d. 1651) are more strictly literary. In his *Proginnasmi* [*Exercises*], he judges the greatest Greek, Latin, and Italian writers with unrestrained freedom and seizes the opportunity to make sometimes sound and unhackneyed new precepts of art. He adopted the name — made up out of Greek, Latin, and Hebrew — Udeno Nisieli ("Of no one, except God"), significant of his attitude about liberty during times in which all writers were "of" someone and in the service of some prince.

Tommaso Campanella: Philosopher

Speculative thought finds many representatives in Italy in that age. We consider here a philosopher who is reminiscent of Bruno in the boldness of his thought: Tommaso Campanella, born at Stilo in Calabria in 1568. He was a Dominican and teacher of philosophy in Rome, Florence, Padua, and Bologna; he made many enemies for himself with his anti-Aristotelianism. He was accused of conspiracy against the Spanish government, imprisoned, and kept in jail for almost thirty years. When he was freed, he went to Paris, where he died in 1639. Campanella was a poet: rough, but often very original, whether stating the principles of his philosophy or narrating his soul's experiences and the wretchedness of his life. Especially, however, he was a philosopher. He sought the way to certainty, not in the Aristotelian dialectic of the schools, but in revelation and in experiment (and therefore he admired Galileo, to whom, from his prison cell, he sent an *Apologia* [*Defense*] for Galileo's use. He sought to reconcile philosophy and faith, but his system is not the clearest, nor the most thought out; nor did the philosopher scorn the occult sciences, which then were finding a gifted upholder in Girolamo Cardano, a doctor and mathematician of Pavia. Campanella believed in an upheaval of all the classes of society in a near future, but he believed that that upheaval would be started or prepared by a universal monarchy, which should be Spain's. These concepts are developed in the *Discorsi ai principi d'Italia* [*Addresses to the Princes of Italy*], who, "for their own good and that of Christianity must not speak against the monarchy of Spain," and are found also in the ample treatise *Della monarchia di Spagna* [*On the Monarchy of Spain*]. Campanella is fiercely opposed to heretics, as is apparent in a *Dialogo politico contro Luterani e Calvinisti e altri eretici*. He wants the world to be a great convent, where everyone must live according to the Catholic rule, supported by the scepter of the king of Spain. The state is everything, a principle that he teaches clearly in a sort of novel or social romance *La Città del Sole:* a city that is imagined to exist on the island of Taprobana and is inhabited by a colony of refugees from India who have escaped from the inhumanity of the Magi and the tyrants. In that hypothetical city, individual property is suppressed; eurythmy, order, and maximum uniformity reign. The highest citizen, the metaphysician, is both sovereign and high priest, with three ministers at his side, symbols of the three divine attributes: power, wisdom, and love. The first governs the actions of the citizens; the second, their thoughts and beliefs; the third, their affections. The state rules everything: education, religion, and even weddings.

Galileo Galilei: His Life and Principal Works

In the first half of the seventeenth century, all the indomitable and productive energy of Italian thought finds expression in Galileo Galilei, whom we can not bypass although that great man belongs much more to the history of the sciences than to that of letters. Galileo was born in Pisa in 1564. His father planned to make him a doctor but, in that time, medicine was quackery and empiricism. The youth, eager for truth, preferred to devote himself to that science which is truth absolute: mathematics, which later appeared to him as the cipher or the alphabet by which the laws of nature are revealed. Nature, which everybody sees and which speaks to so few, spoke to him from the time when, in the cathedral of Pisa, observing the swinging of a lamp, he divined the law of the isochronism of the pendulum, a law later applied to the exact measurement of time, to the great advantage of astronomy and geography. Also in that time, while reading the fragments of Archimedes, he discovered the law of the specific gravity of bodies, and wrote the treatise of the *Bilancetta,* or hydrostatic balance, to determine gravity or weight. He studied Dante, whom Voltaire called the mathematical poet, delivering two lectures at the Florentine Academy *Sulla figura, sito e grandezza dell'Inferno* [*On the Figure, Site, and Size of Hell*]. He studied, and meditated, without any desire to earn a degree. He was extremely poor, but the Grand Duke Ferdinando I had an idea: he appointed Galileo, at the age of twenty-five, lecturer in mathematics in the university of Pisa. The laws of falling bodies, derived later from physics which he determined in those years, brought down upon the young professor the wrath of the old teachers, who had their own ideas and their peripatetic errors, concerning motion and the laws of motion. In addition, Galileo had no intention to remain silent, to dissimulate; he scorned them. The tempest thundered around his head, but the Venetian senate saved him by appointing him, in 1592, professor of mathematics in the university of Padua.

Galileo remained in that city for eighteen years, and they were the calmest years of his life. There he composed several small works on mechanics, physics, and hydraulics: the treatise *Del compasso geometrico e militare* [*On the Geometric and Military Compass*], the *Discorso intorno ai gallegianti* [*Discourse on Floating Bodies*]. In Padua he made his most marvelous invention, the telescope (suggested to him by the experiment of a Dutch craftsman), with which he succeeded in enlarging objects a thousandfold. With his telescope he climbed up to heaven. He discovered the mountains and the valleys of the moon; he saw that the number of fixed stars was eighteen times greater than had been known up to that time; he found that the Milky Way is a mass of stars. He discovered four satellites circling around Jupiter and, out of gratitude to the Grand Duke of Tuscany, he gave them the name of "Medicean Planets." He discovered the ring of Saturn, the phases of Venus, the spots of the sun; he wrote three letters concerning their origin: they were clouds or vapors emanating from the body of the star. He gave information about many of his discoveries in the *Sidereus nuncius* [*Messenger of the Stars*], a sort of diary of his observations. But homesickness for Tuscany fell upon the Pisan, and he began negotiations concerning appointment to the service of the Grand Duke Cosimo II. In 1610, the Grand Duke, in thanks, wrote to him in his own hand, naming him Chief Mathematician of the University of Pisa, without requiring him to live in Pisa, or lecture there and assigning him an annual stipend of one thousand scudi.

So far as the constitution of the universe was concerned, the discoveries that Galileo was making in astronomy were confirming, more and more, the ancient system that had been restored by the Polish mathematician Copernicus, with new proofs, and which took his name. Having the reputation of supporting the hardy Copernican opinion, in 1611 Galileo came to Rome to find out what was thought of him and against him there and to defend himself. Great honor was paid him, and he was made a member of the glorious Academy of the Lincei [the lynx-eyed: far-seeing ones], founded not long before by Prince Federico Cesi. For the time being, accusations were hushed, and he could return safely to Florence and write some interesting things on the wise interpretation of the Bible and on the limits between science and faith in a letter to Father Castelli in 1613 and in another in 1615 to the Grand Duchess Christine of Lorraine. But the persecutions started up again. In that same year, the Inquisition instituted its first proceedings against him, based on assertions taken from his *Lettere sulle macchie solari* [*Letters on Sun Spots*]. In 1616 he was summoned to Rome. In the presence of Cardinal Bellarmino, he was warned to abandon his opinions that the sun is the center of the world and that the earth moves, opinions judged to be erroneous and heretical because they are contradicted by many passages in the sacred scriptures. He was ordered neither to defend them, nor to hold them, or to teach them in any manner whatsoever. On that occasion, Copernicus' work was placed on the Index. Galileo conformed to the will of those gentlemen: perhaps he thought that it is useless to prove at the cost of martyrdom a verity of mathematics or perhaps his religiousness kept him from rebelling against the authority of the Church in which he believed. After his return to Florence, he informed the Grand Duke of a new way he had thought out of determining longitude at sea, at any point and at any hour of the night. The Grand Duke transmitted this information to the king of Spain, whose maritime power was at that time immense, so that he might profit by Galileo's discovery, but all this came to naught; Galileo then addressed himself to the States General of Holland, also without success. He continued his studies.

A comet that appeared in 1618 gave him occasion to write a *Discorso sulle comete* [*Discourse on Comets*], which has also been attributed to his disciple Mario Guiducci. The comet also prompted a Jesuit, Father Orazio Grassi of Savona, a mathematician of the Collegio Romano, to publish, under the pseudonym of Lotario Sarsi, a small Latin work entitled *Bilancia astronomica e filosofica* [*Astronomical and Philosophical Balance*] in which Galileo's opinions were minutely sifted and derided. Stung by this attack Galileo answered with his most spirited writing, *Il Saggiatore* [*The Assayer*], 1623, a dissertation in the form of a letter addressed to Monsignor Virginio Cesarini, an academician of the Lincei. It is a polemical little work: the experimental method is praised, outmoded Aristotelianism is harshly condemned, and Father Grassi is convicted of gross errors of optics and covered with ridicule. The Jesuit order prepared to avenge its confrère.

But Galileo had been working for several years on his *Dialogo sopra i due massimi sistemi del mondo* [*Dialogue on the Two Principal Systems of the World*—the Ptolemaic and the Copernican]. Because of the eurhythmy of the whole work, the light and shade given to the characters, the clear and precise language, the masterly style, this is not merely the work of a great scientist, it is the work of a great writer. The same may be said of all Galileo's prose writings. The protagonists of the *Dialogue* are two of his dear, dead friends: Francesco Sagredo, a Venetian patrician, who had advised him against leaving Venice, and Filippo Salviati of Florence, who had entertained him richly in his Villa delle Selve. These two are in a discussion with the Aristotelian Simplicius, a defender of the old prejudices (Simplicius was an ancient expounder of Aristotle, but in this work the name is perhaps not without an ironical significance). The dialogue takes place in Venice and lasts for four days. On the first day the subject is the resemblance of the earth and the moon; on the other three the Ptolemaic and Copernican systems are more particularly discussed. The author shows, or intends to show, that he is formulating objectively the ratios of probability equally for the one and the other of the two systems. However, the poor figure cut by Simplicius, the defender of the Ptolemaic theories, leaves no doubt about the real intentions of the book. The book was published, though not without stratagems which procured the permission of the ecclesiastical authority in Florence, in 1630.

The wrath that this book caused in Rome was great, the more so because Pope Urban VIII was given to believe that the figure of Simplicius was a personal mockery of him. While still Cardinal Maffeo Barberini, he had defended the immobility of the earth with the same arguments that Simplicius used. A second trial of Galileo was immediately instituted. On September 23, 1632, the Holy Office peremptorily summoned him to Rome. Close to seventy years old, he tried to avoid the journey, on the basis of the declaration of three physicians that he was suffering from hypochondria and hernia. This was taken by the Holy Office as subterfuge and dilatory tactics; it threatened to have him dragged to Rome in chains. Towards the end of January the old man set out. His second trial lasted five months. The minutes of the appearances of the accused, signed by himself, have been preserved. The first is dated April 12, 1633, the last, June 21. They are a succession and a crescendo of the humiliations of a man who was proud by nature. The principal accusation made against Galileo is that, notwithstanding the warning of 1616, he had continued to sustain and to teach the Copernican system. At first Galileo defended himself: Cardinal Bellarmino had told and written him that the opinion of Copernicus could be held as a hypothesis, humanly speaking. If in that admonition back in 1616 he had been warned not to teach that system, he had forgotten the prohibition. Then, however, he gives way. He denies being a supporter of the Copernican system. In the *Dialogue* he had stated what there was in favor of that system, and what was contrary to it. He recognizes, indeed, that certain arguments favorable to that system are put in a stronger light than are those unfavorable to it. He admits that the wise conclusions of Simplicius pass unnoticed in the multitude of those favorable to Copernicus, but in another day which he will add to the *Dialogue* he will not fail to make amends. Dated June 22, 1633, the sentence of condemnation sums up the accusations brought against Galileo, beginning in 1615, and concludes that he had given cause to be suspected of heresy by having "held and believed false doctrines contrary to the Sacred Scriptures: that is to say, that the sun is the center of the Universe and does not move from east to west, and that the earth does move and is not the center of the universe." The judges were disposed to temper the penalty, provided the guilty man "abjures, curses, and detests" the above-mentioned errors. Meanwhile the *Dialogue on the Two Principal Systems* was prohibited; the guilty party was condemned to imprisonment at the pleasure of the Holy Office, and for the space of three years, he was required to recite the penitential psalms once a week. Galileo abjured.

When the sentence had been passed, he remained in prison at the pleasure of the Pope, and his prison, in truth, was the palace of the Grand Duke on the Trinità dei Monti, where the French Academy of Fine Arts is located today. Then he was permitted to go to Siena in the care of his intimate friend, Ascanio Piccolomini, archbishop of that city. Then he went to a villa of his own, at Arcetri, and the Grand Duke in person came there to visit him. Finally he was permitted to return to Florence. He did not write another word on the Copernican system; but from the sky, so perilous for him, he came back to stay on earth. He became blind; he lost his adored daughter, Sister Maria Celeste, a nun in San Matteo d'Arcetri, many of whose affectionate letters to her father have been preserved. All the more fervently he immersed himself in his studies and in meditation; in those last years he thought out and composed the *Discorsi e dimostrazioni matematiche intorno a due nuove scienze* [*Discourses and Mathematical Demonstrations on two New Sciences*], these too are in the form of dialogues spread over four days and have the same interlocutors as in the *Dialogo sui due massimi sistemi*. In it Galileo expounds very lucidly the main principles of mechanics, hydraulics, acoustics, and other divisions of physics which, in this work, for the first time assumed the character, the method, and the dignity, of a science. Illustrious disciples collaborated with Galileo in his ever youthful and alert old age: Evangelista Torricelli of Faenza, inventor of the barometer; Benedetto Castelli of Brescia, a Benedictine, the father of the science of waters; Vincenzo Viviani, Florentine, an architect, founder of the Academy of *Cimento* or Experience — the first scientific academy in Europe — and an affectionate and diligent biographer of his teacher. These men were all sharp observers and clear and correct writers. And so, in the midst of these his real sons, Galileo died in 1642. The Grand Duke ordered that he be buried in Santa Croce, the temple of Italian glories. Viviani, who gave up his wish to be buried near him, took care of the monument.

The Second Half of the Century: The Principal Forms of Poetry

Lyric Poets

In the second half of the century, a tendency to restore good taste and common sense to poetry is already visible;

later this tendency is consciously formulated and affirmed. Chiabrera has a more numerous following than Marini; but lyric poetry is given to high-flown and Pindaric forms which often degenerate into pomposity and rhetoric.

Alessandro Guidi of Pavia lived in Rome in the circle of the former queen of Sweden, Christina, a convert to Catholicism, and Clement XI, and died there in 1712. In his overweening pride, he demanded burial near Tasso's tomb in Sant'Onofrio. He left a pastoral drama, *Endimione* [*Endymion*], based on the mythical loves of that shepherd and the moon. Written on commission for Christina and possibly including some verses written by her, it was highly praised by that reformer of poetry, Gian Vincenzo Gravina. Of Guidi's numerous canzoni, the one which greatly impressed young Alfieri was famous: *Alla Fortuna* [*To Fortune*], in which the poet appears stoically indifferent to the favors and the "slings and arrows" of that fickle goddess. Others are panegyrics addressed to powerful personages, still others are reworkings of the *Homilies* of Clement XI.

The Milanese Carlo Maria Maggi (d. 1699), secretary of the senate of his city and professor of Greek followed in his youth Marini's footsteps, but corrected himself early enough to be considered one of the restorers of good taste. Today he is more praised for his comedies in the Milanese dialect than for his poems in the grand style; because of his comedies, he may be considered the creator of the mask of Meneghino. [Meneghino, adj.: Milanese; noun: Milanese dialect; here a comedy figure representing the popular Milanese type, pleasure loving, good-hearted and extremely sententious.] Another Milanese poet, the Jesuit Tommaso Ceva (d. 1737), was highly extolled. In a Latin poem, *Philosophia nova-antiqua,* he fought the new philosophies of Descartes and of Gassendi and, once more, the Copernican system. He was more felicitous in the *Puer Jesus* [*Young Jesus*], a poem that narrates the story of the boy Jesus with much truth and tenderness.

The Florentine Vincenzo da Filicaia was perhaps more of a poet than any of the preceding. Like Guidi, he lived in Rome at the court of the former Swedish queen. He died in Florence in 1707. The threatened capture of Vienna by the Turks in 1683, and the liberation of the city by the valorous John Sobieski, King of Poland, inspired Filicaia to write some *canzoni* that are perhaps the most eloquent and lofty of that century. He wrote many other poems, of which the many on religious themes are noteworthy as are the others in which he speaks of his own misfortunes: they are full of sadness and Christian resignation.

After Galileo, however, scientists were more honored in Tuscany than poets. If some spontaneous poet arose, he was usually a man of science as well, like Francesco Redi of Arezzo, a doctor and illustrious naturalist, earnest student of Italian literature and a professor at the University of Florence (d. 1698). Overly famous among his many lyrics is the dithyramb (as the Greeks called a panegyric in praise of the gods) *Bacco in Toscana*. Bacchus, after having extolled wine, the giver of forgetfulness, enumerates the qualities and the defects of many wines, praising that of Montepulciano above all others. Little by little, as he samples the many wines, the god becomes tipsy; the changing, jumping, and mobile meter of the poem follows the staggering of the intoxicated deity.

Alessandro Marchetti of Pontorno near Empoli was a fine mathematician, professor of mathematics at Pisa, where he died in 1714. His translations of the *Aeneid*, of Anacreon and especially of the Latin naturalist Lucretius' poem *On the Nature of Things* are more worthy of remembrance than his original verses. The audacious antireligiosity of the text did not permit his translation to be published in Italy. Three years after the translator's death, Rolli had it printed in England.

Satirical Poets

The political and civic wretchedness of the Italians in those years of servitude and the presentiment or desire of a restoration, which became full awareness in the following century, strengthened in the late seventeenth century that satirical current that had already been so full in the seventeenth century.

Salvator Rosa of Naples, died in Rome in 1673 after a most adventurous life. He was a magnificent painter of gloomy landscapes and magnificent scenes in the manner of Michelangelo Caravaggio, and he was a violent poet in six satires in tercets: *La Musica, La Poesia, La Pittura, La Guerra, La Babilonia, L'Invidia,* [*Music, Poetry, Painting, War, Babylon, Envy*]. He lashes out at the coarse tastes and the effete customs of the time, especially in corrupt Rome (Babylon) : consequently these satires were printed abroad sooner than in Italy and after the author's death.

More noted was Benedetto Menzini, a priest of Florence who, persecuted at home, found protection in Rome with Christina of Sweden and Clement XI; he died there in 1704. In the footsteps of Filicaia and Guidi, Menzini "pindarized" abundantly. His *Poetica* in five books, in tercets, is significant; it defends traditional poetry and opposes the futility of seventeenth-century poetry. His twelve *Satire* are somewhat declamatory and very obscure, either due to allusions to persons and customs or because of abuse of dialectal phrases or idioms. However, they are sometimes quite lively: for instance the third, in which the poet bewails being refused a professorship at Pisa; or the ninth, in which the poet speaks against the greed of ecclesiastics.

The satirical temperament par excellence of the time was that of Girolamo Gigli of Siena (d. 1722, Rome) whose program was to combat academicians and hypocrites of any sort. He gained popularity with the very felicitous comedy *Don Pilone,* which is considerably analogous in spirit and in action to Molière's *Tartuffe* and, like that play, is an energetic tirade against sanctimony. Later he staged *La sorellina di Don Pilone* [*Don Pilone's Little Sister*] suggested to him by his troubles with his wife. Afterwards he devoted himself to publishing the works of his great fellow citizen Saint Catherine and to a *Vocabolario cateriniano* [*Dictionary of St. Catherine's Language*] in which he avails himself of any pretext to vent his dislike of the academicians of the Crusca and the Florentines. The Academy took violent revenge. The book was put on the Index and burnt by the public executioner. Its author lost his teaching chair in Siena. He left a *Gazzettino* in manuscript and unfinished; this is a collection of fanciful letters of the author or *Avvisi ideali* [*Ideal Warnings*] about an imaginary troop of Chinese amazons, who come to Europe to get married. In these writings Gigli wanders over many subjects, all prohibited in those times: against courts, bigotry, and untruthfulness.

Writers of Art Prose

The second half of the seventeenth century does not have great writers, but it does have great men of letters who find their development in the Jesuit school. Father Daniello Bartoli filled the age with his personality. Born in Ferrara in 1608, he entered the Society of Jesus at an early age, anxious to devote himself to the missions in India. The Fathers, though, could not bear to lose such a magnificent literary genius, and they wanted him back home to teach and study. They called him to Rome to write the history of the Company, which by that time had been in existence for a hundred years of success and was powerful and overpowering. After a life of piety and study, he died in 1685. He wrote on many subjects. In several books he busied himself with linguistic questions in opposition to the overly rigid Cruscan academicians, and he put together a book called *Il torto e il diritto del "Non si può"* [*The Right and the Wrong of the "You Can Not"*], in which, with his great knowledge of Italian literature, he demonstrates how there is hardly a construction or phrase that one can not use on the authority of excellent writers. He wrote on physics and on natural history in the vein of the Old Aristotelian method already overthrown by his contemporaries; he wrote books of piety, such as *La povertà contenta* [*Contentment in Poverty*]. His most considerable work is the *Storia della Compagnia del Gesù* [*History of the Company of Jesus*] consisting of the *Vita di Sant'Ignazio* [*Life of Saint Ignatius*], of the *Asia* (that is to say, the history of the conversion of the Indies, Japan, and China to Catholicism), of the *Inghilterra,* and of the *Italia.* In this history, or story, or romance, which, with the utmost seriousness, he relates the most extraordinary miracles, there is no research into sources, no individuality of thought. On the other hand, Bartoli is a perfectionist of style. Even Giordano and Leopardi, who indeed had no liking for the Jesuits, considered Bartoli an incomparable prose writer. To us today, who ask first of all if a writer has a soul, Bartoli does not seem to be a writer but a virtuoso of the word, a great master of language that he digs up from the most forgotten archives, which he knows in all its mysteries, and displays and parades on every occasion, and even when there is no occasion.

With Bartoli another Jesuit is to be remembered, whom tradition considers the greatest Italian sacred orator: Paolo Segneri. Born at Nettuno near Rome in 1624, he became a disciple of Pallavicino. On entering the Company, Segneri devoted himself with the enthusiasm and conviction of an apostle to preaching. In the greatest cities and equally in the humblest towns, he preached, although he never was favored by good health and became somewhat deaf in the year of his maturity. Princes wanted the famous orator in their courts; he lived for a long time in Florence, at the court of Cosimo III. Then he was named personal preacher to Innocent XII and preacher to the Sacred College. He died two years later, in 1694. He wrote many works for the teaching and the edification of the Catholic people, such as the *Incredulo senza scusa* [The Inexcusable Unbeliever] and *La Manna dell'anima* [Manna of the Soul]. His *Quaresimale* [Lenten Sermons] are especially famous. Naturally for a Christian of today Segneri's oratory seems somewhat antiquated. The straining for effect is too apparent, and one looks in vain in his work for those living lyrical pages that show humanity seen from above, that do not leave us the strength to criticize, to doubt, to smile, and that, whether or not we are believers, force us to listen to the profound voice of a conscience. But compared to the orators or rather the historions of his age, Segneri is admirable for the clearness and seriousness of his arguments, the warmth of his conviction, and the dignity of his language. He is as sincere, and therefore as eloquent, as he was permitted by the insincerity and the rhetoric that then abounded.

Among the many who, in the second part of the seventeenth century, devoted themselves to the sciences that were then being born, Lorenzo Magalotti (d. 1712) has a place in literature. Born in Rome of a Florentine family, he was a great favorite of the Grand Duke Ferdinand II, who had him accompany the Duke's son Cosimo in his travels to the various courts of Europe. This was a joy to Magalotti, who was very fond of traveling and observing. A sudden distaste for the world caused him to enter a cloister, but after five years he was once again back in the world. His knowledge was encyclopedic: he wrote about his own travels, or those of others; he also wrote on science, and his greatest work was *I Saggi di naturali esperienze fatte nell'accademia del Cimento* [Essays on Natural Ex-

periments Performed at the Academy del Cimento], of which he was secretary, the founder having been Viviani as mentioned above. His *Lettere famigliari* [*Intimate Letters*] were quite celebrated; they were intended especially to combat atheism and to show that everything concerning man is a mystery that the sciences are powerless to destroy.

G. B. Vico

To bring this chapter to an end, I take pleasure in telling of the man who was perhaps the greatest genius among Italian thinkers, Giambattista Vico. I include him here because, although Vico's writings were published in the first decades of the eighteenth century, his thought continues the Italian philosophical tradition which the eighteenth century broke with because of its love for the easier French and English speculation. Although it is pregnant with very modern intuitions, it stands in denial of Cartesianism, which even in Italy was being widely cultivated toward the end of the seventeenth century. Vico was born in Naples in 1668, the son of a humble book dealer, and he lived a poor life. He did not suffer the persecutions that often increase the stature of their victim by making him conscious of his worth, but the continual straits of indigence, which stifles energy, and the silent anguish of feeling his own greatness and having to beg for the praise, approbation and even tolerance of mediocre men he did suffer. He studied jurisprudence wholeheartedly, for in the history of the law he saw the philosophy of the human race in action. For nine years he was relegated to a small town in the wilds of the Cilento district in the province of Salerno, as educator of the nephews of Monsignor Rocco, bishop of Ischia. Solitude depresses men of little genius, who have need of everybody and of everything; it strengthens geniuses, who experience in it the joy of learning to know themselves and of hearing their own thoughts. In that solitude Vico read, meditated, and developed in mind and spirit. On his return to Naples, he obtained a professorship of rhetoric at the University, on a very low stipend. He aspired to a chair of jurisprudence, but although he had already written profound essays on the history and philosophy of law, he was considered "unsuitable." He did not persist in his requests, and he did not complain. On the contrary, he blessed providence for granting him more leisure to devote to the work that he had been sternly meditating for twenty years: the *Principi di Scienza nuova* [*Principles of New Science*], which came out in 1725. The public was unaware of the book and the official scholars paid only the usual semi-official compliments to the author. Vico appeared satisfied. As an intelligent and innovating monarch Carlo III of Bourbon, who had come to the throne of the Kingdom of the Two Sicilies, appointed Vico royal historiographer. The promotion came too late. In those last years he was as one who had outlived his time. A cancer had taken from him his tongue and his eyes. He died January 20, 1744. In that year he had succeeded in completing the third edition of his *Scienza Nuova* and was able to die in peace.

The *Principi Di Scienza Nuova Nazioni* [*Principles of New Science*] English translation, *New Science*, 1948

It is not easy to give even the most summary idea of this work. It is a work that is obscure because of an excess of thought content. A spirit of perpetual travail is felt in it; before it has elaborated one idea, it is already intuiting a new one. Therefore, the work was revised, three times apparently, but in reality five or six, and the last revision differs substantially from the first in several points. In Vico, the historian and the philosopher oppose and overwhelm one another continually, although Vico is substantially a philosopher and only occasionally a historian, which explains the numerous inaccuracies of fact. He does not aim at the single event but at the idea expressed by that event: he does not aim at concrete history, but at the historical idea.

The thinkers of the seventeenth and eighteenth centuries devoted much study to the origin of law: a problem that was transferred from the field of theory into the practical; that is to say, their theories became criticism of laws actually in force and became the reason for the revolutions of the new times. Under different names, that problem was dealt with throughout Europe, and before long Rousseau, with the intent to create conflict, would take it up in his *Social Contract.* It was also constantly present in Vico's consciousness. He alone, among his contemporaries, saw that law comes into being without man's being aware of it, and it accompanies man in his evolution from the state of animality to the state of civilization. He saw that law is innate, but develops, and when law is perfect, then society too is perfect. The origin of law is therefore merged with the origin of society. The history of the society that takes shape is the history of the formation of law. In order to know the origin of law or, rather, its progress from its origin to its full explication, it is necessary to know that history of the society which has never been written directly: the history that we call *prehistory* and that Vico called *the age of fable.*

A large part of the *New Science* is concerned with the reconstruction of this prehistory or age of fable. That age is studied by Vico in various and new aspects. He gives an historical value to the Greek and Latin myths as the imaginative expression of actual facts. He considers words in their primitive meaning as surviving documents from past events and extinct institutions. He believes that the life of peoples passes through the various phases of the psychological life of individuals, passing from an age strictly of the senses to an imaginative age, and culminating in an age of reason just as traditions of the fabulous age have penetrated into the history of the formed and perfected societies, as the great rivers continue flowing for a long distance after they reach the sea. Vico attributes an extraordinary importance to these traditions, these scraps and fragments of prehistory, and interprets them in a manner peculiarly his own. Finally he goes back to the age of fable by studying the institutions and the characteristics of the Middle Ages, for he believes that the Middle Ages represent the prehistory of the modern age.

Vico insists on the study of Roman history, which he considers almost a typical history, and he interprets it with entirely new intuitions, which later historians adopted as their own and more or less continued. Thus he considers the history of Rome as legendary, down to the Second Punic War. Vico examines Greek history with as much genius as he showed in studying the Romans. Greek mythology offers him illustrations of progress of various kinds, the various social and juridical forms of the Hellenic state and of all states. The Homeric poems are for him the historico-poetical expression of the customs, the beliefs, and the institutions of primitive Greece. For him, Homer never existed as a person. Homer is but a symbol, a figure of the poet of the primitive age: Achilles is the symbol of strength; Ulysses of prudence; Agamemnon of kingliness; and so on. In short, Homer is one of the many Greek myths. This theory of the nonexistence of Homer was later taken up clamorously by German critics using arguments that their Italian predecessor had already presented in one of the six books of the *New Science*.

Vico believed that all societies pass, and must pass, through the various conditions or steps through which the Greek and the Roman societies passed. Although created by the free will of mankind, society always begins with a monarchical and theocratic form. The perfect form follows, the equilibrium of all the elements that make up the society: the *republic*. From this state, society passes on to the *oligarchy,* which is the government or the supremacy, as the case may be, of the few who put their personal interests above or opposed to that of the state. A dismal period of disorder and of anarchy follows, from which the wearied citizens free themselves, conferring full powers upon a single ruler: so that the *empire* is born. In such ways, through trials, successes, and errors, providence works to educate political man.

Vico was the first to see the enormous importance of that which we call the economic factor in history. Though hidden under the most fanciful and picturesque wrappings, the materialistic interpretation of historical fact is clear in Vico: the idea of historical fact has had and still has many followers in our age, although such interpretation has proved to be insufficent to explain the most significant moments of history. Vico reduces all Roman history to an economic struggle between patricians and plebeians in which the contests for equality in law are in reality contests only for economic equality. For Vico, the first embryo of society is contemporaneous with the first ownership of property, and with the first agrarian struggles between the *heroes* (which to his mind signify simply owners, proprietors) who give the *famuli* [servants, slaves] their fields to work, and the *famuli,* who wish to possess the cultivated fields. The first senates are a league of proprietors against whom the workers are becoming ever stronger and more threatening. The workers find their organ in the *comitia* and their representative in the tribune. For Vico, innumerable myths are the poetic expression of this gigantic, implacable struggle between those who have and do not want to lose it, and those who have not and would like to have. Thus, Vico sees Apollo, who in the name of Jove smites the giants, the sons of the Earth, as the figure of the Patriciate who, in the name of God, crushes the workers of the fields. Tantalus, who dies of thirst in the pagan hell while having water up to his chin, is the hungry worker who sees before his eyes the ears of grain, the crops, and the fruits that shall not be his. The teeth of the dragon that Jason, the winner of the Golden Fleece (that is, for Vico, the golden grain), throws on the soil and from which armed men shoot up, are the teeth of the plow that cultivates the fields, and those armed men are the workers, who rise up to exact their own rights.

7.
The Eighteenth Century

Poetry in the First Half of the Eighteenth Century

The Arcadia

In the first half of the eighteenth century, poets propose to reproduce simplicity and naturalness in opposition to the artificiality of the preceding century. At least this was the program of a celebrated academy of poetry which, with the name of *Arcadia* (region of Greece celebrated as pastoral and poetical), arose in Rome in 1690. It was centered among several men of letters who had gathered around the former Queen of Sweden, Maria Christina. I shall spare my readers the childish story of the foundation and precepts of that academy and of its "colonies" spread throughout Italy. It lasted for a whole century, during which time it was no longer permissible to write poetry except under the double name conferred by an Arcadian colony, one indicating the person of the poet, the other his place of origin. The Arcadia was an encouragement to poetical cowardice, already too common in Italy; and nothing else can be expected from a poetical "academy" — a contradiction of terms, since nothing is more personal and more antiacademic than poetry. The preference given to the false world of pastoral poetry, the total lack of daring in thought in those assemblies of abbés, of nobles, of ladies, and courtiers, made the poetry of the Arcadian school a synonym for poetry without sinews and without dignity. In reality, however, the Arcadia should not be judged so summarily and as a unit. The Arcadians followed various currents. Those of the South were sentimental and melancholy; those in Tuscany, continued comic and farcical poetry. Lombardy had poets full of bourgeois common sense. The declamatory poets of the late seventeenth century were not without followers in the Arcadia because, basically, the Arcadia was also rhetorical. There was a desire to renew poetry, but first consciousnesses had to be renewed and purged of the misconceptions inflicted by several centuries of intellectual and political servility.

Some Poets of the Arcadian Age

Poets worthy of the name, are a rare sight among men; they are in inverse proportion to the number of versifiers, or pseudo-poets. These latter were innumerable in the Arcadian age, and all of them had some fame in their time and in their province. We have touched on some of them in speaking of the late seventeenth century: Guidi, Filicaia, Maggi. Now we shall add a few names. There were many women among them. Standing out from the others was Faustina Maratti, the wife of Felice Zappi of Imola: He was graceful; she was the stronger, especially in that sonnet that describes maternal affections. The mathematician Eustachio Manfredi (d. 1734) versified in Bologna with an austere purity that at times is reminiscent of the *Vita Nuova*. Niccolò Forteguerri, a native of Pistoia who lived as a courtier in Rome (where he died in 1735), made a name for himself with the last of the poems coming down from the *Furioso,* the *Ricciardetto,* which is prevailingly comic in character and occasionally satirical. The *Cicerone* by the priest Gian Carlo Passeroni may be paired with the preceding. Passeroni was born at Lantosca near Nice, but he lived in Milan, where he died of old age in 1803. He uses his narration of the life of Cicero as a pretext for a thousand digressions on his own times, whose private and public customs he analyzes and criticizes with plebeian mockery. Consequently, the enormous poem, perhaps the longest in all Italian literature, still has some value for the history of eighteenth-century customs. Passeroni was a moralist by temperament and found natural nourishment in fables, for which the age was greedy; following the example of La Fontaine, he wrote seven volumes of them.

Alfonso Varano, prince of Camerino, a Ferrarese nobleman (d. 1788), stands apart from others in his *Visioni* in tercets. In this work the very religious poet extols God the avenger, who sends his scourges upon a corrupt world: the Lisbon earthquake; the pestilence of Messina. He imitates Dante in meter, manner, and obscurity, but certainly not in poetic impetus. He finds in the Bible his inspiration for demonstrating how false was Voltaire's widely shared opinion that it was impossible to write poetry on Christian and religious themes.

The Veronese, Scipione Maffei, whom we shall discuss later, sought to give dignity to tragic poetry. He was opposed to the tendency to imitate French drama, represented especially by Pier Jacopo Martelli of Bologna (d. 1727). With simplicity of line and language, Maffei composed *Merope,* a tragedy in blank verse, on maternal love, which even today cannot be read without emotion.

A unique personality and a noble physiognomy characterized Paolo Rolli, a Roman who lived a long time in England, at first in the household of Lord Steers Sembuck, afterwards as preceptor of the royal family of George II. He died at Todi in 1765. He translated Milton's *Paradise*

Lost into Italian, as well as Vergil and Anacreon. He composed several hendecasyllables of his own and others in the style of Catullus, as well as odes and felicitous *canzonette* [canzonets: little songs, or the words thereto]. The canzonets reproduced the lovers' laments, or analyses of unconquerable passion, with facile sentimentality rather than the deep seriousness that ordinarily characterizes Petrarch's *canzoni*. The preferred meter is the *ottonario* [verse line of eight syllables] or the *settenario* [line of seven syllables] in short, melodic strophes, their musicality being heightened by song.

The most successful lyric poet of the first half of the eighteenth century was the Genoese abbé Innocenzo Frugoni, who reigned over literature at the court of the Farnese and the Bourbons in Parma and died there in 1768. His attitude was normally that of a man inspired by Apollo, and he declared that he had seen many of the enterprises of his heroes while in a state of ecstasy. Most of his innumerable poems are panegyrics of princes and of members of their courts; many are exercises and declamations based on ancient history, both sacred and profane. Though he did not disdain light or trivial poetry, he wrote many lyrics in the grand style. He especially enjoyed using a thundering, sonorous blank verse that attracted many imitators, as so often happens with fashions in bad taste.

Pietro Metastasio

In reality, the only poet in the first half of the eighteenth century was Pietro Metastasio, perhaps because his was the most spontaneous expression of the tastes and feelings of his age and he was sincere in portraying so much falseness. He was born in Rome in 1608, into a poor family, and his real name was Trapassi. He improvised, as was the fashion at that time, and the boy improviser attracted the attention of the erudite Gravina, who took him into his household. Like the Greek scholar that he was, Gravina transmuted the prosaic name of Trappassi into the more dignified surname of Metastasio and undertook to make him into the poet of his heart's desire. Gravina set the youth to studying law and made him learn Cartesian philosophy, which was his own. At his death, Gravina bequeathed all his possessions to Metastasio. Metastasio quickly squandered his inheritance and went to Naples as the assistant of a lawyer. But he had been born under a lucky star. On a solemn occasion at court, he produced the *Orti Esperidi* [*Gardens of the Hesperides*], a *cantata* (the name generally given to one-act melodramas involving mythological persons) that greatly pleased a famous actress, Marianna Bulgarelli, nicknamed La Romanina, who played the role of Venus. La Romanina fell in love with the author, who wrote for her his first melodrama, *Didone abbandonata* [*Dido Forsaken*], which was passionate although not free of the comic ingenuousness and coarseness that still contaminated the genre. His work scored a tremendous success. The poet followed his patroness to Rome; there he conceived the idea of raising the melodrama to the dignity and respectability of the tragedy, and he wrote *Catone*. Corpses were not acceptable on the stage of that day, and the play was a failure. Metastasio went back to his melodramas of love and intrigue and had triumphal successes. Then Charles VI called him to Vienna to succeed the Venetian Apostolo Zeno as Imperial poet. The Imperial poet had to be ready to compose for any event involving his royal patrons and especially to write dramas for the court theater. Metastasio was just the man: he accepted gladly and lived in Vienna from 1730 on, satisfying the desires of Charles VI and Maria Theresa. Conditions were favorable for him to produce, and he produced in quantity and to the admiration of everyone. In his old age, he was invited to collaborate on the *Encyclopedia,* but refused; he was what we would call today a conservative. He died at the age of eighty-four, in 1782.

In his lifetime, Metastasio was extolled as the greatest of poets; a few decades after his death he was already forgotten, or else reviled. The consciousness of the public and its conception of art were completely changed. Metastasio is *the* poet of the first half of the eighteenth century, just as the melodrama was the representative poetical genre of that voluptuous, languid, sentimental age, of that elegant society unencumbered by any depth of thought and which asked of its theater the intoxication of love's dream. Although it might accept the heroic, it was on condition that it be reduced to the proportions of an idyll. In the theater it found poetry, scene painting, and the dance joined together in the superior unity of music, which then had such competent masters as Porpora, Cimarosa, Paisiello, and Gluck. The melodrama of Metastasio is also completed by its music and subordinates itself to music's necessities. A simple reading of the dramas is insufficient for a just evaluation.

Considered in its extrinsic makeup, his melodramas are normally composed of three acts; the characters speak in blank verse, or in series of hendecasyllables or seven-syllable lines freely rhymed. When they must express the rush of passion or pass judgment on something they speak in rapid little strophes, which are called *ariette* [little arias] in the plays.

Love faced with difficulties and crowned with success is the theme of most of the Metastasian melodramas. But there are generally two pairs of lovers, thus making it possible to present the principal ranges of singers' voices. The events of one couple intersect the incidents of the other pair, and in the variations of this interplay lies almost all of the action. A sure knowledge of the impulses of the heart and in particular of the feminine passions, a ready and tender sensibility, a clear and precise expression, an always spontaneous eloquence: these are the principal endowments of Metastasio, together with a musicality that to today's tastes seems too facile and cloying. Situations are not developed in depth; the characters pass with the greatest of ease from one sentiment to a contrary one with such ingenuousness or childishness that it is impossible to read even the most serious melodramas without smiling.

Besides some enchanting *canzonettas* of love, Metastasio wrote over seventy melodramas; among those which became most popular and most famous after the *Didone* are the *Olimpiade, Attilio Regolo, Temistocle, Clemenza di Tito,* the latter imitated from the *Cinna* of Corneille.

Critics

In the first part of the eighteenth century, criticism in the literary fields tends to be related to the new philosophic systems coming from France and England. An effort is made to study the artistic product according to reason rather more than according to the oracle of Aristotle, Horace, and the other masters of poetics and rhetoric. Among the new critics was Metastasio's teacher, Gian Vincenzo Gravina, of Roggiano in Calabria, a counselor-at-law who lived most of his life in Rome, dying in 1718. In two books, *Della ragion poetica* [*On Poetic Reason*] he uses the philosophy of Descartes in forming rational judgments of poetry. It is Gravina's belief that poetry should be substantially a reproduction of reality and aim at instructing by images and allegories; this in itself is an insufficient concept which confuses poetry with science and reality, but its purpose was to give to art a seriousness that had been lacking too long a time. In *Della Tragedia* [*On Tragedy*], he urges a return to simplicity and naturalness and an end to romantic love that formed such a large part of dramas. He urges basing plays on subjects of common interest; he combats what he considers a genre false by its very nature, the melodrama, the very genre in which his disciple Trapassi was to gain so much glory (so much for disciples following in the footsteps of their teachers!). So Gravina wrote serious tragedies on plots derived from Roman history and in meters that tried to imitate the Greeks. He was not a poet and his prosaicism was unbearable.

Other thinkers, less famous than Gravina, explored the problem of poetry and its nature with perhaps a greater sense of truth. In his treatise *Della perfetta poesia,* Ludovico Antonio Muratori studies the imagination as the inspiration for the poetic work: he subordinates the laws of interest and of emotion to imagination and not to whim, as was customary in the preceding century. In extremely obscure writings, the Paduan, Antonio Conti, traces the poetic phantasm back to a copy of the original Ideas according to the system of the Platonists and recognizes the special importance of imagination, even in the scientific field. On the contrary, Francesco Maria Zanotti of Bologna, following the theories of the Sensists (Sensationalists), reduces poetry to a mere play and pleasure. The Marquis Giuseppe Orsi of Bologna (d. 1733) merits special praise for his defense, in a series of dialogues of the poetical capacity and dignity of the Italian language against the strictures of a French Jesuit, Father Bouhours who, in *La Manière de bien penser* [*The Way to Right Thinking*] had exaggerated the accusations of artificiality previously leveled against Italian poetry by the supreme French dictator of good taste, Boileau. Several Italian noblemen who were writers of that time joined in the polemics started by the Marquis Orsi. Today's criticism places Giulio Cesare Becelli of Verona (d. 1750) in a special light: in his *Novella Poesia* [*The New Poetry*] he was the first to affirm the independence of Italian poetry from the classics; he proclaimed a liberty of inspiration and form that caused him to be considered a precursor of the Romantic school.

Historians and Writers on Various Subjects

The objective of a great number of the writers of the eighteenth century was to publicize and to argue in favor of the new ideas; for them history was no longer dead material but a weapon. Here are a few of those many erudite authors:

Ludovico Antonio Muratori, mentioned above, was of Vignola near Modena. He was a priest, and a librarian first, of the Ambrosiana of Milan, then of the Estense in Modena, where he died in 1750. His stature as a historian is greater than as a critic. The special object of his research was the Middle Ages, until then a period far more disdained than known. He collected all the chroniclers, known or unknown, who had written about Italy from 500 to 1500, and published them with prefaces concerning the life and times of each. The series was called *Scriptores rerum italicarum* [*Historians of Italy*]. The last of its twenty-five volumes was published a year after Muratori's death in Modena in 1750. His *Antiquitates italicae medii aevi* [*Medieval Italian Archeology*] consists of dissertations on the customs and institutions of the Italian Middle Ages and is a supplement and commentary on the *Scriptores*. These were works of interest to professional historians, but Muratori wanted to write for everyone. For the general cultured public he composed *Gli Annali d'Italia* [*The Annals of Italy*] which considers the period from the beginning of the vernacular era down to 1749. It was a vast and assiduous history in which the author is not satisfied merely with narrating but formulates his most honest judgment of events, including those touching the Church: his judgment is inspired by a high Christian and humanitarian morality. In his desire to spread the light of knowledge, Muratori did not restrict himself to history. His works number more than two hundred. Along with other philosophical works he wrote the *Filosofia pei giovanetti* [*Philosophy for Young People*] and a treatise on the imagination. In religion, his book combatting superstition, *Della regolata devozione* [*On Well-ordered Devotion*], aroused the anger of the Jesuits against him; his essay on public hygiene, *Del governo della peste* [*On Control of Pestilence*] was a highly beneficial work. He entered the field of oratory with a treatise *Della sacra eloquence* [*On Sacred Eloquence*] which decries rhetoric in the pulpit. Concerning the economic conditions of states, his treatise on *La felicità dei prìncipi* [*The Happiness of Princes*] expressed the opinion that the prince's happiness is obtained only through the happiness of his subjects; his *Riflessioni sopra il buon gusto nelle scienze e nell'arti* [*Reflections on Good Taste in the Arts and Sciences*] indicates his position on reforms in the field of teaching and was published under his Arcadian name of Lamindo Pritanio.

Muratori was a soul of Christian mildness. On the contrary, another historian, Pietro Giannone of Foggia, was harshly polemic. He spent his youth in Naples as a lawyer. His *Storia civile del regno di Napoli* [*Civil History of the Kingdom of Naples*] forced him into exile. For a time he was in Vienna, Venice, Milan, and Geneva; finally he was treacherously delivered into the hands of the King of Sardinia who, to please the Roman Curia, held him prisoner at Fenestrelle, Pinerolo, and Turin. He died in prison in 1748. His *Civil History* deals with the age of the author; it was a time in which states were trying to free themselves from the bonds of the Church and become autonomous. Giannone shows how many unlawful ways the Church used to impose itself upon the kingdom, which it still considered as a vassal state. And this gives the author an opening to study the constitution of the primitive Church and to regret that it had deviated from the spirituality and the poverty of former times. To be sure, in the development of his thesis, Giannone was not overly scrupulous in his examination of the facts, nor did he refrain from borrowing and copying from earlier historians without acknowledgment. The work was combated and opposition drew from the author a long *Apologia* [*Defense*] in which he reiterates his antiecclesiastical ideas, which are expressed more distinctly in his *Triregno* [*Triple Kingdom*], and in the *Autobiografia*, which he wrote in prison.

Comparable to Muratori in the scope of his erudition, but differing from him in his vivacious nature, was the Veronese Count Scipione Maffei (d. 1755) whom we have mentioned already as a reformer of tragedy. His major work is the *Verona illustrata*, that is, the history of his native city as read especially in its monuments. This work offered him scope for every sort of digression; such as that on ancient theaters. He touched on every subject: literature, chivalric art, natural philosophy; he was always bent on combating prejudice of any sort.

The vast work *Della storia e della ragione di ogni poesia* [*On the History and the Reason for Every Poem*] by Francesco Saverio Quadrio (d. 1756) is of special interest to students of Italian poetry. Although belonging to the following generation, the Jesuit Girolamo Tiraboschi of Bergamo (d. 1794) has more in common with the great men of learning of the first half of the century. He was Muratori's successor as head of the Estense Library at Modena. His *Storia della letteratura italiana* [*History of Italian Literature*], which would be better named History of Italian Culture, extends from the Etruscan age down through the seventeenth century. However lacking it may be in critical value, it is nevertheless extremely worthwhile for the quantity and sureness of its biographical and bibliographical information.

The knight errant of the culture of the eighteenth century, the man who made it accessible to noble and bourgeois alike and to the world of elegance, was the

Venetian Francesco Algarotti who traveled over half of Europe, educating himself in the then customary manner. He became singularly esteemed by Frederick II of Prussia, who made him a count and made sure that he would be buried in the cemetery of Pisa, the city in which he died while still in the prime of life (1764). He wrote prolifically and with a certain lightness of manner that appeared to be elegance on travel, literary questions, fine arts, and poetry. His *Newtonism per le dame* [*Newtonism for Ladies*] is perhaps his most important work. It is a series of dialogues in which he instructs a lady in the optical theories of Newton, which were full of novelty at that time.

Remarks on the Second Half of the Eighteenth Century

A whole ferment of reforming ideas in the field of morality and social relations characterizes the second half of the eighteenth century. This ferment was favored by the rulers and particularly by the enlightened government of Austria in Milan, and in Naples by Carlo III of Bourbon. A struggle against the clergy who were invading the rights of the state, propaganda for culture, attempts to increase public wealth: these were some of the main points of the ardent reforming. Italy needed to come abreast of the more energetic nations. The major French and English writers were read eagerly in Italy. The poets of those nations were placed on a level with the Italian classics in the cult of literature, or completely replaced them. It was a revolution in the best sense of the word; a revolution that developed with the consent and the aid of the foremost men of letters with programs both bold and high-minded. After a few words about the principal representatives of that movement, we shall talk about the writers who translated the innovating spirit of the times into art forms.

Philosophers and Reformers

Milan and Naples were the cities where the new ideas found the warmest welcome. The Milanese writers were mostly concerned with the practical solution of the problems, while the Neapolitans were content to engage in theoretical research.

The initiator of the reform in Milan was Pietro Verri (d. 1797). He was particularly interested in public finances, the science that teaches the state how to increase its wealth. In that century the greatest problem was production: all possible means for increasing it were pondered, from the increase of agriculture and industry to the increase of the population, from the freedom of trade to new tax systems. We have the *Storia di Milano* [*History of Milan*] from Verri's pen, various writings on statistics and diverse articles on moral Sensistic philosophy that were printed in *Il Caffé,* the *Coffee House,* a periodical that he founded, which lasted only two years (1764–1766), and which debated important economic, moral, and literary questions. It was supposed that the editors met for discussion in a Milanese café or coffee house, hence the name of the periodical. Alessandro Verri (d. 1816), although much younger than his brother, was more famous than he for his novels, such as *Saffo, Erostrato,* and, the most important, *Notti romane al sepolcro degli Scipioni* [*Roman Nights at the Tomb of the Scipios*]. The burial place of the famous Roman family had recently been discovered in Rome, and the influx of curious foreigners was considerable. Alessandro imagines that he too visits the tomb, at night. His torch is extinguished, and, left in darkness, he has a vision in which he sees the shades of famous ancient Romans: Cicero, Caesar, Brutus, and others, who discuss politics, liberty, whether the republic is preferable to a tyranny, and so forth. That is to say they debate political questions most interesting to the men of the late eighteenth century. These discussions continue for several nights, on the last of which the shades take a tour around the new Rome under the guidance of Alessandro, comparing it with the ancient city. The final statement of the book is on the superiority of Christianity to paganism; like so many novels of the time, the work has a didactic character and a conservative purpose. In our day it seems intolerably declamatory; to Alessandro's contemporaries, it appeared admirably eloquent.

More sober in style but far more important was the work of Count Cesare Beccaria, another Milanese (d. 1794). He was the author of *Dei delitte e delle pene* [*On Crimes and their Punishments*], which was translated into all the European languages and became the basis for new penal legislation. Following the spirit of reason and the humanitarian attitudes of the century, he assumes the defence of the guilty facing their judges, and in the delinquent, he sees the right of the man. Dealing first with procedure, he insists that the accused be given all the means for his defense, that he shall not be imprisoned before the proper time, nor subjected to torture, which is as useless as it is cruel. He insists further that the function of judge shall be separate from that of accuser, and that laws shall be written and unchangeable, their application not subject to the will of the judge. Passing on to an analysis of crimes, he believes that the crime is proportional to the real damage that is inflicted on society by the delinquent. Nor should a man be punished for his opinions. The punishment inflicted should force the guilty party to compensate society for the harm that he has caused it; hence the approval of Beccaria for the pain of *obligatory servitude,* which later ages called forced labor. The death sentence should be abolished as the most unjust and the least efficacious, save possibly in some cases for reasons of state. The author would like to see the state eager to prevent crime rather than repress it; among the means of prevention, he considers public education the best.

In Naples, Ferdinando Galiani from Abruzzi (d. 1787) was a shining light. For many years he was a secretary of the embassy in Paris. He added French *esprit* to Neapolitan vivacity, which breaks out entirely in a comic opera written in collaboration with G. B. Lorenzi, *Socrate immaginario,* which was judged, perhaps too indulgently, to be a masterpiece of its kind. Just as Don Quixote, as a result of reading romances of chivalry, came to think he was a knight errant, so here a poor provincial barber, by dint of hearing philosophy discussed, believes that he has become Socrates and tries to duplicate the life of that philosopher. He creates about himself the environment which surrounded Socrates, even including Xantippe; from all this, many comical and exhilarating situations arise which his contemporaries enjoyed all the more when they more clearly discerned in Socrates the parody of a master of contemporary erudition, Father Saverio Mattei, eulogizer of the Greek world and translator of the *Psalms.* But Galiani merits much more praise for other writings, especially for his treatise in dialogue form, *Della moneta* [*On Money*], which dispelled numerous errors concerning the ways, all very bad, by which states and private persons sought to meet the serious economic situation. Many of Galiani's numerous letters in French and Italian have been preserved; addressed in great part to a lady of rank in France, they present a good picture of his character. In Naples many of his shrewd sayings and maxims are still current.

Antonio Genovesi of Salerno, a contemporary of Galiani, was professor of financial science at the University of Naples, where he died in 1769. He was a simple-hearted man of immense learning. His most significant works are on philosophy, and in them he endeavored to temper Christian teachings with the dictates of French and English sensism. He was the first man both to lecture on philosophy from a professional chair in the Italian language and to write on philosophy in Italian; this was due to the need for cultural propaganda then current. He gathered the best of his philosophical and moral teachings in a book intended for the general public, *Diceosina* [*Justice*], which is read even today with admiration for the wise thinking and courageous attitudes of the philosopher.

It is fitting to record here the Neapolitan prince, Gaetano Filangieri, who was the author of a work left unfinished after the fourth of the seven books that had been contemplated: *La scienza della legislazione* [*The Science of Legislation*]. In it the author deals systematically with the social, economic, and political questions of greatest interest to his age: population and ways to increase it, agriculture, and the penal system. The things said about popular education in the fourth book can still be read profitably: the author claimed that education should be a responsibility of the state until the student's eighteenth birthday and that it should aim not only at giving him a profession, but a character and a soul. The fundamental mistake of Filangieri and other contemporary writers on reform was to rely too much on the operation of laws and to forget the concrete nature of man. His untimely death in 1788, at the age of thirty-six, saved him from the scaffold, upon which many of his companions in thought and faith died in the repression of the Parthenopean Republic.

Critics of the Second Half of the Eighteenth Century

The critics were more negators than builders, and more iconoclasts than critics. The most violent and likeable of them was Giuseppe Baretti (d. 1789) of Turin: the first, in order of time, of the many vernacular writers which Piedmont was later to give to Italy. His restless disposition did not allow him to loll in the placid Italian states; he preferred London, where he made a living by giving Italian lessons and writing for the newspapers. From there he made long trips: one to Portugal, Spain and France, which he described in his *Lettere familiari* to his three brothers; another to Italy in 1760, which was the most important, because he settled down in Venice and from there he launched the issues of the *Frusta letteraria* [*The Literary Scourge*]. He attacked powerful living writers, and venerable dead writers, wherefore the periodical was suspended by order of the Venetian government, especially when Father Appiano Buonafede directed his *Bue pedagogo* [*The Pedagogical Ox*] against Baretti, who replied with poetry. Thereupon Baretti returned to London, which became his permanent domicile. Now famous, he was appointed secretary for foreign correspondence of the Royal Academy of Fine Arts, and in his last years he enjoyed an annual pension of eighty pounds sterling from the king.

Many of his writings are extant. Among the most significant are: a French discourse in defense of Shakespeare against Voltaire's attacks, which is one of Baretti's best thought-out and modern writings. *The Italians* (An Account of the Manners and Customs of Italy, London 1768) is a book in English aimed at Dr. Samuel Sharp who in *Travels in Italy* had calumniated Italy. In reply, Baretti eulogizes the culture and intrinsic goodness of the people, the wise customs of the nobility, and, from an excess of zeal, he defends some serious blemishes, such as the practice of the *cavalieri serventi* [ladies' men]. But Baretti's most important work is the *Frusta letteraria*. Baretti judges books of literature and of philosophy in imaginative language, equidistant from the slovenly indeterminateness of the Frenchifiers and the insipid elegance of the Tuscanizers, with breeziness and an enthusiasm that sometimes are reminiscent of his beloved Cellini. He occasionally touches on books of science, which were appearing in Italy or had recently appeared.

The criterion from which the censor moves is not so much aesthetic or scientific, as it is practical. England had taught him that literature should above anything else be socially useful, and Italian literature seemed to him, in large part, the work or play, of time wasters. The Arcadia, therefore, was the frequent object of his bile, but he did not spare the useless versifiers, the useless — as they seemed to him — archaeologists, or the dangerous metaphysicians; for basically he was a conservative. Therefore, he eulogizes Genovesi, detests Verri and his *Caffè,* and makes a pitiless analysis of Goldoni's comedies, which he considers immoral as well as buffoonish. Among contemporary poets he praised Parini, because he considered him both moral and useful; but Metastasio he considered unsurpassable. He derided the Tuscans, conceited about their vocabulary, which to him seemed much less rich than English. Of the older Italian poets, he cared little for Dante, but he esteemed Ariosto highly as a pure poet. His aversion to French writers is notably constant, especially to the most famous and productive of them, Voltaire.

On the contrary Melchiorre Cesarotti, a prolific writer and an abbé of Padua, was an extreme Francophile. A professor of Greek and Hebrew in the university of his native city, where he died at an advanced age in 1808, he was principally a translator or rather, an adapter. One of his favorites was an English writer, James MacPherson, who had published the songs of an ancient Scottish bard named Ossian, who was supposed to have lived before the Christianizing of Scotland. Regardless of the objections that burst forth concerning the authenticity of those poems, they won the European public to whose new aesthetic needs they provided an answer. They were no longer satisfied with the now antiquated machinery of mythology and could be appeased only with melancholy, lyricism, and rapidity of the saga. Cesarotti translated these poems into Italian with versification as sonorous as Frugoni's, and added learned and critical notes, in which he appeared to prefer the words be translated to those of Homer. In the eighteenth century, and in France especially, Homer had more detractors than admirers. To show what Homer was, Cesarotti made a very flat, literal prose translation of the *Iliad*. To demonstrate what Homer should have been or could have been, he made a translation of the poem in blank verse or, rather, a reckless reworking in which the principal character is Hector (the poem in fact is called *La Morte di Ettore* [*The Death of Hector*]). His death is a punishment for not having prevented Paris from keeping possession of ravished Helen. Cesarotti disapproved of Homer's morality; therefore the capricious gods are removed in his reworking, or considered mere instruments of a very just god, whose name is Fate.

It is said that to refute those who accused him of not knowing the pure Italian language, that is to say, the academic elegances, Cesarotti translated the greatest Greek orator, Demosthenes, into that language. Certainly, he had no scruples about Frenchifying the Italian language, as his cultural world was French. He justified his way of writing in the *Saggio sulla filosofia delle lingue* [*Essay on the Philosophy of Languages*], in which, having posited the principle that languages change with the civilization of nations and through the commerce of one nation with other peoples, he discusses the means of regulating those changes. He imagines academies in each province that would accept or refuse new words: a roughly practical solution of a substantially ethical problem. Cesarotti also wrote poetry. In his old age, he wrote an epic composition in praise of Napoleon, the *Pronea* [*Providence*], which extols the Corsican as the man destined by God to govern and bring back peace to the world. His more modest poems are less rhetorical; for example, the *Genio dell'Adria* [*The Genius of Adria*], *Il Cinto d'Imeneo* [*The Belt of Hymen*], and others.

The Jesuit from Mantua, Saverio Bettinelli, was no less petulant than Cesarotti but considerably less talented. He was a professor in the *Collegio dei nobili* at Parma, a traveler throughout Europe, and an acquaintance of Voltaire. He died quite old in 1808. He wrote endlessly: among his writings is a sensible poem against "collections" of poems that it was customary to write for every great or small occasion. He was especially fond of versisciolti, which he published together with those of Algarotti and Frugoni, with the modest title of *Versi di tre eccellenti autori* [*Poems of Three Excellent Authors*]. Pompously and unpoetically he speaks of *Viaggi* [*Travels*], *Commercio, Caffè, Tabacco,* of a visit to Naples including the inevitable eruption of Vesuvius, of ever so many things: he thought that originality lay in the subjects. He earned unenviable celebrity with the little book that was the preface to those poems: *Lettere virgiliane* [*Vergilian Letters*] in which it is imagined that Italian poets are discussed in the Elysian Fields under the chairmanship of Vergil. Faint approval is allotted to a few of Petrarch's poems, as well as Poliziano's and Ariosto's. The hardest blows in the "Vergilian Letters" are struck against Dante, whose poem Vergil considers absurd in its development and barbarous in its expression; only two or three of Dante's cantos can be saved but only with great difficulty — the famous ones, perhaps the only ones Bettinelli knew. This judgment is not surprising. The eighteenth century hated Dante, as it did Homer and Shakespeare; it wanted works "in good taste" and did not comprehend poets of genius. The resulting scandal was great, and Gaspare Gozzi made a worthy reply. Bettinelli did not retract and repeated his strictures in the *Lettere inglesi* [*English Letters*], remarking that it was necessary to save the young from the vice of imitation and the cult of idols. These *English Letters* are much more worthwhile than the *Vergilian*; in them it is imagined that an English gentleman travels about Italy in order to learn the language and reports on literary conditions in the peninsula. Good things may be read about the lack of real literary and cultural life in Italy, a lack scarcely concealed by the overnumerous "academies." The sympathies of the author are all for English poetry, but only for the mannered and smooth poetry of the eighteenth century. Bettinelli's *Saggio sull'entusiasmo* [*Essay on Enthusiasm*] is noteworthy: for him enthusiasm or inspiration is the true source of poetry, and he traces its characteristics at length. A work which was highly praised was his *Risorgimento d'Italia negli studi, nelle arti e nei costumi dopo il 1000* [*Italy's Revival in Studies, Arts and Customs after the Year 1000*]. It is reminiscent of Voltaire's *Le Siècle de Louis XIV* in its development. It is a description of the progress of the human spirit between the Middle Ages and the *Risorgimento (Revival)*, paying much attention to customs and culture and little to political and military events, which previously constituted the bulk of history.

Art Writers and Autobiographers

Venice, the oldest and most conservative of the Italian republics, accepted the new ideas with much moderation and remained faithful to the classical literary tradition. Count Gaspare Gozzi (1713–1786), was the principal representative of this tradition. A Venetian, he came from a noble family which had become impoverished. He was the father of a large family by his wife Luisa Bergalli, a bluestocking somewhat lacking in judgment, and his life was therefore largely a struggle to make a living. Once, in a fit of extreme depression he tried to commit suicide by throwing himself from a window into the Brenta river. Later, the position of Reformer of Studies in the University of Padua gave him a certain security, although he had wanted a chair of Greek at that university.

The many translations of foreign writers — either his own, or under his name — such as the novellas of Marmontel and the *Death of Adam* by Klopstock, and some of his own comedies or tragedies imitated from the French theater, are among the numerous writings with which he busied himself to earn a living. What he did best was journalism: he was his own "collaborator" on the *Gazzetta Veneta* [*Venetian Gazette*], 1760–1961, strictly a local publication and of interest to anyone wishing to study Venetian customs of the period; with broader views and frequent literary and philosophical discussions, he undertook the *Osservatore* [*The Observer*]. It is made up of events witnessed by the editor, moral novellas, dialogues in the manner of Lucian, and portraits which recall the characters of Theophrastes and La Bruyère. All this is written without much vigor, but in a good style and with great clarity. The work won wide circulation, first with the public and later in the schools. Gozzi did not do very well with a complicated allegorical novel entitled *Il Mondo morale* [*The Moral World*]. His *Difesa di Dante* [*Defence of Dante*] is worthy of praise, if for no other reason than that Dante is seen here not only as a great poet but as a great conscience, contrary to the views of Bettinelli. The *Sermoni,* poems in blank verse, in which the author relates events of his own life and tells of customs of his time, including numerous half-jesting, half-melancholy observations, are perhaps the finest and most personal of his writings.

Carlo Gozzi (d. 1806), Gaspare's younger brother, wrote almost as much but never acquired as much grace or became as famous. He wrote a comic poem, *Marfisa bizzarra,* full of personal allusions to his literary enemies; but he is more noted for his *Fiabe* [*Fables*]: *L'Amore delle tre melarance* [*Love of Three Oranges*], *L'Augellin Belverde* [*The Little Bird Belverde*]; *Re Cervo* [*The Stag King*]; *Turandotte,* which was adapted by Schiller, which was made into an opera by Prokofieff, and by Puccini in his opera *Turandot,* and other fables: *Il Corvo* [*The Crow*]; *La Donna Serpente* [*The Serpent Women*]; *Zuobeide, I pitocchi fortunati* [*The Fortunate Beggars*]; *Il Mostro Turchino* [*The Turquoise Monster*]; *Zeim re de' Genii* [*Zeim, King of Genii*]. The *Serpent Woman* was the source of Wagner's first opera, *Die Feen*. All these fables were intended for stage presentation, partly written out and partly scenarios for treatment as comedies in the vein of the Commedia dell 'Arte. They are lively scenarios of puerile tales. He composed them in opposition to Chiari and Goldoni, the two playwrights who monopolized the theater in Venice, thinking — and he demonstrated factually how right he was — that all it took to fill the theater was puppet spectacles or *teatro dei piccoli* as they are called in Italy today. In his autobiography, to which he gave the curious title of *Memorie inutili per servire alla vita di Carlo Gozzi* [*Useless Memoirs on the Life of Carlo Gozzi*], he discusses the conditions of the theater in Venice, the causes, the purpose, and the success of his fables, together with information about his life, his domestic troubles, and his reactionary ideas.

The eighteenth century produced an abundance of autobiographers and adventurers. Lorenzo da Ponte of Ceneda (1749–1838) attracts some attention: after long residence in Venice, Vienna, and London, he went to America and became the first to disseminate knowledge of Italian literature there. He was professor of Italian at Columbia University, which purchased his library. He wrote the librettos of three of Mozart's operas. But the prince of the autobiographers and adventurers of the time was Gian Giacomo Casanova (1725–1798), a Venetian whose life was an incredible romance, especially after his flight from the Piombi (leaden-roofed prison) of Venice, where he had been incarcerated as a sorcerer. He was familiar with all the courts of Europe and he engaged in enterprises and swindles of every sort. He ended up in Venice, as a spy of the state Inquisition, where he died at the end of the century. He left his *Mémoires,* written in French, in which he reveals with the utmost boldness, magnificent qualities as a narrator and describer.

A Cynical Poet

Giovan Battista Casti, a priest from Montefiascone, was likewise an adventurer. He lived in a great many places: at the court of Vienna, where he took part in a mission to Petrograd; in Milan, where the pungent sensuality of his *Novelle* [*Novellas*] found a tough adversary in Parini. The Revolution carried him to France, and he died in Paris in 1803. He began his writing career with *I Giuli tre* [*The Three Juliuses*], a series of farcical sonnets. And his facile approach to writing — plebeian in its facility — was always his best quality or his worst defect. His *Novelle* were widely read; in them, in concentrated form, is all that is most shameless in the Italian novella writers and in the *Contes* of La Fontaine. On the other hand, his *Poema Tartaro* [*Tartar Poem*] had few readers; in it, under the pretence of narrating the events of the Second Crusade, the poet describes the kingdom of Catherine II of Russia, her libertinage and her mania for French reforms. *Il Re Teodoro* is the liveliest of Casti's melodramas: it is a presentation in satirical form of the undertakings of Theodor, Baron Neuhoff, a celebrated adventurer who attempted to make himself king of Corsica in the eighteenth century. The most thoughtful of Casti's works is a poem in sestinas, *Gli Animali parlanti* [*The Talking Animals*]: an enormous apologue. The author imagines that the animals conceive ways to govern themselves wisely but little by little court intrigues appear — the deficiencies inherent in any constitution are the weakness and wickedness of men. The first edition had the honor of being prohibited by First Consul Bonapart, who tolerated no discussions of a political and philosophical nature.

A Sicilian Poet

The best of the numerous poets who, in Sicily more than elsewhere, preferred their dialect to the national language can be found in the second half of the eighteenth century. He is Giovanni Meli (d. 1815) of Palermo, a doctor at Cinisi and later, in recognition of his poetical talents, professor of chemistry at that university. Little or nothing of the ideas and turmoil of the new times is evident in his work. He is a conservative, reactionary, and put on his guard by innate scepticism against any innovation or daring. This attitude can be seen in some of his good-humoredly satirical poems such as *Le Origini di lu munnu* [*The Origins of the World*], a satire against metaphysics, *La fata galanti, Don Chisciotti e Sanciu Panza, Puisii* [*Poems*] *e favuli morali*. Meli is truly a poet when he sings of the life and occupations of the countryside in the little pastoral poems and love songs: *Odi, Anacreontici, La Bucolica*. It is old poetic material, but recreated by an ingenuous poetical soul that is all spontaneity and feeling. However, connoisseurs remark that Meli's language, its words, as well as constructions, is sometimes more literary than popular: a sign of the times which demanded more elegance from poetry than truth.

Minor Poets

Aurelio Bertòla of Rimini (d. 1798) became known for his numerous fables into which he distilled much wit and wisdom. His *Poesie campestri e marittime* [*Rustic and Sea Poems*] were found equally pleasant. He was among the first to make German poetry known to Italians with his *Saggio sulla bella poesia alemanna* [*Essay on the Beautiful Poetry of Germany*]; his idol was the Swiss pastoral poet Salomon Gessner. However, more of a poet than Bertòla was Ludovico Savioli of Bologna (d. 1804) another native of Romagna, whose songs of love bearing the Ovidian title of *Amores* were widely read over a long period. They have the facility and the felicity of the Latin poet. A frugal and refined maker of sonnets, graphic or representative, was the follower of Frugoni, Giuliano Cassiani of Modena (d. 1778), to whom as an artist both Alfieri, in his lyrical poetry, and Foscolo owe something.

Carlo Goldoni

His Life

One of the principal poets of the age is Carlo Goldoni who, close to the midpoint of the century, accomplished the form of the Italian comedy. When quite old, Goldoni wrote his *Mémoires* in French, in which he gave a detailed account of his life and his art. He was born in Venice in 1707 into a family where the gay and open-handed generosity of his grandfather encouraged good humor and a passion for the theater. His doctor-father sent him to Rimini to follow a course of humanistic studies and philosophy, but he ran away in company with some players, who went along the Po River with him as far as Chioggia, where his mother was staying. He needed to be equipped to earn a living, however, and he was registered in the faculty of law at Pavia as a scholar in the Collegio Ghisleri. A satire that he directed against the ladies of the city caused him to be expelled from the institute. Thereafter he obtained some employment in chancery in the tribunals until, after the death of his father, he decided to obtain his diploma. This he succeeded in winning at Padua, the morning after a night of gaming. He then engaged in practice as a lawyer, and he was not lacking in the talent, fluency of speech, or the ability required in that profession. His heart, however, was in the theater. He was assiduous in attendance at performances, and he was not too proud to appear himself in some plays: in Milan, for example, where he was in the service of the Venetian resident assigned to the Austrian government. He also played in Venice, Verona, where he became the poet of the Imer company, and Genoa, where he followed the company and married Nicoletta Conio, with whom he lived in perfect accord to the end of his days. After his marriage he devoted himself to more serious activities. He was consul of the Republic of Genoa in Venice, a lawyer at Pisa, and when he was acclaimed as an Arcadian, he had many clients. But the Medebach Company was playing at Leghorn, and he became its poet. Since the company was compliant to his suggestions, he conceived the idea of making use of it to impose, at last, his long-cherished reform of the comic theater. Goldoni succeeded in having many of his comedies performed at the Sant'Angelo Theater in Venice, from 1748 on, fascinating the public with his novelties and with his fecundity which, in the comedy season of 1750–1751, enabled him to compose sixteen plays. Then, for about ten years, he worked for the San Luca Theater, where he presented his best works and put his reform into full operation.

Goldoni found adversaries who gave him no truce. A Brescian with a mania for writing, Pietro Chiari — a Pindarizing lyricist, a novellist of great and plebeian effect, on the type of Madeleine de Scudéry, and a bombastic, tearjerking dramatist as well — held the field; at the same time Carlo Gozzi made mock of both Chiari and Goldoni. In his *Mémoires,* either from meekness or indifference, Goldoni does not even mention these competitors. Distaste for such struggles may well have mingled with his inborn liking for travel and the hope of finding a more decorous way of spending his later years when, in 1761, he agreed to go to Paris as director of the Italian Theater, the *Comédie italienne.* In Paris he composed some twenty-four comedies in French or Italian. Some were *a soggetto* (cf. below), as his players preferred, others were fully written out. *Le bourru bienfaisant* [*The Rough Diamond*], which Voltaire admired, and *Le fastueux avare* [*The Magnificent Miser*] were particularly well received. Having been favorably noticed at court, he was appointed to teach Italian to the Dauphines, the daughters of King Louis XV. Goldoni speaks with moving tenderness of the kindness of those princesses and with enthusiasm for Paris and its wonders. He knew Voltaire, became a friend of Diderot — formerly accused of plagiarizing his comedies — and risked a visit to Rousseau who, no friend of the theater, did not receive him very cordially. In Paris he calmly and happily grew old until, during the Revolution, the pension assigned to him by the court was revoked by the Convention. This was restored to him in February 7, 1793, at the behest of the French dramatist Marie-Joseph Chénier, but it was too late. The more-than-octogenarian poet had died the previous day, February 6, 1793.

The Goldoni Comedies

Goldoni was born for the theater. While still too young to have developed a sense of reality, he attempted the lacrymose or the heroic tragedy, such as *Belisario, Rinaldo ardito,* or the Metastasian melodrama, and more successfully, *opera buffa,* with *De gustibus non est disputandum* and *Il signor Dottore.* But his proper field, and his triumph, was comedy. Already in the previous century the *Commedia dell'arte* had taken precedence over the classical comedies; they were called *"dell'arte"* both because they were composed by professional "artists" or comedians, and because the actors followed only *a soggetto,* more or less a given outline or scenario, and in the performance they improvised — the cleverer their wit and the more unexpected their antics and buffoonery, the louder they were applauded. Miming had an important place in these plebeian performances, and certain typed characters, which met with particular favor, became fixed as *masks:* personages who constantly represented certain characteristics, who were more distinct the more the situations or environments into which they were introduced were alien or opposed to them. The audience recognized them by their special makeup. The most famous, at least in Venice, were Pantalone [Pantaloon], the affable, miserly old merchant; Brighella, the roguish trickster; and Arlecchino [Harlequin], the country lad turned servant. All the characters had some flavor of the masks and their conventionalities: the gallant lovers (Florindo and Rosaura); the affectionate and sly maids (Corallina, Smeraldina, Colombina), and so on. The plots of these *commedie dell'arte* were complicated no matter how common; great *coups de théatre* or sensational stage tricks and effects were frequent; brawls, braggadocio, ungainly stumblings about, and buffooneries of all sorts were in profusion. The endings of the plays were usually weddings. Judging by the great favor which they enjoyed all over Europe, it is permissible to conclude that the *commedie dell'arte* must also have had their good qualities of spontaneity and sprightliness. It is certain that some of the leading players were great artists in their way; for example, Sacchi, who was so highly praised by Goldoni himself.

Goldoni wanted to replace the comedy "of art" or "subject" with what he called the "comedy of *character*" that is to say, he wished to portray a world of reality, at least to the extent permitted by theatrical limitations, along the lines used by the ancient comics and by Molière. This ambition of his was really another aspect of that need of rationality, of a return to simplicity, to good sense, and to nature, which animated the eighteenth century. On the author's part, it was the ambition to give comedy to Italy just as others were trying to give her tragedy.

With the tenacity that characterizes peaceable men, Goldoni proceeded slowly with his reform. It was necessary to cool the liking of the public for the old genre; it was necessary to persuade the self-centered actors who were proud of their ability to improvise, to repeat the words of their poet and not to speak on their own. Goldoni began by writing only the principal parts (as in *Momolo Cortesan*). Four years later he found it possible to write a whole comedy, *Le donne di garbo* [*The Gracious Ladies*], but he never freed himself completely from the influences of the *Commedia dell'arte*. Retention of the masks (even in some of his best plays), the lack of the unity of place observed in the classical comedy and in Molière, the division into three instead of five acts, the ending with the usual marriage, the moral recited by the last character, and the pranks of the servants survived in Goldoni as characteristics of the old comedy. It was possible for Cesarotti to say, not entirely unjustly, that "Goldoni has written only four or five comedies: the others are farces to amuse the common people." It is to be noted, however, that truly original writers build, as Ariosto did, upon the foundations of others: they do not destroy, rather they assimilate and transform.

Voltaire defined Goldoni rather well by calling him the painter and son of nature. The Goldonian comedy is a piece of life brought upon the stage: now the turbulent life of the people, more often petty bourgeois life. Goldoni is infatuated with that life, which he knows in all its aspects or, rather, in the numberless varieties of its few aspects. His women especially, whether girls in love or wives who know the ways of the world, or wise mothers, or servant girls who understand and know, are drawn with a thoroughly Venetian liveliness in their special mixture of grace and ingenuous mischievousness. Those comedies were born all around the author, rather than within him. They are reality caught in action. Therefore there is no falseness in the dialogues (unless it is some invasion of moral elements), and it necessary to come to Manzoni to find anyone as spontaneous. His affection for the bourgeois world keeps Goldoni from stepping over the line into satire, which forms such a large part of the repertoire of illustrious comic writers, such as his much admired Molière. His constant tone is that of gaiety and hilarity; his greatest virtue is directness and verity. Therefore, in what may be his finest comedies, he employed the Venetian dialect, either in some characters or in all: Goldoni felt that the bourgeois world could find direct expression only in its own language. Toward the end of his life, he preferred prose to verse, although he made wide and not always good use of the verse-form of the French comedy, the double septenarius.

"Little about the prince, nothing about God" was the motto of the conservative Venetian republic: Goldoni never satirized the princes or the courts, and never brought any churchman upon the stage or mocked superstition; yet he portrayed it humorously in certain pages of his *Mémoires*. For all that, the plays show the effects of the changed times. The decadent patrician class, run down or impoverished, appears often on the stage. Opposite it, and looked upon with lively sympathy, are the commoners with their, as Carducci would say, "plebeian soundness." In one comedy, *La Guerra*, inspired by the wars in Lombardy for the Austrian succession, amid which the poet found himself, he voices the humanitarianism of the times by deploring the profession of arms. In another, *Le donne curiose* [*The Curious Women*], he goes in for mockery of secret societies which were then producing impostors and mystifiers, such as the famous Cagliostro and Casanova.

The comedies of Goldoni, properly so-called, number over a hundred. Lively scenes are never lacking, even in the mediocre ones tossed off in haste. Among the best, we would include *La Bottega del Caffè* [*The Coffeehouse*]; *L'avventuriero onorato* [*The Honored Adventurer*], in which the author alludes to himself; *Le Smanie per la villeggiatura* [*The Mania for Holiday Resorts*]; *La Villeggiatura;* and *Il ritorno dalla villeggiatura* [*The Return from the Holiday*] in which especially lifelike is the portrait of the lady who, in poverty, must carry on the customs of the rich; *La finta ammalata* [*The Woman Pretending to be Sick*], a merry mockery of doctors, reminiscent of *L'Amour* mèdecin and *Le malade imaginaire* of Molière; *Il campielo* [*Small Square in Venice*], and *Le baruffe chiozzote* [*Brawls in Chioggia*], both of which are animated pictures of the life of the Venetian lower classes; *Sior Todero brontolon* [*Mr. Todero the Grumbler*], the annoying, good, old man, a theme recurring later in *Le Bourru bienfaisant;* *Il ventaglio* [*The Fan*], admirable for the complexity of the plot; *La Locandiera* [*The Innkeeper,* or *The Hostess*], which is the eternal story of beauty that conquers all pride, and yet, the story in its ingenuousness — or perhaps because of it — still occupies the stages; *I rusteghi* [*The Rustics* or, rather, *The Boors*], Goldoni's masterpiece (made into an opera by Wolf-Ferrari on a libretto by Giuseppe Pizzolato: *I Quattro Rusteghi*) portrays four old men of outmoded austerity who wish to arrange marriages between their offspring without the intended "betrothed" even knowing each other, but the women are stronger than their truculent husbands and succeed in making the rights of the heart and good sense triumphant.

Giuseppe Parini

His Life

Born at Bosisio in Brianza in 1729 to a spinner of silk, this son of the people, of the working class that was looked down upon at that time, never denied his origin. Indeed from it he drew the deepest inspiration for his poetry of the battle for democracy, in the best sense of that word. Obliged by domestic necessities to become a priest, he never did anything that might bring dishonor upon his habit. He lived all his life in Milan. He was a friend of Passeroni, who was a collaborator of the *Caffè,* and kept his mind open to whatever new or noble attracted a following in the Lombard capital. His poverty led him to accept the situation of preceptor in families of high rank and to suffer in them the humiliations then inherent in that employment. Thus he came to know in its reality what the aristocratic world was like, a world on which, in his poem, he was later to wreak such a long and merry vengeance. That poem, *Il Giorno* [*The Day*], made him famous and feared. Count Firmian, a minister of the Austrian government of Maria Theresa, to whom it was important to free the reform government from the impediments of a parasitical and reactionary old nobility, chose to protect the daring poet. He entrusted Parini with the editing of the *Gazette of Milan* and also gave him counselling concerning the reform of the schools, which Parini wanted to see freed from the ecclesiastics whom he believed to be incapable of understanding the civilizing office of letters. Firmian appointed the poet to a professorship of literature in the Palatine schools and later, after the suppression of the Jesuit order, to a post in the gymnasium (high school) of Brera, from which Parini could make known his principles of literature and literary criticism to great numbers of auditors. For Parini, the death of Firmian meant the loss of any protection. His chair was not taken from him, but he was allowed to live, lame and half-blind as he was, in extreme poverty, which never affected his integrity. When the French reached Milan, the poet of liberty, who had always refused to eulogize Maria Theresa, was made a member of the Municipal Council of the new republic. However, that was not the liberty for which Parini yearned. Above any political revolution there was for him one moral law, one human right, which had to be respected. He withdrew from that office. Death overtook him in his seventieth year, in 1799, when the Austro-Russians, for a single year, before Napoleon's victory at Marengo, had restored the old Austrian government. Parini's last poem was a sonnet of greeting and of warning to those fierce restorers.

"Il Giorno" [The Day]

This poem is one of the outstanding works of humanity and art production in the second half of the eighteenth century. In it the poet assumes the rôle of preceptor to a young man of the nobility, a role which he had so often filled in reality; he teaches his pupil how to spend the day (hence the title of the poem, which smacks of parody of the *Works and Days* of Hesiod). He accompanies the young man during every moment of his day and is present at all his shows of vanity and of mean or cowardly actions. It is understood that the poet-teacher maintains a constant attitude of irony and speaks with a calmness which he loses a few times. He speaks with a preceptive, magisterial, and epic solemnity, which is well adapted to stressing the futility of that society, while the perfection of the blank verse, the frequent picturizations, and the mythological episodes are exquisitely attuned to the lordliness and the elegance of the aristocratic environment in which, ideally, the preceptor lives. He makes evident his profound knowledge of all the rules of high society and his will to see them impeccably executed; the sillier or more iniquitous they are, the more zealous he shows himself in their observance, pretending to adopt as his own the scorn which the gay blades of the time ostentatiously heaped upon the laws of morality and the most venerable traditions.

The poem is divided into four parts. *Il Mattino* [*Morning*], published in 1763, and *Mezzogiorno* [*Noon*], published in 1765, are complete; *Sera*, or *Vesporo* [*Evening*] and *Notte* [*Night*] are fragmentary. In the *Mattino* the teacher watches over everything that concerns the first hours of the "young lord" (generally referred to as *giovin signore*). The latter awakens at midday, wavers between coffee and chocolate, receives his first visits in bed — among them, those of his dancing master, French teacher, and music master. Then he proceeds to the most serious business of the day, which is dressing; during this proceeding, while still in the hands of his hairdresser, he reads or skims through his favorite books: for example, Voltaire' *La Pucelle,* or the very licentious *Contes of La Fontaine.* Finally, in the hall of his forebears, who were men useful to society and look down on him severely from their frames, he girds on his sword, goes down between two lines of servants and leaps, frowning, into his waiting carriage. The coachman whips up his horses, caring not a whit about crushing pedestrians and staining the street with plebeian blood; there are laws, but his master will take care of him against any laws. With that image of blood the *Mattino* comes to an end.

In the *Mezzogiorno* the young lord has reached the goal of his drive: the house of the lady whose recognized *cavaliere servente* [lady's man or squire] he is. In this custom, so widespread among the upper class, Parini saw the ultimate moral degradation of a class which he yet would have liked to lead back to its past dignity; he returns to the subject several times but in the most satirical language. The "young sir" is thereupon admitted into the circle of the young heroes who form a crown around the lady, although not without first having been greeted at the threshold by her husband. When he has played the comedy of love and jealousy with her (for it is the absolute lack of true passions, even evil ones, which makes these inane Parinian personages repugnant documents of a dead society), the hero leads his lady to the repast which forms the principal scene of the *Mezzogiorno* and takes his seat beside her, unless, on that day, there is some illustrious guest, some cynical and disgusting patrician adventurer, for in that case the place of honor would belong to the guest. The poet says little or nothing about the dishes served, for the subject would be too trivial, but he does take note of the various types of diners. Among them are the big eater and the vegetarian, a curious antithesis: the latter does not deign even to sample the meats, out of humanitarianism and the desire to appear to be a philosopher. His loud declamations against the barbarism of slaughtering animals awaken a sad memory in the lady: remembrance of the day when a servant dared to bestow a kick upon her little bitch, her "virgin puppy." But the impious fellow was expelled from that house and from every other house, and finally was reduced to begging alms on the streets. As between a man and the little dog, the dog was far more precious than the man to the humanitarian heart of the lady. Nor are the other subjects discussed at the table less interesting. Atheistic philosophy, trade, eulogies of France and England as opposed to Italian stupidity, these are some of the arguments; here the knowledgeable lady joins in, for women knew science too, and even mathematics had lost any abstruseness for them. Afterwards they all go into the coffee room. The beggars, those beaten in the battle of life and who used to come to hospitable doors to receive the remnants of the feast, must content themselves now with sniffing from a distance: an awful flight of imagination, full of prophecy and of threats. With the noisy game of *trictrac,* an invention of Mercury to allow two lovers to reveal to each other what is in their hearts without the jealous husband overhearing, the *Mezzogiorno* comes to an end: livelier, more nimble, more fully satirical than the *Mattino.* Clearly the poet is now sure of himself and of his public.

We have only a long fragment of the *Sera.* Here the Corso is pictured, the drive of the "young sir" and his lady in his carriage: the picture is animated by various ancient and recent types of the nobility. Then there are the social visits, which take us ever further into the hypocrisy and falseness of the society flailed by the poet. Of the *Notte,* also, which would have shown us the hero at the gaming tables and the theater, only fragments exist. One which portrays the dark and fearsome night of the steely times of the past in contrast with the luminous gay nights of the eighteenth century, is a marvelous piece of description Why Parini left these parts of his *Giorno* incomplete and never published them is difficult to explain. It might have been due to the artist's dissatisfaction, since it is known how he worked and reworked his lines: several versions of the published parts of the poem exist. Perhaps moral reasons prevailed. In the latter years of the poet's activity, when the rest of *Il Giorno* should have come out, it may have seemed useless cruelty to pursue a social class which, in exile, in the prisons, and on the scaffolds of France was expiating its misdeeds and shortcomings.

The *Odi* [*Odes*]

Parini's temperament, more reflective and meditative than given to enthusiasms, found its perfect expression in the bitter and elegant irony of *Il Giorno*. He succeeds less well in the *Odi* in many of which he is fighting for the same civilized and humanitarian ideals as in that poem. *La vita rustica,* a eulogy of the country life, free of servility, which the poet hopes to lead in the fields; *La salubrità dell'aria,* antithesis between the healthfulness of Brianza and the unhygienic conditions in Milan; *L'impostura,* in a style between the comic and the satirical against the always lucky divinity: either it reveals itself in the figures of Numa Pompilius, Alexander, Muhammad, or the more typical ones of the poet's age, the doctor and the hypocrite; *L'educazione,* for his noble pupil Carlo Imbonati, in which it is taught that nobility is a result of virtue and not of noble blood; *L'innesto del vaiuolo* [*Vaccination*], in support of the new and much combatted remedy against the frequent epidemics of smallpox; *Il Bisogno* [*The Need*], a lively statement of the principle that the laws should prevent rather than punish crimes, many of them committed because of dire need; *La Musica,* against the horrible custom of mutilating boys to make singers of them. These are what might be called the social odes of Parini, in which meditative study is felt rather than impetus, élan, and art. But in seriousness of content, vigor of expression, and in the very directness of their speaking to the intellect rather than to the ear, they stand high above the lyric of the period, futile, facile, and melodious. The author is more eloquent when he plucks the moral chord of his lyre, as in the powerful ode *La Caduta* [*The Fall*] where, to a peasant who advises him to make his poetry pay financially by prostituting it to the base instincts of the powerful, he responds with the pride of the poet and the man offended in the deepest of feelings: his dignity. No less meaningful, even though less beautiful, is the ode *A Silvia* [*To Sylvia*] in which, concerning a very free fashion lately come from France called *à la guillotine,* he stresses how necessary decency is in a woman and how, by licentiousness, she passes rapidly into the most frightful corruption. He also composed lyric poems which, while perhaps not love poetry, show his fervent and passionate devotion to beauty. These are from the heart of a poet already for advanced in years, yet they are among the most spontaneous; for example, *Il Dono* [*The Gift*], about the tragedies of Alfieri given to him by a lady — the poet paints the contrast between the images of delight awakened by the lovely giver of the book and the somber ones which accompany the reading of those tragedies. Still more tender is the ode *Il Messaggio* [*The Message*] about another lovely lady who sent a request for news of his ailing health. He reveals how exquisite an artist he can be in the last of his odes, *Alla Musa* [*To the Muse*]. In the close of this Sapphic ode he extols himself as an "Italic swan who, for his good friends, on high scorns the cowardly malevolent crowd": lines wherein lies the salient characteristic of the poet, so democratic in spirit, so austere in conscience, and so aristocratic in his art.

Parini's prose writings are no longer read. *I Principi fondamentali e generali delle belle lettere applicati alle belle arti* [*The Basic and General Principles of Literature Applied to Fine Arts*], a résumé of lectures given at the Brera, repose on a sensist philosophy which no longer suffices for our aesthetic requirements. His *Discorso sulla poesia* [*Lecture on Poetry*] still presents some interest for the new dignity which Parini sees in it, and the *Dialogo sulla nobiltà* [*Dialogue on Nobility*] presents a dialogue between a poet and a ruined nobleman who occupy the same tomb. The poet derides the presumptions of the noble and affirms the equality of all men: a prelude to *Il Giorno*. Besides, not all of Parini's poetry is read now. There are poems of gallantry, trivial ones, and some for special occasions, as was the Arcadian social custom; there are even some comic ones, as required by tradition. However, even in his minor and fragmentary things the new conscience is ardently affirmed, as in the blank verse of the *Auto da fè* against the tortures of the Inquisition, abolished by Maria Theresa; in those on *La Guerra* which despises wars of conquest; and in the *Sciolti al consigliere De Martini* [*Blank Verse Addressed to Councilman De Martini*] which very clearly express the ethical intentions of the author of *Il Giorno*.

Vittorio Alfieri

His Life

Alfieri spoke about himself at length in the *Vita scritta da esso* [*Life Written by Himself*], a book in which the proud author first pictures himself as the slave of every dissipation, then the master of his will, with the inaccuracies and omissions inevitable in one who wants to publish his own defence rather than his confessions. But it is salutary for youth to read that book, so inwardly true and so substantially heroic.

Vittorio Alfieri was born in Asti in 1749 to a family of hereditary counts. The poet, a hater of tyrants, was proud of his noble blood all his life, although he claimed it imposed more duties than rights. As a boy he was sickly, melancholy, and choleric. He studied first in the *Collegio* of the nobles in Turin, then in the academy, eight years in all, which he called years of noneducation. He learned nothing; his heart found no nourishment in a purely mechanical instruction which spoke neither to the feelings nor to the reasoning faculties. Yet during those years he did much reading: French novels; *The Thousand Nights and One Night;* and Fleury's *Ecclesiastical History,* which contributed considerably to his scepticism with regard to religion. Ariosto filled him with enthusiasm.

He came out of the academy an ensign in the provincial regiment of Asti; but Alfieri detested the profession and the discipline of arms. Since he was his own master, he devoted himself to traveling, which kept him occupied for some ten years. It was one way of giving vent to the obscure and powerful need of action which tormented him and quieting the melancholy that often assailed him. Furthermore, in his travels he observed nothing. Only great architectural creations profoundly fascinated him; it was the only form of art for which he seemed to enjoy. He also enjoyed the solemn aspects of nature, such as the sea and the mountains. On his first voyage, he looked at Milan; Florence, where he meditated before the tomb of Michelangelo in Santa Croce; Rome; and, center of every joy, Naples. From there he went back to Rome and, by way of Bologna, to Venice. Then he traveled across all Upper Italy to Genoa. Without losing any time, he embarked at Genoa for Marseilles and hastened on to the Paris of his desires; the city made a very unpleasant impression on him and he was soon off to London. He immediately became enthusiastic about London and England. There he seemed to have found that industrious activity in the men, that proudness of character, that liberty in political life, which he had vainly sought elsewhere. Before long he was in Holland, where he plunged into one of his stormy, troubled love affairs, which narrowly missed ending with his suicide. Finally he returned to Italy.

Only a few months later he again fell prey to ennui. His boredom drove him to depart on a second voyage, longer and more complicated than the first. He began with the Germanic countries; at Schönbrunn, in the Imperial gardens, he saw Metastasio make the customary "little genuflection" to Maria Theresa and refused to approach him; in Berlin he was presented to the great Frederick, the general in command of that horrible barracks, as Prussia seemed to him. "The king spoke those four usual words according to usage. I observed him closely, staring respectfully at him eye to eye and I thanked Heaven for not having made me born his slave." Then, off through Denmark and, afterwards, Sweden, where the traveler admired the cleanliness of the houses and the dark majesty of the winter landscape. Here he abandoned himself to the fun of sleighing. Then, crossing a frozen sea, he reached Finland, from which he arrived at Petersburg. Russia appeared to him a land of barbarians masked as Europeans: a nation aping France. He refused to be presented to the famous Catherine II — "philosophizing Clytemnestra" — nor did he continue on to Moscow but, crossing Germany and Holland, he made his way back to his beloved England. In London he lost his head completely over a woman who was absolutely unworthy of his love. From it there ensued a duel with her husband and, on the husband's side, a suit for divorce. There was a scandal and Alfieri found it advisable to leave England. Back in Paris, he refused to meet a great man, one as proud as he: Jean Jacques Rousseau. Passing the Pyrenees he entered Spain. Crossing the deserts of Aragon, which harmonized with his melancholy, he rode ahead of his retinue and reached Madrid alone. The ill humor of the wanderer increased. One evening he had a beastly quarrel with his faithful servitor Elia who, in arranging his hair before going to bed, had pulled a lock of it. Then from Madrid he went to Lisbon: here the Abbé di Caluso, employed in the embassy of the king of Piedmont, read him the *canzone* of Guidi *Alla Fortuna* [*To Fortune*]. Alfieri listened, quivering with enthusiasm; he knew he was born a poet. Thereafter he always cherished warm feelings towards that excellent man. Finally he returned to Turin.

So ends the period which Alfieri calls that of the travels and of dissoluteness. It would be wrong, however, to believe that in those years of his early manhood (at the end of his second voyage he was barely twenty-three) Alfieri had done nothing but dissipate his energies. In those travels he had acquired experience of men and things; he had tempered his energies. Not only had he loved women, and horses as well, but he had learned English and Spanish passably well. The future writer of tragedies had heard the master works of European theater in the principal playhouses. In addition, he had read the sceptical philosopher, Montaigne, with great diligence and Plutarch, with great enthusiasm; later he had grown fond of the Italian classics, which he had acquired during his last stay in Paris. In truth he had learned more than a regular course of studies or familiarity with learned men could have taught him and he had kept his originality.

"A third love net," as he called it, in which he remained for a good four years, was awaiting him upon his return. One day, while tending his love, who was ill, he conceived the idea of killing his boredom by dashing off some scenes on the fatal passion of Anthony for Cleopatra which, in its effects, resembled his own. Out of this came a tragedy, which was presented one year later (1775) at the Carignano Theater. The author had written a farce to follow the tragedy, *I Poeti,* making fun of himself in it, so little did he hope for a success. On the contrary, his success was great, and Alfieri thought his road and his vocation were plainly indicated. He proposed to give to Italy the tragedy which she lacked: a magnificent ambition. Tragedy, more than any other poetical form, filled his overpowering need for action; in a manner of speaking, it was a substitute for action, and the theater was the most direct means of proclaiming the ideas of rebellion and of liberty which were roaring within him.

He dedicated himself to his new life with the impetuosity and will which he brought to whatever he did. He forced himself to forget French; he compelled himself to read the Italian classics in order to learn the language; he learned Latin. When one is only twenty-seven, everything is possible. To "dispiedmontize" himself in customs and language and to breathe freer air, he traveled in Tuscany. In Pisa he submitted his first tragedies to the learned professors there, but they could make little out of them. He went to Siena; then Florence, where he met Luisa Stolberg, the Countess of Albany, young wife of old Charles Edward Stuart, the unlucky former pretender to the throne of England now given to debauchery. He loved her for the rest of his life, and he resolved to remain forever in Florence, giving all his possessions to his sister and contenting himself with the income. To follow his beloved he went off on several more travels; without her he could neither live nor compose. He followed her to Rome, where a cardinal (Henry Duke of York, the brother of Charles Stuart) had her shut up in a convent. Alfieri's love affair and his ideas raised a scandal in the city; he avoided expulsion from Rome by departing precipitately by way of Siena, Venice, and Milan, where he met Parini; then he returned to Florence. From there he made another voyage to England, for pleasure and to buy at least fourteen English horses. Meanwhile the courts had pronounced the Countess separated from her husband. He rejoined her in Alsace, where she had relatives and connections; he followed her to Paris, where he lived for more than three years, until the outbreak of the Revolution.

First he eulogized, then hated the Revolution as the triumph, not of free men, but of freedmen. When he lost the funds which he had invested in banks in France and, later, with difficulty salvaged the Parisian edition of his tragedies, he returned with the Countess to Florence. He made that city his permanent home, dividing his time between studies (it was then that he learned Greek) and hatred of the French. Death came to him in his fifty-fourth year, in 1803. He was laid to rest in the temple of Italian glories, in the church of Santa Croce. His Countess commissioned the famous sculptor, Antonio Canova, to create a monument to him there.

The Tragedies of Alfieri

In rare moments of extraordinary emotion, Alfieri saw, like a flash of lightning, his tragedies take form in synthetic outline. With his soul filled with this vision, he would then make a prose draft (the first tragedies in French, the rest in Italian); he would leave them in this unfinished, redundant condition, for a time, occasionally quite long. Then, in moments of renewed inspiration, he would strip off all superfluity and versify them.

In its origin, then, the Alfierian tragedy is a creation of impetuous and ardent inspiration, like any work of high poetry; it preserves the stamp of the original synthesis which is the same as saying the stamp of its intrinsic unity. This fact explains several characteristics of that tragedy. It explains the traditional unities of time and place, which for this author are not extrinsic and to which he rigidly adhered as the great French tragedians had done. It explains the elimination of all unnecessary and insignificant characters (which the French tragic writers had not eliminated, with the possible exception of Voltaire), such as tutors or guardians, confidantes or nurses; the suppression of all situations not directly related to the fundamental motif of the drama. Therefore the Alfierian tragedy has only a small cast of characters. The personalities of the character reveals itself in aroused dialogues or in brief monologues. Also, there is generally nothing arbitrary in the action; it is the manifestation, the logical expression of the characters and of their passions. These are the real and only motive forces of the drama; not blind chance, as is often the case in Shakespeare, and not destiny. The action starts immediately, at the beginning. The antecedent facts are made known as occasion offers and with utmost brevity. The protagonist appears in the second act: his physiognomy is already known from the developments of the first act, and interest in him is already keen. In the opinion of the author, who was his own most objective and severe critic, the fourth act is the weakest one of all, the one in which the action sometimes slackens; in the fifth, the catastrophe bursts forth unexpectedly. It is the densest and shortest act.

The struggle between liberty and tyranny, the eulogy of the free man, who conquers at the end or, more often, succumbs, this is the dominant motif of many of Alfieri's tragedies. The free man gathers within himself the superior qualities: pride and courage; but almost always his loyalty brings about his ruin. The tyrant is portrayed quite profoundly: brooding, shrewd, ironical, and cynical. While the presentation of the free man is reminiscent of Plutarch, who was for Alfieri's age the book of heroes, the delineation of the tyrant owes much to Machiavelli and Tacitus, no less well known to the poet. In that terrible world, love affairs are infrequent, but there is never any lack of women's roles: mothers, wives, and daughters, all tenderly feminine. For Alfieri, tragedy is synonymous with action: action to arouse in the Italians the desire for the heroic and its glorification: heroism as the only road to the rebuilding of consciences. Therefore he is the hidden protagonist of his tragedies, hidden but constant, and his theater is filled with him, his angers, his ideas, and his passions. His style, that is, his expression is all his own, all responsive to his purpose of shaking the flabby fibers of his hearers, to reach them deeply within, and not merely to win their ear, and to make them reflect and not to amuse them. His poetic line is rarely melodic but often harmonic dry but far from prosaic; is sometimes sublime in the concision, as in the great tragedians.

In approximately chronological order, the tragedies are: *Filippo, Polinice, Agamennone, Oreste, Virginia, La congiura dei Pazzi* [*The Pazzi Conspiracy*], *Don Garzia, Maria Stuarda, Rosmunda, Ottavia, Timoleone, Antigone, Merope, Saul, Agide, Sofonisba, Mirra, Bruto primo, Bruto secondo;* in all nineteen, to which are to be added *Alcesti seconda,* a consequence of the translation of the *Alcestis* of Euripides, and the *tramelogedia,* as he called it, *Abele* [*Abel*].

Filippo, in which the struggle between Philip, the cruel King of Spain and his noble son Carlo is not only the sruggle between the spirits of tyranny and those of liberty, but, on the father's side, jealousy of the father toward a son who loves his stepmother, formerly his betrothed. This play, and *Oreste,* are among the most nearly perfect tragedies of Alfieri. In *Oreste,* the rigid Greek myth of Orestes is humanized somewhat, in that Orestes consciously kills his mother's paramour Aegisthus, then blinded by rage, he unknowingly slays his mother Clytemnestra, who has come on to defend her lover. *Don Garzia,* is a dark and bloody story of the Medici family; *Merope* is written in emulation of the very tender play of Maffei; *Mirra* deals with the mythical, wretched love of Myrrah for her father, for which she suffers in silence a long time and then, at the very moment when a word betrays her, kills herself. But, the consensus over the years is that Alfieri's masterpiece is *Saul:* a tragedy which, the author narrates, came to him in a rush.

In it, in the guise of the ancient king of Israel abandoned by God to be a prey of the Evil One, a suicide on the field of battle against the Philistines, the author portrays in gigantic forms not the tyrant but himself, with his exaltations and his repressions, his furies and his despairs. For the first time in a great work of art, man is presented as the wretched victim of his own overwhelming ego: the romantic man.

Other Works

Contemporaneous with the tragedies, and with the same impetuosity, Alfieri wrote some important prose works. They were important not so much for evaluating the reform of tragedy (for which all the concepts may be read in a *Lettera al Calsabigi* and in the *Considerazioni sulle sue tragedie* [*Reflections on His Tragedies*] as in showing the new importance as apostle of liberty and molder of consciences which was to be attributed to the writer. The three books of *Del principe e delle lettere* [*The Prince and Literature*] are all aimed against the evil of patronage, an ulcer that would never permit the restoration of Italian literature to health. The same patronage, ever since the fifteenth century, had been granted by princes and rulers to writers, who thus became hired slaves; whereas liberty is the air the writer must breathe — the writer must proclaim useful truths to his nation, create public opinion, and represent the only hero possible in times of servitude. Even more vehement is his treatise *Della Tirannide* [*On Tyranny*], in which he defends the thesis that the tyrant is most dangerous when shows himself to be enlightened and well disposed toward favoring the progress of his states; this with manifest allusion to the princely reformers of the time. In the *Panegirico di Plinio a Traiano* [*Eulogy of Pliny Addressed to Trajan*], the author refashions the panegyric in his own way by imagining that Pliny exhorts the emperor to renounce his rights to the empire, now that he has insured its peace and order, and to become again a plain Roman citizen, an act which would be his purest act and his greatest glory. In the dialogue *Della virtù sconosciuta* [*On the Unknown Virtue*], Alfieri imagines his conversation with the ghost of his recently deceased Sienese friend Francesco Gori; he eulogizes that man of ancient virtue and asks his permission to dedicate to him the tragedy *La Congiura dei Pazzi*, which in great part was the outcome of discussions with that fervent though obscure lover of liberty.

Alfieri's prose writings are warm, eloquent, personal, and they exercized no less influence than the tragedies. They became the code, the laws which the great spirits of Italy who came after him followed when they resolved that the Italian tradition should be preserved and the Italian conscience renewed as the first condition of political renewal. Such spirits were Foscolo, Santarosa, Niccolini, Mazzini, Gioberti: all men filled with the ideas of Alfieri, especially in their consideration of literature as a civil priesthood, a ministry. Similarly the epic poem *Etruria vendicata* [*Tuscany Avenged*] was conceived in the spirit of the tragedies, being the narration of the assassination of Alessandro de'Medici at the hands of Lorenzino, whom the author makes a hero. The poem is not without scenes of great effect and moving and satirical passages, but taken as a whole it is much more declamation than poetry.

His lyrical poems are more praiseworthy, even having made some critics believe that Alfieri was born more poet than tragedian. Certainly, he wrote innumerable verses, almost all of them inspired by different moments of his life and of the times, as he relates in his autobiography. Those which express his love and his melancholy, his fundamental pessimism, are beautiful and profound. His political rhymes are very rhetorical, such as the five Pindaric odes; *America libera,* on the American Revolution; and the odes *Parigi sbastigliato,* concerning the taking of the Bastille, which the poet, then in Paris and then a revolutionary, eulogized.

Satires and Comedies

In truth there is something violent, forced, and cerebral in the Alfierian poems. These qualities are most apparent in the *Satires,* written in a period when the poet's ardor for liberty was growing fainter or, rather, he was feeling the great difference that existed between his own concept of liberty and that which he saw being put into practice every day. There are seventeen *Satires* including the one used as prologue and deriding the ladies' men (the *Cavalier servente veterano*). In tercets of Dantean harshness, he examines the customs, the currents of ideas, the political forms of the times, inveighing fiercely even in cases where Parini smiled ironically. Among the more significant satires is the very short one, *I, Re* [*The Kings*], who are to be destroyed, to be sure, but only by the peoples who no longer need them; also *La Sesquiplebe* (plebe, populace one and a half times: sesquipopulace) in which the aristocrat strikes at the hated middle class; *Le Leggi* [*The Laws*], impossible or useless to enslaved populations, and in Italy perverted to the protection of delinquents; *L'Educazione* which pictures the emptiness of the patrician education and the moral wretchedness of the preceptors, held in less esteem than their masters' coachmen; *L'Antireligioneria* [*Antireligiousness*] directed against Voltaire; *I Pedanti* [*The Pedants*], is a witty mockery of the Crusca academicians and others of their ilk, with whom the poet was more than once at odds; *I Duelli,* a custom which Count Alfieri desires to see continued; *La Filantropineria* [philanthropy, with a pejorative ending], a disparagement of the humanitarian spirit of the times; *Il Commercio* which seems to the poet to be the coarsest and most detestable of social activities; and then *Le Donne* [*Women*], who in themselves are neither good nor bad, but are what men make them.

Certainly, the tendency toward violence in Alfieri was very pronounced ever since the time, when he had barely passed his twentieth year, he wrote the *Esquisse du Jugement universel* [*Outline of Universal Judgment*] in bad French, and revealed himself in many *Epigrammi* hurled, as occasion demanded, at his enemies, mostly literary, and against the hated French. He gathered the epigrams written against that nation, with some sonnets and prose compositions, together with his imaginary defence of Louis XV facing the convention, into a small volume entitled *Misogallo,* which was published posthumously. Even in his reactionary exaggerations and inability to understand the Revolution at its true worth, he did much to spread the idea that the Italians should have faith in themselves and make ready to act on their own behalf.

To the last years of an Alfieri now turned sceptic and perhaps even reactionary, belong his unfortunate and very strange comedies. Four have a political theme: *L'Uno* [*The One*] against monarchical government, of which the protagonist is Darius who, with the consent of the priesthood and for the good of the people, becomes king of the Persians; *I Pochi* attacking aristocratic rule — here the two protagonists are the Gracchi brothers, whom the poet does not see as defenders of the people but as ambitious men striving to rule; *I Troppi* [*The More than Enough*] aimed at democracy, impersonated by an imaginary mission of Athenian ambassadors to Alexander the Great in Babylon. At their head is Demosthenes, the famous defender of Hellenic liberty, who does not resist any longer than his companions the splendor and the charm of royalty. *Tre veleni rimesta, avrai l'antidoto* [*Mix Three Poisons, You'll Have the Antidote*] is a heavy, fantastic allegory, which submits that the least evil of political consitutions is one which combines in itself the typical forms of government: monarchy, oligarchy, democracy, each one checking the harm done by one form with that of the others — supposedly the constitution of old Venice and of England. The fifth comedy has a moral theme: *La Finestrina* [*The Little Window*], aims at showing by a mythological fiction what poor things even great men would be if they could be seen inside: if, as in the comedy, a little window might open into their hearts. *Divorzio,* the sixth, is a social comedy, the satire of a marriage of convenience in which the marriage contract, in accord with the custom of the times, is encompassed by so many clauses as to leave the wife free of any submission to her husband, turning an apparent marriage into an actual divorce. The reading of the contract takes up the entire fifth act and is the most spirited part of the comedy.

We shall conclude the section on Alfieri by adding that his enthusiasm for the ancient literatures, which he revered as models and his desire to satiate himself with their masterpieces, as he expressed it (*invasarsi* is the word he used), led him to try his skill at translations, first from Latin and later Greek. He translated the *Aeneid* from the Latin, but his translation of Sallust was more highly esteemed; from the Greek he did the *Alcestis* of Euripides and *The Frogs* of Aristophanes.